Praise for 'It's a

Steve Chilton is a committed runner and qualified athletics coach with considerable experience of fell running, and a marathon PB of 2-34-53. He is a long-time member of the Fell Runners Association (FRA). In a long running career he has run in many of the classic fell races, as well as mountain marathons and has also completed the Cuillin Traverse. He works at Middlesex University, where he is Lead Academic Developer.

Steve's work has been published extensively, particularly in his roles as Chair of the Society of Cartographers, and Chair of the ICA Commission in Neocartography. He is heavily involved in the OpenStreetMap project (osm.org), having co-authored *OpenStreetMap: Using and Enhancing the Free Map of the World*.

It's A Hill
Get Over It

Steve Chilton

The Guides race: rounding the flag on Silver Howe
(Photo: Illustrated London News)

SANDSTONEPRESS
HIGHLAND | SCOTLAND

First published in 2013 in Great Britain
and the United States of America:
Sandstone Press Ltd
PO Box 5725
One High Street
Dingwall
Ross-shire
IV15 9WJ
Scotland.

www.sandstonepress.com

This edition published 2014.

Editor: Robert Davidson
Copy editor: Kate Blackadder
Index: Jane Angus

The publisher acknowledges subsidy from Creative Scotland towards
publication of this volume.

ISBN: 978-1-910124-17-8
ISBNe: 978-1-908737-58-8

Cover design and typesetting by Raspberry Creative Type, Edinburgh
Printed and bound by Ozgraf, Poland

To mum and dad, who made me what I am,
and would be very proud.

In many ways fell running has more in common with cycle racing than it does in other athletic events. The sport tests not only the competitor's stamina but also his or her courage and skill as the runners descend at speed across uneven and often slippery surfaces. You might expect that coming down the slope they would pick their way gingerly as if descending stairs. Far from it. The minute they hit any section that is less than perpendicular, they immediately go flat out. At times this is just how they end up – flat out. The St John ambulance men are kept busy at fell races.

Harry Pearson in *Racing Pigs and Giant Marrows*

Lakeland fell runners are not ordinary men. Remarkable fitness and stamina are required to race up a fellside, and tremendous muscle control and judgement are needed to race down. Lakeland breeds such men, and has been doing since long before the days when records began to be kept at the local sports meetings.

Harry Griffin in *Inside the Real Lakeland*

Contents

List of Illustrations

27. Kenny Stuart winning the Glasgow Marathon
28. Rossendale Fell Race – Jeff Norman leads Dave Cannon in 1970
29. Phil Davidson, Bob Graham and Martin Rylands at Dunmail Raise, June 13 1932
30. Billy Bland at the end of his record-breaking BGR in 1982 Rob Jebb leading from the Addisons on Reston Scar, 2012
31. Rob Jebb leading from the Addisons on Reston Scar, 2012
32. Alistair Brownlee leads brother Jonathan and Javier Gomez in the 2012 Olympic Triathlon in London

Photo credits

Prelim	Illustrated London News	Plate 17	Neil Shuttleworth
Plate 1	Cumbria Libraries	Plate 18	Dave Woodhead
Plate 2	Cumbria Libraries	Plate 19	Pete Hartley
Plate 3	Cumbria Libraries	Plate 20	Pete Hartley
Plate 4	Cumbria Libraries	Plate 21	Neil Shuttleworth
Plate 5	Dave Woodhead	Plate 22	Ben Nevis Race Association
Plate 6	Lancashire Evening Post Ltd	Plate 23	Colin Dulson
Plate 7	Lancashire Evening Post Ltd	Plate 24	Pete Hartley
Plate 8	Pete Hartley	Plate 25	Neil Shuttleworth
Plate 9	Pete Hartley	Plate 26	Pauline Stuart
Plate 10	Helene Whitaker	Plate 27	Pauline Stuart
Plate 11	Tommy Sedgwick	Plate 28	Jeff Norman
Plate 12	Tommy Sedgwick	Plate 29	Abraham Photographic
Plate 13	Tommy Sedgwick	Plate 30	Copyright holder unknown
Plate 14	Cumberland and Westmorland Herald	Plate 31	Mike Cambray
Plate 15	Westmorland Gazette	Plate 32	Moira Chilton
Plate 16	Westmorland Gazette		

Maps

All maps in the book were compiled and drawn by the author. Map data is derived from the OpenStreetMap dataset which is available under an ODBL licence (http://www.openstreetmap.org/copyright). The contour data is derived from Andy Allan's reworking of the public domain SRTM data (http://opencyclemap.org/).

Acknowledgements

There are many people to thank for various supporting roles in the production of this book. Firstly, I must thank Moira for understanding (I think) why sometimes I suddenly had to dash to the Lake District alone for the weekend to follow a lead, or why we had to interrupt our holiday to divert to some obscure café, only for me to say she must amuse herself whilst I interviewed someone she had probably never heard of.

When encouragement was much needed in the early days of the project Kirsteen Macdonald was usually available to massage the fragile ego of a nervous proto-author over a coffee. The Lake District trips often involved short stays at what I ended up thinking of as my writer's retreat, to which Mike Cambray and family always welcomed me back.

I would like to thank various friends for the loan of their copies of *Fellrunner* and *Up and Down* magazines, and in particular to thank Nick Barrable for always willingly digging out back copies, or photocopies, of *Compass Sport* magazines or articles therein.

Almost any serious research will involve libraries to some extent or other, and this was no exception. To the staff of the British Library newspaper library in Colindale and the British Library in St Pancras I'd like to offer a huge 'thank you' for being there, and for providing such a superb service. I also spent many a productive day in Kendal public library, and really appreciated the support of the staff there, particularly Jackie Faye who helped source photographs and articles which I might never have found. The sweets that staff in the Local History section shared one day were part of what made working there such a joyous experience.

Many people have both helped trace photo reproduction rights, and then give them where possible (individual photos are credited as appropriate). Pete Richards, who is Keswick AC website guru, provided some seriously time-consuming help with tracking photo copyrights and providing important contacts. Pete Hartley, Dave Woodhead, Neil Shuttleworth, Colin Dulson, Tommy Sedgwick, Jeff Norman and Pauline Stuart also kindly searched out photos when leads took me to them and their photograph collections.

Every effort has been made to contact copyright owners, authors and publishers, and appropriate attribution to original sources has been noted.

I would particularly like to thank those who gave up their time to be interviewed, or check material in the draft of this book. I often felt that I was skating on thin ice, with just a book synopsis under my arm, and no previous 'form' as an author (which has got to be a pretty convoluted metaphor). A massive thanks to those I interviewed, for taking me at face value and for having faith in the outcome. I do hope I haven't misrepresented any of you.

Then things started getting serious, and it was time to show someone the first draft of the manuscript. Celia Cozens was that first critical friend and she did a superb reviewing job. She made some significant structural suggestions and knocked some pretty rough edges off in the process, and still came back to agree to carry out a proof read for me later.

Especial thanks are due to my second critical friend, Alan Durant. He brought his considerable experience in the field to bear on my working manuscript. His comments resulted in a major structural and stylistic redraft which, I am sure, has resulted in a more readable book.

The completed manuscript was reviewed by the publisher's own reviewers, who came back with some more suggestions for improvements. The final manuscript was then read by Sarah Rowell, and she provided a view from within the sport and some very useful pointers as to where I might have strayed slightly in my research. For this, and for providing a cover quote for the book, I am eternally grateful to her. John Blair-Fish reviewed a couple of chapters when I posed questions on topics in his field, and in the process helped me to correct some inconsistencies. Any remaining errors are mine.

Finally, I would like to express my grateful thanks to all at Sandstone Press, especially my editor Robert Davidson who has guided me patiently through the process of bringing this, my first book, to press; Kate Blackadder for her proofing skills; and Heather Macpherson for cover design, typesetting and organising the photo section. I would specifically like to thank the following for granting permission to quote passages from works written or published by them:

The Fell Runners Association for permission to use a number of quotes from their committee and AGM minutes.

Andy Styan, Ross Brewster, Harvey Lloyd, Alan Bocking, Tony Cresswell, John Blair-Fish and Rob Jebb for permission to quote from race reports they wrote for *Fellrunner* magazine.

The estate of Nan Shepherd and the publisher for permission to quote from *The Living Mountain: A Celebration of the Cairngorm Mountains of Scotland*, Canongate Canons (2011).

Simon and Schuster for permission to use a quote from Boff Whalley's *Run Wild*, Simon and Schuster (2012).

Aurum Press for permission to use three short quotes from Richard Askwith's *Feet in the Clouds*, Aurum Press (2004).

Glossary/acronyms

AAA	Amateur Athletic Association
BAAB	British Amateur Athletic Board
BAF	British Athletic Federation
BGR	Bob Graham Round
BMC	British Mountaineering Council
BOFRA	British Open Fell Runners Association
BUCS	British Universities and Colleges Sport
carbo-loading	A carbohydrate-loading diet is a strategy to increase the amount of fuel stored in your muscles to improve your athletic performance. Carbohydrate loading generally involves greatly increasing the amount of carbohydrates you eat several days before a high-intensity endurance athletic event. You also typically scale back your activity level during carbohydrate loading.
CEGB	Central Electricity Generating Board
CFRA	Cumberland Fellrunners Association
CIME	Coupe Internationale de la Montagne
fartlek	Means 'speed play' in Swedish, is a training method that blends continuous training with interval training. The variable intensity and continuous nature of the exercise places stress on both the aerobic and anaerobic systems. It differs from traditional interval training in that it is unstructured; intensity and/or speed varies, as the athlete wishes.
ECCU	English Cross Country Union
FRA	Fell Runners Association
GR 20	A long-distance trail (Grande Randonee) that traverses Corsica diagonally from north to south.
IAAF	International Association of Athletics Federations
ICMR	International Committee Mountain Running
ITU	International Triathlon Union

KIMM	Karrimor International Mountain Marathon
LAMM	Lowe Alpine Mountain Marathon
LDMTA	Lake District Mountain Trial Association
LDSMRA	Lake District Search and Mountain Rescue Association
LAMM	Lowe Alpine Mountain Marathon
NCU	National Cyclists' Union
NCAAA	Northern Counties Amateur Athletic Association
NIMRA	Northern Ireland Mountain Running Association
OMM	Original Mountain Marathon
OS	Ordnance Survey
PB	personal best (time) for an event
PYG track	The PYG Track is one of the routes up Snowdon. It is possible that it was named after the pass it leads through, Bwlch y Moch (translated Pigs' Pass) as the path is sometimes spelled 'Pig Track'. Or, maybe because it was used to carry 'pyg' (black tar) to the copper mines on Snowdon. Another possible explanation is that the path was named after the nearby Pen y Gwryd Hotel, popular amongst the early mountain walkers.
RWA	Race Walking Association
SHRA	Scottish Hill Runners Association
SLMM	Saunders Lakeland Mountain Marathon
Supercompensation	In sports science theory, supercompensation is the post training period during which the trained function/parameter has a higher performance capacity than it did prior to the training period.
SWAAA	Southern Women's Amateur Athletic Association
UKA	UK Athletics
WAAA	Women's Amateur Athletic Association
WMRA	World Mountain Running Association
YHA	Youth Hostel Association

Introduction

It was a lovely day on the fells. I was going up beside the wall on the steep side of Birk Knott when suddenly I collapsed to the ground and couldn't go on. I gave myself a stiff talking to and struggled upwards. A friendly face, and a sugar rush from a proffered Mars bar, revived me enough to shuffle down the fell and complete the Three Shires Fell Race in a distinctly mediocre 2 hrs 53 mins 52 secs.

Earlier in the day I had pitched up at the Three Shires Inn full of bravado and looking forward to competing in this classic Lake District fell race. Facilities were limited, to say the least, and you mingled with the stars as you registered and submitted yourself to the required kit check. There was a rumour buzzing around that an Olympic champion had turned up to run. Was this to be my first victory over an Olympic champion? Turn up on the start line and you are there to be beaten, I reckon. OK, so beating the 1976 Olympic 400m champion Alberto Juantorena (so far the only athlete to win both the 400 and 800m Olympic titles) in the London Marathon a couple of years later may be no big deal, but you get the idea. (At least he had negotiated London's kerbs better than he had the track kerb at the World Championships, where he injured himself by falling over it and ended his career.) Maybe Steve Ovett was turning to the fells to show an even more impressive range of distances and events than he had already achieved. Maybe Seb Coe was coming across the Pennines to show the value of all that hill work in the Rivelin Valley. Well no, it was Chris Brasher, some 32 years after he had won gold at the 1952 Olympics in the steeplechase.

The race started with a steady stream of runners ascending Wetherlam via the side of Birk Fell, then through Swirl Hawse to Swirl How. We then dropped down to the Three Shire Stone (marking the boundary join between former counties of Cumberland, Westmorland and Lancashire) on top of the Wrynose Pass. Then choices start to come into play. Ascending sharply up Pike of Blisco and choosing between contouring around via the road under Side Pike, or dropping south of Blea Tarn and facing the stiff ascent of Lingmoor Fell can make a lot of difference to your result. I had chosen wrongly, and faltered on the steep slope.

I wondered why I was suffering so badly. I was a reasonably conditioned marathon runner (with a PB (personal best) of 2 hrs 34 mins to come the next year) and, unlike my friends who would sit and watch Live Aid, I was to spend that weekend completing the two-day Karrimor International Mountain Marathon in the eastern Lake District. The winner that day completed the Three Shires in a time about an hour less than mine. Subsequently, Gavin Bland set the present course record of 1 hr 45 mins 8 secs in 1997. What I wanted to know was: how could these guys be so fast, what were they like, how did they train? More particularly, why was it that a bunch of guys called Bland, all from the same extended family from in and around Borrowdale, had set so many of the fell race course records in the Lake District (and other areas), many of which survive to this day?

Twenty-seven years later I set out to find out.

The particular questions I have drawn attention to above may not *all* be answered in the resulting book. My plans gradually changed as I started to undertake the necessary research. Over time, my project turned into a desire to go beyond such particular questions and to write a broader history of fell running. The end result is still, I hope, an in-depth study of fell running's frequently neglected history. It is also now an account of some of the greats of the sport, as well as a description of some of the values which give the sport *its* distinctive character. Because of this broader scope, I felt it was best not to present the development of the sport chronologically, or through the vehicle of my own experience, or through the eyes of other runners. Rather, the sport's historical development is explored more as a series of linked themes and topics, some but not all of which follow an overt timeline.

Fell running has, in my view, been poorly served by the publishing industry. Finding *any* books to read about the sport has always been a struggle, even in the best-stocked bookshops. The sport just hasn't been that well documented. You could say that Bill Smith may have already written its definitive history, but a lot has changed since his influential *Stud marks on the summits* appeared in 1985. You might think Richard Askwith's more recent *Feet in the Clouds* covers the sport's history comprehensively, folded between the author's own efforts in training and races, and finally his Bob Graham Round (BGR, see Chapter 15). Even Askwith's journalistic, auto-biographical examination is inevitably not a history of the sport. Boff Whalley's still more recent *Run Wild*, another important book about what makes fell running the sport it is, is really a celebration, concentrating on what the author believes 'running can be – unpredictable and surprising'.

Very few early books gave much guidance to those wishing to participate in the sport. James Fixx's 1977 best-selling book *The Complete Book of Running* was for a while a huge influence on people taking up running. Fixx had a few words to say on the taking up of the sport:

> Entering a fell race is simplicity itself … Training for the fells, on the other hand, is not so simple. More than once, runners who are acclaimed on the track have swaggered to their first fell race, only to be publicly humbled as their muscles turned to tapioca under the relentless punishment of the high places. Like runners everywhere, the best fell runners have their training secrets and superstitions. But there is at least one incontrovertible principle: To race well on fells you've got to do lots of training on them.

As we go through the history and the individual stories we will see how true this is, and also some variations on the training approaches that have been taken, even amongst the leading participants.

Bruce Tulloh's *The Complete Distance Runner* was published in 1983, and offers a mere three paragraphs on fell running (note that like Fixx he is offering also a 'complete' coverage of running). Tulloh says of fell running:

> This might be considered a form of cross country, but actually it is more of a religion. Some southerners maintain it is more of a disease, and that you will only take up fell running after being bitten by another fell runner, which is not unlikely, as they are a bunch of animals!

Later on, two publications appeared which covered training for fell running. Firstly, the British Athletics Federation published *Fell and hill running* by

Norman Matthews and Dennis Quinlan in 1996, and then in 2002 Sarah Rowell's *Off-Road Running* was published, which included examples of training programmes from well-known runners.

While acknowledging the excellent work of these authors, this book is an attempt to do something else. It brings together various facets of the sport, and looks at them from different perspectives. As successive themes and characters are explored, the book aims to give both a historical view and an idea of what participating in this fantastic and very different sport can offer.

A phenomenon as historically complex as fell running, and as relatively non-institutionalised, needs this kind of attention. I have written about many aspects: the people who run; the sport's organisations and rules; its techniques and conventions; its dangers and rewards; and its relation to other apparently similar or closely related sports. The particular themes I have chosen range from the sport's early days and domination by gambling and professionalism, through the development of a full race calendar, to the sport becoming 'open' at last. There are also details of the fight for control of the sport and of the development of international fixtures in recent years.

There is more to any sport than its competition element. I know of many participants in fell running, for example, who train but don't ever race. They are happy just to enjoy the scenery and the mental and physical release running on the fells can give. There is much in my account of the sport for such people; but for those who do race, or who prioritise the competitive dimension, the book also includes detailed sections on championship winners, on course record breakers, and on the phenomenal endurance fell challenges that have been set, and beaten, over the years. Downsides of the sport are also touched on, like the fortunately infrequent fatalities, and individual or institutional disagreements.

Finally, fell running does not exist in isolation, and some coverage of the similarities and differences between fell running and marathon running, and those who succeed at both, is included. Similarly, those who compete at a high level simultaneously in fell running and in other related sports are discussed. Perhaps most important of all are the different kinds of participants in fell running: journeymen (and women), characters, record breakers, and innovators are all covered. Particularly highlighted for obvious reasons are the early giants of the sport, as well as those I consider all-time greats.

My mix of themes is brought together from a wide range of sources, both historical and contemporary. In order to present some important personal perspectives (other than my own) on what might otherwise seem a rather fact-laden read, I have spent a significant amount of time interviewing some of the sport's leading proponents. Their reflections offer an interesting counterpoint to some of the recorded history. In some cases, their reflections even give a somewhat different slant to 'facts' reported in the published secondary sources. The gaps that open up should not be seen as revisionist, but more an acknowledgement that there are usually (at least) two sides to any story. If the resulting picture of some situation or event does not ring true to any particular reader, I can only say I have checked details with participants in such events as much as I possibly could. If any errors have crept in then *mea culpa*. Please feel free to contact me to discuss any such errors or omissions, and where I have an opportunity to do so I will correct them.

My background as the author of this book is both that of an academic and of a long-term participant in the sport of fell running. This isn't an especially common combination, so it is worth exploring how I came into fell running and why I thought I should – and could – embark on writing the sort of account of the sport's history outlined here.

My start came early, though not in an obvious or direct way. At school I followed an older brother who was academically very accomplished. At one point I was directly told by a teacher that I was 'not as good as him'. That scarred me for life, but also got me going! My brother John was also an excellent cross country runner, so instead I took up race walking. I carried on playing football and eventually went to study a vocational (i.e. non-academic) course in cartography at Oxford Polytechnic. This period of my life is now recalled to others as 'when I was up at Oxford'.

My father had run at a reasonable standard at school, and then played football. He was not especially sporty by the time I was growing up, although he was still a mainstay of his work's sports club. He played cricket until fairly late in his life, and then continued in a managing and administrative capacity.

Finding my own way, I did the usual teenage stuff of going out exploring on foot and by bike, being brought up in the glorious Devonshire countryside. This was at a time when parents allowed their children to go about unsupervised all day long.

The day after my last exam in Oxford, a bunch of lads from the course threw sleeping bags and tents in a car and drove to Snowdonia. On day one we headed from the campsite at the north end of Llyn Gwynant straight up the flank of Gallt y Wenallt, something I probably wouldn't do now as it was phenomenally steep and a wee bit scary. We were only young.

Several years of fell walking followed, getting more and more serious and including half-heartedly ticking off the Wainwright summits as they were done. A good friend, 'Skipper' Dave Allen, worked at Butharlyp Howe Youth Hostel and encouraged me also to go out running with him on the Lakeland Fells each time I visited. Occasionally this was in the company of Jon Broxap, who was a YHA warden at the time. There was no intention on my part to race – just to cover more ground. We also used to sit on the summits and take in the view.

Failing eyesight saw an end to football for me, and a consequent increase in girth due to some poor lifestyle choices at this time. Some friends were entering the *Sunday Times* Fun Run and this inspired me to get fit enough to do that. At a mere 2.5 miles it was no real problem. Chris Brasher's instigation of the London Marathon in 1981 had also caught my imagination and I did a certain amount of training, and completed the event in a seemingly easy 3 hrs 5 mins. Four years of greatly increased training, facilitated by joining Barnet & District AC, gave me a PB of 2 hrs 34 mins 53 secs for the Marathon in 1985.

Soon after my 1981 marathon I had already started seeking new running challenges, and in that context the thought of fell racing came into my mind even though I wasn't really in a position to do much decent fell training. No matter. My first race was Butter Crags, in June 1981. On that day I remember being especially impressed that one of the leading runners had gone straight back after the race to repair the wall where runners had awkwardly scrambled over it. Having enjoyed that race, I sought out similar fell races whenever I could, including most of the classic fell events. Joining the Fell Runners Association (FRA), I also followed the top-end of the sport closely, which was very competitive during that era – and I must admit I sometimes think back (possibly overly) fondly on the period as the best of times for the sport, with its uncomplicated race diary, amazing races and fast times.

Orienteering was also among my interests then, and led me to have the confidence to try some of the longer navigation events such as the OS

(Ordnance Survey) Mountain Trial, the KIMM and the Saunders (as they were called at that time). One thing you do find out in taking part in the two person/two day mountain marathons is how you REALLY have to get on with your chosen partner – particularly when the going gets tough, usually on day two. Partnering with Mike Cambray turned out to be a good combination for me. I brought running fitness, whereas he probably had superior mountain craft – but amazingly we seemed to gel into a pretty efficient team. I can still recall the savoury pancakes he had made for one of our overnight camps.

I never achieved anything in orienteering, but enjoyed it immensely nevertheless. On reflection, I never achieved anything really in fell running. Looking back though I particularly enjoyed courses like the Fairfield Horseshoe the most: medium length and runnable. I kept going back whenever I could.

Time moves on. A hip replacement, which 'may' have been necessitated by years of hard training, put an end to racing. It was perhaps appropriate that my last race was the World Vets Fell Running Championships when it was held at Keswick in 2005. Running, in its own odd way, has led to writing. Some of the friendships made during my time in the sport became instrumental in making further contacts, which resulted in turn in interviews drawn on in this book. An informal network also built up of people only encountered recently, including some people only ever met virtually, and these people facilitated much of my research, gave access to further contacts again, and extended my ability to find previously unknown material sources and ownership of photo rights.

In the academic work that has paralleled my running career, I have written quite extensively on my area of expertise and interest (principally cartography). Writing this book has definitely been something completely different. I feel my passion for the sport and my academic instincts have jointly allowed me to produce a book that – I hope – strikes a balance between historical facts and the personalities behind them. I would like people both to appreciate the outstanding achievements of leading exponents of the sport and also to feel that fell running is something they could themselves enjoy, at some level or other from armchair to summit.

In writing this book it has also been my hope that it will go some way towards showing my appreciation for all the good times I have had on the fells, and will also serve as a thank you to people in the various networks I have identified who helped bring this material together. Perhaps the resulting work may find its place somewhere alongside the three outstanding books referred to at the beginning of this introduction, adding to the sport's *oeuvre* and possibly inspiring others to write about their particular interests – exploring and reflecting on this sport or indeed on other subjects.

CHAPTER 1

Early Days

It's a hill. Get over it.
Seen on the back of a runner's t-shirt

Fell running can easily be distinguished from other athletic events, in that it takes place not on a track or on roads but off road, over rough country and preferably with considerable amounts of ascending and descending, usually over some significant hills or mountains. There are organised fell races, certainly. It should not be assumed that fell running has to have a competitive element to it. Where there *are* races, they may also involve mountain navigation skills, since a race may involve participants finding their way from one checkpoint to the next, often over terrain that has no paths to guide the way. Thought of in this way, fell running is probably not a sport for everyone. It can give fantastic benefits, both physical and metaphysical, to those who take part.

There is much detail in this book of races, records and achievements. Not everyone sees it as being as competitive as that. There are those who are happy just being out in the fells. I certainly know of athletes who never take part in fell races, but who might call themselves fell runners, if asked. An interesting view on the competitive urge is expressed by Nan Shepherd in her excellent treatise on a life lived in the Cairngorms, *The Living Mountain*. She gives these thoughts on the matter:

> To pit oneself against the mountain is necessary for every climber:
> to pit oneself merely against other players, and make a race of it,

is to reduce to the level of a game what is essentially an experience. Yet what a race-course for these boys to choose! To know the hills, and their own bodies, well enough to dare the exploit is their real achievement.

She does admit on the very next page that it is 'merely stupid to suppose that the record-breakers do not love the hills'.

Early feats of endurance such as those of the Greeks carrying news of victorious battles may at a stretch be seen as precursors. A traditional story relates how Pheidippides, an Athenian messenger, ran the 26 miles from the battlefield at Marathon to Athens to announce the Greek victory over Persia in the Battle of Marathon in 490 bc with the word 'Νενικήκαμεν!' (we were victorious!). He then promptly died on the spot. Being a messenger was a respected and well-rewarded occupation at this time. According to Thor Gotaas[1], there was then no word for 'amateur', the nearest being *idiotes*, an unskilled and ignorant individual.

The story about Pheidippides is incorrectly attributed in most accounts to the historian Herodotus, who recorded the history of the Persian Wars in his *Histories* (written in about 440 bc). In its detail, the story seems improbable. The Athenians would have been more likely to send a messenger on horseback. Possibly they might have used a runner, as a horse could have been hindered by rough terrain encountered on the journey. It is difficult to be sure. Either way, though, no such story actually appears in Herodotus' account.

As with the Athenians, there are also early records from Scotland of runners crossing the hills as the only way to spread urgent messages. Given the potential importance of such messages, clan chieftains organised races among their clansmen to find the fastest men to carry out the task. The details of their circumstances are highlighted in this excerpt by Michael Brander from his *Guide to the Highland Games*, where he notes that:

> In the wild and mountainous highlands, where no roads existed, and peat bogs, boulders and scree were likely to slow down or cripple even the most sure-footed horse, by far the quickest means of communication was a man running across country. The 'Crann-tara' or fiery cross was the age-old method of raising the clansmen in time of need. It was made of two pieces of wood fastened together in the shape of a cross, traditionally with one end

alight and the other end soaked in blood. Runners were dispatched to all points of the compass and as they ran they shouted the war cry of the clan and the place and time to assemble.

The earliest fell race that we have details of was that organised by King Malcolm Canmore (literal translation Big Head), who was King of Scotland in 1064. As a way of identifying suitable candidates for these message-delivering duties, a race up Creag Choinnich (or Craig Choinich), near Braemar, was put on by Canmore. The race was won by Dennisbell McGregor[2] of nearby Ballochbuie. He received a prize consisting of a 'purse full of gold' and a sword. In a recent article about that race, in the *Scottish Mountaineering Club Journal*, Jamie Thin offers this description of proceedings:

> All the challengers set off led by the favourites, the two elder Macgregor brothers, but at the last moment the third and youngest Macgregor brother joined the back of the field. The youngest brother caught his elder brothers at the top of the hill and asked 'Will ye share the prize?' The reply came back 'Each man for himself!' As they raced back down the hill he edged into second place and then dashed past his eldest brother. But as he passed, his eldest brother despairingly grabbed him by his kilt. But slipping out of his kilt, the younger brother still managed to win, if lacking his kilt!

It can be argued that McGregor was perhaps the best rewarded professional racer ever, if we take into account how minuscule the prizes in professional races were by comparison, even centuries later.

King Malcolm Canmore, it seems, had a more general love of sport, too. He had already earned respect for his hunting and fishing activities. Alongside his contribution to running in particular, his enthusiasm also helped create the forerunners of modern-day Highland Games in Scotland.

As well as the races to aid the search for messengers, there are more recent precedents, whereby endurance was both tested and admired. The exploits of nineteenth-century 'pedestrians' such as Robert Barclay Allardice, Corky Gentleman and the Flying Pieman provide some of the earliest formal endurance records.

One of the most famous pedestrians was Robert Barclay Allardice, who was known as Captain Barclay. He was born in August 1777 at Ury House, just outside Stonehaven in Scotland. He became the sixth Laird of Ury at the tender age of 17. Despite his noble upbringing, he was one of the strongest men of his generation, something which seems to have been a family trait. Members of his family were known for their achievements in activities such as wrestling bulls, carrying sacks of flour in their teeth and uprooting trees with their bare hands. J.K. Gillon wrote of Barclay[3]:

> In 1809, at Newmarket he accomplished his most noted feat of endurance walking. This involved walking one mile in each of 1,000 successive hours. In other words Barclay was required to walk a mile an hour, every hour, for forty-two days and nights. Barclay started on the 1st June and completed his historic feat on the 12th July. His average time varied from 14 minutes 54 seconds in the first week to 21 minutes 4 seconds in the last week. Over 10,000 people were attracted to the event and Barclay picked up substantial prize money for his efforts. Variations on the 'Barclay Match' were attempted throughout the century.

Wagers on the feat were estimated at around 16,000 guineas (*valued at over half a million pounds today*)[4]. In 2003 a team re-created the 1,000 mile challenge, and finished it off by running the London Marathon. They achieved the 1,000 mile target easily. However, when it came to running the marathon they struggled because they had actually lost fitness during the event.

Despite being famous for pedestrianism, Barclay was also acknowledged as an accomplished stagecoach driver. He is credited with taking the London mail coach to Aberdeen single handed, which required considerable endurance, as he had to remain seated for three days and nights. Captain Barclay died of paralysis in 1854, a few days after being kicked in the head by a horse as he tried to break it in.

It wasn't just the British that took up pedestrianism. In 1879, an American called Edward Weston was mobbed by so many British fans that he fell just short of completing a 2,000- miles-in-1,000-hours walk around England. Along the way he delivered lectures about the health benefits of walking. He was given a police escort whenever he went into major towns and cities in his trademark hat and boots. His career stretched over 61 years, from 1861 to 1922. He was a star on both sides of the Atlantic, at a time when pedestrianism was a sport which hundreds of thousands of people turned out to watch, and he was the focus of the betting of huge sums of money.

Weston's endurance capability and remarkable powers of recovery led doctors to study what he ate and how much he slept, even taking samples of his urine and faeces. It was during those studies that one of the most controversial parts of Weston's career came to light. Doctors noticed a brown stain on his lips after a race and discovered it was down to his chewing of a coca leaf, the source of cocaine. The incident is one of the first known examples of drugs being used to enhance sports performance.

When he died in 1929 Weston was 90 years old. At that time, the life expectancy for males in the US was just short of 56. During the last two years of his life, though, he was in a wheelchair, after being hit by a modern invention that he considered something of an enemy – the motor car.

Returning to the earliest recorded foot races, there are stories of competitors being naked. Similarly, the earliest Olympians supposedly competed in the nude, adorned only with olive oil. Personally, I can't imagine how I would deal with the distraction of un-restrained 'equipment' when trying to run a race. I still have all too vivid memories of spectating at a cross-country event when a clubmate had to pull out when leading the race, due to a clothing malfunction opening him up (literally) to a possible charge of indecent exposure.

Imagine then the scene described in *Miss Weeton: Journal of a Governess, 1807-1811*:

> there followed a foot race by four men. Two of them ran without shirts; one had breeches on, the other only drawers, very thin calico, without gallaces [braces]. Expecting they would burst or come off, the ladies durst not view the race, and turned away from the sight. And well it was they did, for during the race, and with the exertion of running, the drawers did actually burst, and the man cried out as he ran 'O Lord! O Lord! I cannot keep my tackle in G-d d-n it! I cannot keep my tackle in'. The ladies, disgusted, everyone left the ground … it was a gross insult to every woman there.

There are also other early endurance running exploits to be noted outside the United Kingdom. There used to a saying 'to run like a Basque'. At the end of the eighteenth century the mountain dwellers from the Basque region used to hold two-man races, around which much betting took place. They favoured fairly long distances, anything from six miles to around 15 miles. The events were not held over fixed routes, but had fixed starts and finishes. The participants developed excellent fitness, navigation and resourcefulness as they negotiated the very hilly courses used for these events.

Some running 'characters' were also appearing in the New World. The Flying Pieman was the nickname of William King, who was born in London in 1807. He emigrated to Australia in 1829, landing at Sydney. By 1834 he had begun cooking and selling meat pies around the Hyde Park cricket ground and along Circular Quay. He was known as 'The Flying Pieman' because of the practice whereby he offered his pies to passengers as they boarded the Parramatta steamer. He would then run the 18 miles to Parramatta with the unsold pies, and offer them to the same passengers as they disembarked. He also twice managed to beat the Sydney to Windsor mail coach on foot, a distance of just over 32 miles.

Moving on through history, we see that organised fell running has its real roots in the mid nineteenth century. It was in northern England that fell races started being established in the mid-1800s. The first races as we know them now were those that were incorporated in local events, being just another test of physical prowess. They would take place alongside events such as wrestling, sprinting and throwing the hammer or tossing the caber (a Scottish speciality). In Scotland, the community aspect was borne out by the cultural and agricultural activities that were taking place on these occasions, which were more akin to the fairs or agricultural shows in England. Fell running has developed into one of the toughest branches of athletics, with its emphasis on endurance and rough terrain.

Two of these earliest local events were held in Yorkshire, at Lothersdale in 1847 and Burnsall in 1850. In the Lake District the Grasmere Sports were first held in 1852, incorporating a fell race (the now famous Guides Race), as well as Cumberland- and Westmorland-style wrestling and hound trailing. The term 'guides' stemmed from the experienced fellsmen, such as fox hunters and shepherds, who guided the early-nineteenth-century tourists engaging in lengthy walks and explorations in the mountains. In the early days these 'guides' were often the only fell race contestants, as they raced to prove their superiority, and thus enhance their employment prospects. The races were virtually exhibition events staged for the guides to display their fell racing talents to appreciative gatherings at the shows. Sometimes they took the form of handicap foot races around an undulating course.

In Wordsworth's *Guide to the Lakes* he describes an excursion to the top of Scafell with a shepherd guide, and he is later recorded as watching fell racing. One of the most famous of the early guides was Will Ritson, who was landlord of the Wastwater Hotel (now the Wasdale Head Inn) in Wasdale, and noted for his tall tales. He has a bar named after him in the pub, and is the inspiration behind the World's Greatest Liar competition[5].

In some cases cycle racing also featured intermittently in the programmes. Having watched grass-track racing at sports meetings I can see a certain similarity with chariot racing, with their tight circuits. Furthermore, looking at the old photos of events like Grasmere you can imagine a gladiatorial aspect to the cycle events with their tightly packed large crowds pressing in on the oval arena. The early fell races were designed for the benefit of spectators, and were usually held over a direct course encompassing fields, walls, streams and whatever obstacles were around. They usually led to a tough climb up the adjacent fell or crag as far as a prominent marker point on the skyline and then straight back down again.

Like Wordsworth, Dickens was known to have attended these festivals, which were held in places like Windermere and Ambleside, as well as at Grasmere. In Ambleside it was the Cycle Club which originally promoted the first Ambleside and District Amateur Athletic Sports in 1892. The organisers proudly declare on the event website[6]:

> Many events with our type of location have switched to mountain cycling, however here at Ambleside we have retained track cycling around a 300m circuit which ensures that the sport remains exciting for the spectators. Both the Senior and Junior events are also handicapped which helps to ensure that every race is closely contested.

There had been an Ambleside Sports held in 1886 to celebrate the Golden Jubilee of Queen Victoria. Although there seems to be no evidence in contemporary reports of a fell race, the event was repeated in 1887, and a fell race is noted. There appear to have been no sports for four years until the aforementioned Amateur Athletic Sports were held in 1892. These were held under the then current cycling and athletics rules, and the committee banned professionalism and gambling of every description. However, prizes to the value of £35 were donated by local tradesmen (*worth well over £2,000 today*).

Details of these events now started to appear in historical records. One such example is Marjorie Blackburn's booklet *Our Traditional Lakeland Sports,* which documents Ambleside and its Sports in fascinating detail. In it she notes, with regard to the fell race of 1892:

> for this there were 14 entries, but only about eight started. The course should have been across the river, and over the two highest peaks at the Ambleside end of Loughrigg, but owing to the floods it was deemed risky to cross the beck, so the course lay out of the field over the two bridges and up by Brow Head. Prizes: 1 – tea service, value £2 [£119]; 2 – castors, value £1 [£59]; 3 – opera glasses, value 10s [£30].

However, there is some uncertainty around the exact origins and dates involved in events like Grasmere being established. One account is given in *Reminiscences in The Life of Thomas Longmire.* Here J. Wilson (referring to Grasmere) wrote:

> It is somewhat difficult to arrive at the exact time when these noted sports were really established, as they emanated and gradually developed from the old rustic wrestling contests, for most insignificant prizes, which were inseparable from the annual Sheep Fair, held on the first Tuesday in September ... As the Guides Race is the most popular feature of the programme, that may be taken as the foundation, and was started at the September Fair in 1869[7] held under the stewardship of Mr W.H. Heelis and Mr J.F Green, and it is mainly due to the last named gentleman, that the Grasmere meeting has attained the proportions and popularity it has done, and of which he still is, and has been from the first, Honorary Secretary and Treasurer. There were 10 entries in the first Guides Race won by G. Birkett, with W. Greenop the 'Langdale antelope' second.

The next year saw the establishment in Scotland of the New Year Sprint, which is one of the longest standing athletics events in the UK. The Sprint has been staged in Scotland on or around New Year's Day every year since

1870. It is a handicap race over 110 metres. Competitors, whether amateur or professional, now race for prize money totalling over £8,000. The New Year Sprint, formerly known as the 'Powderhall', is a unique event, as it represents the last of the old galas. The format, however, remains unchanged. Races are handicapped to try to ensure close finishes, and betting adds to the enjoyment of the spectators.

The prizes at these early events might have generally been insignificant, but the betting was serious and that produced many issues. Both the pedestrians and the sprinters were embroiled in a world of gambling, which they shared with early fell runners. The days of huge betting coups and malpractice are long gone, but the tradition, spirit and atmosphere remain. It is still a big deal to win the 'Big Sprint'.

One particular event of this era achieved great notoriety. 'The Race of the Century' was how the newspapers of the day billed the world championship challenge race between Harry Hutchens and Henry Gent in 1887. With 15,000 spectators packed into West London's Lillie Bridge stadium, the two runners were forcibly removed from the dressing-room, bundled out of a side-entrance and spirited away in separate carriages. When their non-appearance was announced, the crowd tore down the wooden stadium buildings, ripped up the perimeter railings and burned everything that they could get their hands on. The spark, it transpired, had been the bookmakers being fearful of being cleaned out after discovering that Gent had broken down in training. 'They stood over me in the dressing-room with open knives and bottles,' Hutchens told *The Sporting Life*. 'They swore they would murder me if I tried to run.' The burning of Lillie Bridge prompted the demise of pedestrianism, but not gambling and professionalism. The stadium had been the venue for the early 'Varsity' athletics match between Oxford and Cambridge Universities, which had been held at Lillie Bridge from 1867 to 1887.

The earliest fell races were invariably professional, in that the winners were awarded cash prizes. The first prize might exceed a week's wages and at a major meeting, such as Alva, far exceeded it. The races also attracted bookmakers and gambling. By the 1911 Ambleside Sports betting was allowed quietly ('and no shouting by the bookmakers'). The continued influence of the bookmakers at the sports meetings may be judged by Marjorie Blackburn reporting in *Our Traditional Lakeland Sports* that as recently as in 1981 there was a serious problem when:

all four hound trails had to be called off after reports off sheep worrying in the Cumberland Fells. A hound, which had gone missing two months previously was thought to be the culprit. On the day of the Sports the bookies, not to be outdone, bought in portable TV sets to cover the afternoon's horseracing.

There was also unfortunately sometimes malpractice in evidence, because of the betting involved. One such example is noted by rock climber Ron Fawcett[8] in his autobiography Rock Athlete:

Fell running is in my blood, in a way. Grandad Bate was a good runner in his youth, and locally very successful ... There is a big race in Embsay, every year in September, and a story in the local press had tipped Grandad as worth a few quid at favourable odds. So a local bookie headed off a possibly disastrous day for the bookmaking fraternity by getting Grandad drunk. Needless to say he didn't win.

The pecuniary rewards available were considered immoral by the 'gentlemen' supporters of the amateur concept, and when the (AAA) Amateur Athletic Association[9] came on to the scene their objective was to rid athletic sport of this influence, causing other problems on the way, as we will see. The history of some of the earliest races is included in Chapter 3, but first we look at the professional/amateur divide, which at one point looked like ripping the sport apart.

CHAPTER 2

Professional versus amateur

Training can get on a man's nerves
Alf Shrubb

It can be quite difficult to get a clear picture of the amateur and professional divide in the sport of fell running, as often the lines have not been clearly drawn. The sport has moved from being dominated by professional races, through two parallel codes, to now being an integrated open sport. In the early days the professional races tended to be shorter, and the rise of the amateurs increased both the number of, and range of lengths of, races that were being organised.

Confusion reigned at times. For example, the 1877 and 1878 Grasmere Guides Races were contested by professionals alongside amateurs, although the formation of the Amateur Athletic Association (AAA) ended that practice. At Grasmere in 1878 there were two competitions run in parallel over the same course. For the professional event there were only three starters, and for the amateurs eleven. The report quoted in *See the Conquering Hero Comes* lists the three professional finishers as J. Greenop, W. Greenop and W. Scott, with the comment that:

> the race altogether was a fair one especially between J. Greenop and Warburton, the latter of whom is a well-known amateur athlete. He did not know the course and this was a great disadvantage, he, however held his own well in making the ascent, and in coming down, was only some 40 yds behind Greenop who won in 16 min

31 secs. Some of the others who had been toiling up the steep ascent, had scarcely reached the summit when the leaders were topping the wall on their return.

The Grasmere Guides Race was first held in 1868, going to the top of Silver Howe and back. It was a professional race, with £3 (£137) being the first prize. The main reason the guides races were actually held was because the runners were being paid by wealthy patrons to run and provide entertainment. The current 'professional' Grasmere Guides Race record of 12 mins 21.6 secs over the Butter Crags course was set by Fred Reeves in 1978 and is said to be still unbeaten today. To further confuse the situation, there is another course record, established on 16 May 1985 in an amateur event, which is held by Kenny Stuart with a time of 12 mins and 1 sec.

The Grasmere Race has been won by all the greats over the years. Fred Reeves was successful eight times altogether. Bill Teasdale won the event ten times during the 1950s and 1960s – including five consecutive times. In the 'open' era Rob Jebb first won the Senior Guides Race in 2000. He has so far won eight times and been second and third on two occasions. He had six consecutive wins to his credit, from 2004 to 2009, and has equalled the record for the most consecutive victories. Five hundred pounds is still being offered to anyone who can beat Reeves' record.

Early reports of these races provide some fascinating details of these events and the athletes involved. In the earliest days of fell running at Grasmere, when the race went up Silver Howe, it is said the runners used to change their footgear at the summit. They would replace their light boots with a stouter pair. There is also a story of one runner being offered two left boots by mistake and finishing the course barefoot.

Their mode of dress was different too. An old photograph of the Grasmere runners in 1876 shows two of the competitors wearing low shoes and all but one of them wearing what look very like singlets and long underpants, with bathing trunks added. The one exception wears heavy corduroy knee breeches, a pair of braces – and a fine-looking beard. At this time there was an interesting way of finishing the race. The winner was the first man to touch the ground after clearing the wall round the field.

The influence of betting is shown by the fact that in 1878 *Sporting Life* had published a challenge for the considerable stake of £100 (*equivalent to over £4,800*) by John Greenop of Langdale to race 'any man of the World' over the Grasmere Guides course. That year Greenop won to seal a hat-trick of victories. This confidence, together with the subsequent results he achieved, marks Greenop out as the first 'star' of the Lakeland races.

Meanwhile, the Scottish Highland Games scene was developing. Interestingly, the Scots seemed to turn their hands and feet to a host of athletic events during a day's games. This is probably the main reason why many of the older Scottish races, despite the high mountains, are only short hill races. The early Games superstar Donald Dinnie, was both a runner and an all-rounder. While not being a class runner, he nevertheless competed at all the heavy events. He also jumped, ran and wrestled, often beating the specialists. According to the athletics records Dinnie was the first athlete to high jump 6ft in 1868, just before he set off on a tour of America.

There are further examples of the confusion over codes in more recent times. For instance, in 1978, in the *Fellrunner* magazine, Bill Smith reported on a series of Coniston fell races. In April, a 7.5-mile fell race for YHA (Youth Hotel Association) assistants to the top of the Coniston Old Man was won by Jon Broxap. In July the amateur race was held over six miles at the local sports meeting, normally given over to professional events. This was also up the Old Man and was won by Brian Robinson, with Jean Lochhead winning the ladies race over the same course. There was also a 2.5 mile Guides Race which was won by Fred Reeves.

Back at the beginning of the twentieth century, the development of professional races was taking place in both the Lake District and in Northern England. However, difficulty of travelling meant that not many runners raced outside their own immediate areas. One of the first to buck this trend was Tommy Metcalfe, who was from Hawes in Yorkshire. He regularly ran in the Lakes against Ernest Dalzell, Charlie Mossop and Jim Fleming, who were the top locals at the time. Dalzell coming across from Keswick to run in the special race at Burnsall is another example of further expansion of the race fields. Between the wars improved transport, especially motorbikes, meant that Lakeland and Yorkshire runners were able to race each other more often, but there were still two codes in the sport.

Eventually some races actually changed their status. For instance, Stoodley Pike was originally a professional race, and in 1976 was run under amateur rules. John McDonough organised the original race with Rochdale Harriers, and carried on after the change, with the help of Todmorden AC.

The early professional races attracted huge crowds too. In the immediate post-war era Grasmere and Ambleside Sports would attract as many spectators as attended the 1948 London Olympic Games. Despite the huge crowds, the prize money at the professional races was not great. Roger Ingham is quoted in *Stud marks on the summits* as saying that:

> professional is rather a lavish name with which to bestow contestants when certain 'amateurs' can now make a full-time living from sport. Many professionals do not win enough in a season to cover their entry fees, let alone travelling expenses, but they uphold a tradition that dates back well over a century.

In the early 1980s the top prize at the Kilnsey Show was £100, and £75 at Grasmere, while at the prestigious Braemar and Ambleside races the top prizes were just £40. Earlier still, the 1966 programme notes for the Hebden Sports, which offered monetary prizes, referred to the meeting as 'an event that is run by amateurs for amateurs' – clearly a contradiction there. The first prize at Ambleside Guides Race in 1954 was £10.

Despite this, good money could be made at times. Jack Pooley was a professional racer and won a series of races in 1919, including Grasmere on the only occasion he ran there. In *Inside the Real Lakeland* Harry Griffin commented that after winning Grasmere:

> an Australian visitor came up and pressed £50 [*around £1,000 now*] into his hand. Young Pooley said he could not take it, but the visitor insisted, adding: 'I've backed you on every race this season, and you've won me £785 [*over £16,000*], which has paid nicely for my holiday'.

Even the athletes didn't always see a clear division. Some athletes have moved between branches of the sport, and some have probably been oblivious to the very division. Fred Reeves was a notable amateur before 'going professional' and several high-profile amateurs such as Pete Bland and Kenny Stuart had been reinstated after having raced as professionals. There was some considerable resentment expressed at Stuart's reinstatement, especially when he swept all before him so soon after entering the amateur ranks.

Earlier still, development of the amateur races was fuelled by interest from mainstream athletes. Chris Brasher's involvement is documented herein, and he had considerable influence. Derek Ibbotson, the World Mile Record Holder, won Burnsall in 1953. Contrarily, Bill Smith – nominally an amateur – used to enter the Grasmere Guides Race falsely under the name of W. Wilson.

At least throughout most of this time the sport of fell running accepted that there could co-exist amateur and professional versions of the sport, and had procedures for reinstatement. In contrast the Amateur Athletic Association was intransigent for years about allowing those they considered 'professional' to compete in their events. There was the ludicrous case of John Tarrant, who was banned in 1952 for earning the princely sum of £17 as a boxer earlier in his life. Bill Jones' book *The Ghost Runner* details how the AAA insisted that 'reinstatement by the Amateur Boxing Association [ABA] would be necessary before his application to compete as an amateur athlete could be considered'. Bizarrely, Tarrant had never been registered as a professional boxer; he just accepted some money to box locally. Although he never raced on the fells, preferring roads and longer and longer distances, he did train on the Peak District hills a lot when he lived in Buxton. Jones notes about Tarrant:

> Up in the shadow of Combs Moss and Axe Edge Moor, there were days when he never felt tired, when he felt he could run for ever, never happier than when climbing steeply, his mind at war with every sinew until the slope eased and he could allow himself one glance across the hilltops back towards Buxton ... which he reached faster, and with less effort, every time he wrenched on his pumps and braved the hilly air.

In his book Jones claims that Tom McNab had won £5 in the jumps at a 1956 village Highland Games which at the time resulted in a lifetime ban from competing in international athletics. Derek Ibbotson (Burnsall winner in 1953, remember) would personally choose prizes before competing in a race. Jones quotes Ibbotson as saying: 'I could ask for an appearance fee, because there were very few like me who could get a crowd in. The organisers knew what they were going to get, and I wasn't going to turn out for nowt.'

The professional races were usually shorter, and also featured quite small fields, often dominated by the same runners. But, they were run in front of vast crowds, often swelled by many tourists. Fred Reeves won the professional Fell Runners League in 1978 by winning a total of 31 races during the season (remaining unbeaten). Despite that dominance it was quite a season. For instance, at the Ambleside Sports race he won from Tommy Sedgwick, followed by Kenny Stuart. His win was his ninth, thus beating Bill Teasdale's record of eight wins. In the senior Guides Race at Grasmere Sports, Reeves won in the new record of 12 mins 21.6 secs, with previous record holder Sedgwick second, Graham Moffat third and Kenny Stuart fourth, the same positions they held in the Fell Runners League at the end of the season. Reeves, Sedgwick and Stuart also took the first three places at the Benson Knott race held with the Kendal Gathering Gala Sports. At this event there was also held the Men's Coalbag Carrying World Championships, which was won by guides racer Steve Parsons.

When Kenny Stuart was reinstated, his first race as an amateur was the Burnsall Classic. This is, according to the current Fell Runners Association, scheme a category 'A' race, over 1.75 miles, with 827 feet of ascent. It was in August 1982 and was the centenary race. Stuart lost to John Wild by 33 seconds, being roundly verbally abused by some of the crowd, presumably for having the nerve to change codes and forsake his professional career. However, to show his strength, and his racing range, Stuart won the 14 mile category 'A' Sedbergh race the very next day. Confusingly, Stuart had run the Duddon race in May (earlier that year of his reinstatement) and had outsprinted Billy Bland to win after a 21-mile-long tussle. High profile amateur athletes like Joss Naylor and Billy Bland faced a potential AAA ban for competing in this amateur race with Stuart, but it seemed to pass without notice. Actually, Kenny Stuart did not know if his reinstatement would take effect in time for the Burnsall, so he entered the Grasmere Guides Race as a professional and the Burnsall Classic as an amateur, to cover both options.

The professional side of the sport has evolved into 'open fell running'. This is administered by the British Open Fell Runners Association (BOFRA) who run regular short-distance events with a strong emphasis on junior races. The Fell Runners Association was set up in April 1970 to organise the duplication of an event calendar for the amateur sport. FRA now administers fell running in England, being affiliated to UK Athletics. As will be seen this has not been a smooth process. In theory the sport is really open now, with anyone able to run in any races they wish.

FRA's *Fellrunner* magazine, in its 1985 and 1986 issues, carried much correspondence relating to the whole amateur versus professional issue. It isn't pertinent to rehearse that here, as both the tone and sentiments expressed didn't reflect well on the sport and its participants. This discussion, together with international race activities and the introduction of sponsors, was creating cracks – as evidenced by a resignation from the FRA committee and a vote of no confidence in the FRA Chair at the time. It is worth noting the motion that was passed at the 1985 FRA AGM:

> The FRA recognises that in principle there is no difference between amateur and professional in our sport. The Committee is requested by this meeting to seek an end to this distinction by means of negotiation with the AAA (or by any other appropriate means).

However, stubbornness from the professional race organisation BOFRA let this whole situation drag on for a long while yet.

Professionals were allowed to be reinstated as amateurs. By 1986 only seven professionals had been officially reinstated – Pete Bland, Billy Bland, Tommy Robertshaw, Fred Reeves (so going amateur to professional and back to amateur), Kenny Stuart, Graham Moffat and Mick Hawkins. Pete Bland had won Ambleside as a professional in 1968, ten years after a motor bike accident, following which he was told he would never run again.

As an indication of the size of the fields at the time, the 1985 Grasmere Guides race had 48 entries. It was won by Duncan Gillies from Keith in Scotland, with Stephen Hawkins from Grassington in second place. Hawkins was the brother of the then recently reinstated amateur Mick Hawkins.

The FRA committee met in 1986, with AAA suggesting professional races could be included in FRA Calendar, and that there should be a moratorium on athletes (i.e. to open the sport). However, in the summer of 1987 BOFRA were accused of actually being a 'Closed' organisation. The pro/am issue rumbled on. The FRA Committee noted, even in March 1994:

> contact with BOFRA re-established and it is hoped that pro/am problems can be resolved before long. Ideas have been put to BAF

Fell and Hill Running Committee, and if these are endorsed, they will form basis of discussions with BOFRA.

A fuller explanation of this whole messy situation is detailed in Chapter 8, but first we take a look at the development of races over the years, initially in the 1800s.

CHAPTER 3

The early races – the 1800s

*The man who can drive himself further once the effort gets
painful is the man who will win.*

Sir Roger Bannister

It is not possible in the space available to give full histories of all the many
fell races that have been established over the years. This chapter concentrates
on the earliest ones, which in most cases are still being run in a similar way
to when they were first organised, and progresses in a roughly chronological
manner.

In passing, it is worth noting that some of the early races didn't get
properly established and fell by the wayside. Writing in *Cumbria* magazine
in 1975, R.W. Robson bemoaned the demise of several races that he used
to compete in. While acknowledging the continued importance of Grasmere
and Ambleside, he noted the demise of the race at Ullswater Sports to the
top of Heugh's Scar, and the Holme Sports race to the summit of Farleton
Knott. Others included Hilton-cum-Murton, racing to the summit of Roman
Fell, Dufton Pike from Knock sports field, the Bampton Sports race to the
top of Knipe Scar, together with the races at Mungrisdale, Patterdale and
Braithwaite.

The earliest significant event is the Grasmere sports, which were first held
in 1852, with a one-mile 'foot steeple-chase' being held in the field adjoining
the Red Lion Hotel. The six shillings prize money (*worth £17*) was won by
James Fleming of Grasmere. After the first recorded 'sports meeting' in 1852,

the lack of records suggests that either local interest was not high, or that the competition from established events such as The Ferry Sports in Windermere, was too great. Records of similar races exist for 1865 and 1866, but not for 1867.

The first **Grasmere Guides Race** to the top of Silver Howe[10], was held in 1868, and was won by George Birkett in 22 mins, his prize being £3 (*£137*). The programme included wrestling, high jumping, pole vaulting, flat races and a boat race (presumably literally, rather than the drinking variant) – it was a true 'sports' meeting. The venue moved in 1870 to Pavement End. Thanks to the enthusiasm of Joseph Fleming Green, and other like-minded sportsmen, the event became established. Since 1868 the Sports have been held annually, unbroken except for the duration of the First and Second World Wars. These days it is no longer necessary to smear tar and broken bottles along wall tops to deprive would-be spectators of a free vantage point.

There is no doubt that the influence of people like Lord Lonsdale, in inviting northern dignitaries, politicians, bishops, and even royalty on one occasion, to the various Sports had much to do with their success around the turn of the twentieth century. These contacts in high places were coupled with the organising skills of Joseph Fleming Green, who was a local slate quarry owner, and was the Honorary Secretary at Grasmere from the start. This, plus the authority and experience of Colonel Ridehalgh, the first Chairman who had worked on The Ferry Sports, helped to give Grasmere Sports a style which became the envy of other northern events.

The invitation to the likes of Lord Lonsdale[11] to become 'patrons' added lustre and was almost guaranteed to attract large crowds of 10,000 or more to what became the Blue Riband sports event of Northern England. Grasmere was now the place for athletes to compete, and also the place for ladies to parade their new fashions. The three main sports attractions at Grasmere have always been the Fell Race (or more correctly the Guides Race), Cumberland and Westmorland Style Wrestling, and the Hound Trails. Thus the annual Grasmere Lakeland Sports took shape, and by the early 1870s they were very well established. The prize money was not the highest, but what was available was usually spread as widely as possible amongst those taking part.

Early winners here included Robert Lancaster who was very succesful in the 1880s, winning four times. He was followed in the late 1880s by John

Grizedale who won in 1888 and 1890. Grizedale trained for three weeks before the race, with a regime that according to Miller and Bland involved:

> a walk round Thirlmere before breakfast. On the course for the last 14 days walked it twice a day and ran it once a day. Food mostly beef, chicken, eggs, port and brandy[12]. On the day of the race usually two or three light-boiled eggs, tea and toast at 6am and at 1pm a few milk biscuits and nothing more until the race.

The next athlete to emerge was Tom Conchie[13] in 1894, who won Grasmere five times up to the turn of the century. His time of 14 mins 26 secs, set in 1896, was the fastest on that version of the course. Conchie was a very successful runner, also winning at Pooley Bridge (a race no longer run) seven times, and had five wins each at Keswick and Bowness. He worked at the Shap granite works, and frequently performed exhibition runs for visitors at Shap Wells Hotel. He was very prolific, once winning nine events in one day, including two fell races. He also once beat Fred Bacon, holder of the world mile record, in a two-mile track race. It is said that Conchie on one occasion wanted to ensure a soft landing for himself, so laid a bed of bracken the day beforehand at the base of a high cliff he used to leap off on this early Grasmere course. On race day he was descending only to be shocked to discover, in mid air, that an opponent had removed the soft landing overnight.

Complaints about other unsporting behaviour or downright obstruction during the race were not unknown. You ran to the summit of Silver Howe, round the flag, handed over a piece of paper with your number on as proof, then descended on your chosen line over bracken, scree, rocks or whatever lay in your path. The Silver Howe summit was not visible from the sports field, so from 1881 the flag was placed at the second summit, which is slightly lower down. This meant that runners were visible to spectators throughout, and may have reduced the possibility of underhand tactics.

The venue for the Guides Race changed in 1904 to Broadgate Meadow, next to Grasmere Hall, seemingly because of a disagreement over terms with the previous field owner. The course now ascended Butter Crag[14], which is still the turning point. John C. Murray won the first race on the new course, having also won the last three on the previous course.

Ernest Dalzell then dominated the Grasmere Guides race for a few years. Dalzell was a small man, but was utterly fearless with his headlong plunges to victory. He was employed as a gamekeeper at Ormathwaite and mostly trained by walking or using races to get fit. He first won Grasmere in 1905 at the age of 21, and won it seven times in all. The *Westmorland Gazette* reported that 'he used to come down the fell any how, sometimes 'blood up', once carrying his running pumps in his hands'. A report of a race at this time in *Some Records of the Annual Grasmere Sports* notes:

> Dalzell, the winner, is a long way ahead, and comes in hundreds of yards in the lead, having made the round trip in 17 minutes. He is the only one who stands and talks after getting back; the others as they come in fall to the ground in various postures of extreme fatigue and their faces seen through the binoculars, are ghastly indeed. One gritty fellow has come half way down with one shoe lost and the other ankle badly wrenched.

More details of Dalzell's career appear in Chapter 7.

Tommy Metcalfe finished second at Grasmere to Dalzell in 1908, possibly because he had already won the mile beforehand. He had beaten Dalzell at Ullswater and Keswick. In 1910 Metcalfe won the Powderhall half mile.

Grasmere resumed after the war, in 1919 moving to the present start and using the Butter Crag course, with Jack Pooley winning. George Woolcock won in 1920 at the ripe old age of 17 years and one month, and repeated the win the next two years. Woolcock had been working at the Elterwater gunpowder works since the age of eleven. He was another of the great descenders, being nicknamed 'The Flying Devil'. He had an exceptional year in 1922, winning all but two of the 24 fell races he entered. In the latter part of the 1920s the Grasmere race was dominated by Ronnie Robinson, who won it six times, just failing to beat the race record. Robinson had great all round ability, being a winner at many mile and half mile events, yet winning over a hundred fell races in all. Later on, Ronnie Gilpin managed five Grasmere wins in the 1930s, before the war caused a break. Gilpin was also a good track runner, training on both grass tracks and on the fells.

Immediately after the Second World War, Stan Edmondson was dominant at Grasmere for a while. He won three times between 1947 and 1952. Then Bill Teasdale started his reign by winning in 1950, subsequently winning eleven in all. In the 1951 race Edmondson was third at the summit, but came through on the descent, to just beat Teasdale. Edmondson ran once more and then retired at just 27 years of age. In 1965 Teasdale brought Reg Harrison's record time of 13 mins 14 secs, which was set in 1957, down to 13 mins 5 secs. On the record run of 1957 Teasdale and Harrison went round the flag in 10 mins 30 secs, with Harrison recording an outstanding descent time of 2 mins 44 secs. Harrison's descents must have been a sight to see. For the 1962 race it was pouring with rain, and coming down he managed to fall six times, but succeeded in winning the race, just.

The race was then completely dominated for a decade by Tommy Sedgwick and Fred Reeves. The tussles over the Grasmere course between Sedgwick and Reeves in the 1970s are described elsewhere in this volume (see Chapter 7). Their rivalry did result in the record being brought down to 12 mins 57.5 secs by Reeves in 1974, and again by him to 12 mins 50.7 secs the next year. Sedgwick took it to 12 mins 24.8 secs in 1976 and Reeves finally brought it down to 12 mins 21.6 secs in 1978. The table illustrates just how dominant Reeves and Sedgwick were at Grasmere in this period, and how they forced each other to run faster in order to win.

Year	First	Second	Winning time
1969	Reeves	Sedgwick	13-27
1970	Reeves	Sedgwick	13-35
1971	Reeves	Sedgwick	13-19
1972	Sedgwick	Reeves	13-07
1973	Sedgwick	Reeves	13-06
1974	Reeves	Sedgwick	12-57.5 record
1975	Reeves	Sedgwick	12-50.7 record
1976	Sedgwick	Reeves	12-24.8 record
1977	Reeves	Sedgwick	12-40
1978	Reeves	Sedgwick	12-21.6 record
1979	Reeves	Sedgwick	13-07.4

Eventually in 1980 Kenny Stuart broke their stranglehold, taking a 30-second lead on the ascent and winning in 12 mins 37.5 secs. Reflecting on this race, Stuart is quoted in the *Westmorland Gazette* as saying:

> I knew I had to try to burn them off on the way up, so I went
> hard right from the start. Near the top, I thought I might have just

overdone it, but I struggled on alright, and when I looked round I
knew I was safe unless I fell.

Despite the best efforts of Kenny Stuart and others, the 12 mins 21.6 secs
remains the course record for this classic Guides race although Kenny has
recorded 12 mins 1 sec at the Butter Crag race held over the same course.
Incidentally, no Grasmere resident has ever won the Grasmere race.

Although in the nineteenth century the majority of races were professional,
there were also amateur races such as the **Hallam Chase** (in Sheffield). The
Hallam Chase is hailed as the sport's oldest amateur race, being first run in
1863. There is also a claim for the first cross country race of all, over a
ten-mile course the year beforehand. Despite it being amateur, there was
considerable gambling on this race, and sometimes shady events took place
in an attempt to make sure the bookies' favourite actually won. The Chase
is best described as a cross country fell race, which currently goes from
Hallam cricket ground to Stannington church and back, crossing the Rivelin
Valley twice. Although it had originally been held over ten miles, it is now
3.25 miles and is run as a handicap race. It has been held under AAA rules
since 1925. There was a break in 1938, and the war resulted in it not
restarting until 1951. The course record time for the Hallam Chase was set
in 1968. It is 19 mins 42 secs and was set by Hallamshire Harrier Trevor
Wright, who was later a silver medallist in the marathon at the 1971 European
Championships.

West of the Pennines, Rivington Pike has been a magnet for people for
centuries, and has religious connotations. Puritans used to meet there in
secret in the fifteenth century. There is also the tradition, whose origins are
lost in time, but certainly from the early nineteenth century, of locals walking
up Rivington Pike on Good Friday. Around the turn of that century the Pike
Fair was also established at Easter. By the 1960s there were claims of 60,000
visitors to the Pike Fair on the day.

In the 1830s races were held on Horwich Racecourse. However, athletic
clubs were only starting to be formed in the area in the 1890s, and these
tended to hold cross country or trail races (with a paper trail being laid).
Handicap races also took place, often with gambling being closely linked.
There are records from around this time of a race from the Pike *down* to

Rivington and Blackrod School as part of its annual sports day. A time of 3 mins 45 secs was recorded for the winner in 1894. Access through the farms on the lower slopes had to be negotiated for any such event. There were certainly some professional Pike races from the 1880s, with Tommy Gill claiming a record from an 1882 race that started at the Crown Hotel, Horwich.

The current **Rivington Pike Fell Race** was first held on Easter Saturday in 1893, making it the second oldest amateur fell race, although it has not been held continuously. The race originally started from the recreation grounds just west of Horwich railway works, as part of the Horwich Athletic Festival. It was actually held to celebrate the opening of a new wing of the Railway Mechanics Institute, which is still commemorated in the name of the current local club, Horwich RMI Harriers & AC. The original race was run as a handicap and seems to have been run until 1899, and was very much a gambling event rather than an athletic event. It attracted mostly people from a very local catchment area, but often with much gamesmanship because of the betting involved. In his book *Rivington Pike: history and fell race*, P.L. Watson gives a considerable amount of detail of these first seven races. He quotes from the local paper's report of the first race from 1893:

> The athletic sports, held on the recreation ground on Saturday, concluded the celebrations in connection with the opening of the Samuel Fielden wing and extension of the Mechanics Institute … £60 [£3,500] as prize money … 9 events on the programme … 273 entries … encouraging as a first festival … attendance of about 4,000 people (plus people on surrounding streets) … quite a number were attracted to the Pike and on the route there by the Rivington Pike Race … open bicycle races … open sprint, half mile and mile, quarter mile. The Rivington Pike Race brought out a fair number of starters.

The race was won by J. Fearnley from Bolton, with no time given. Completely separate to this series were two other races organised by the Horwich Harriers[15] around this time. In 1894 a closed race only for members of the Horwich and Chorley athletic clubs was held, it being won by Griffiths of Horwich. Then in 1902 Horwich Harriers, who had moved to the Railway Mechanics Institute and changed their name to Fielden Gymnasium Harriers, held a club race up the Pike and back. There is a considerable range of times given for these first events, and it is by no means certain where exactly they each started and finished.

After a break it was revived as an amateur race by Bolton United Harriers in 1929. It was seen as a good event to mark Bolton Civic week. The new race started and finished in Crown Square in Horwich, partly to avoid using the previous start area which was Horwich (now RMI) Harriers territory, and partly to use the Crown Hotel as the race HQ. It didn't go unnoticed locally that it was a Bolton club taking the initiative, not a Horwich one.

One man dominates this period of the history of the Rivington Pike Fell Race. Pat Campbell won nine out of the next ten races, only missing 1933 as he ran the London to Brighton relay race instead. His record of wins still stands. He set a record for this version of the course of 18 mins 6 and 6/16th secs[16] in the second race in 1930. Campbell also represented Great Britain in the two-mile steeplechase in 1934 and 1935.

The Second World War caused another break in the event for a while. As part of the victory celebrations for the war Horwich RMI staged a Pike race in June 1946. Then a War Memorial Gala race was held in 1947, but this didn't lead to regular racing again. The race was revived again by Horwich RMI Harriers in 1953, 1954 and 1955, but these races were restricted to members of the host club. At this time the start was moved from Crown Square to be from the gates by the park entrance at Lever Park Avenue, and the date moved back to Easter Saturday. It was stated that one reason for the races was to beat Campbell's 1930 time, but that is an irrelevance as not only was the course shorter but the intermediate ground had changed considerably.

In 1956 the race was opened out to all runners again, being organised by Horwich RMI from the Crown Hotel, and starting from the Lever Park gates. Bolton's Jack Haslam won in 17 mins 47 secs, which became the *de facto* course record. In the 1959 race Gerry North won convincingly in a new record of 16 mins 48 secs, having already established a lead of 150 yards as he rounded the tower. He actually claimed at a later date that it was probably the ONLY fell race he ever ran in. At this point the times for the race were usually recorded to nearest second, yet in 1967 Alan Blinston recorded 16 mins 47.8 secs for a new record, 4.2 seconds ahead of Ron Hill. In a style typical of the man, Hill had won the Salford 7.5 on the Friday and was running in the Beverley Marathon on the Sunday. In perfect conditions in 1971 Ron McAndrew raced to a new best of 16 mins 30 secs, despite having to pull one shoe back on during the descent.

On account of its reputation the Rivington Pike race has always attracted high quality athletes, with Olympians Ron Hill, Jeff Norman and Alan Blinston amongst those appearing on the winners list. Rivington Pike was Jeff Norman's first ever fell race. Norman says it has a special place in his heart and he recalled that 'Alan Blinston beat me in the first one by a couple of places. On the second one I was three places lower down but beat my time by over a minute. I had my first win in 1973, and then won again 1974.' Jeff Norman is still in the top 20 for times there. He went back aged 60 to get the M60 record, and then went back again at 65 to get that record too. A ladies race was introduced in 1978, at the time over a slightly shorter course. Carol Greenwood holds the women's record of 19 mins 38 secs from 1987.

In 1981 the organisers placed an advertisement in *Athletics Weekly* to try to generate interest in runners to attempt to beat the previous best time of 16 mins 30 secs. It paid off, as John Wild accepted the challenge and was at the very top of his form, having broken two big fell race records already on the previous two weekends. He won with a time of 15 mins 53 secs, in conditions that were described as perfect. It is intriguing to wonder what other fell running specialists like Wild might have done to the record. There is no record of either Kenny Stuart or Billy Bland coming over from the Lakes to run there, but Fred Reeves did so, winning in 1964, although in a time well off the record of the time.

The story of hill running on **Ben Nevis** goes back to 1895. William Swan, a Fort William hairdresser, dog breeder, and sporting man about town, made the first recorded timed ascent up the mountain. This was on, or around, 27 September 1895, when he ran from the old post office in Fort William to the summit and back in 2 hrs 41 mins. The next few years saw a fascinating series of runs achieved by all manner of people. The route to the top then would have been much as it is now, with five miles or so of bridle path, zig-zagging up the mountain, with a gradient of 1 in 5 at some points.

The first Ben Nevis race was held on 3 June 1898 under Scottish Amateur Athletic Association rules. Ten competitors completed the course, which started at the Lochiel Arms Hotel in Banavie and was thus longer than the route from Fort William. The winner was 21-year-old Hugh Kennedy, a gamekeeper at Tor Castle, who finished in 2 hrs 41 mins. The summit Observatory was still in operation and Kennedy's arrival at the summit was relayed to the crowd at the finish by means of a telegram. Within a few months a Mr MacDonald had established a new record for the 'official course' of 2 hrs 18 mins, although not in a race.

Regular Ben Nevis races were organised until 1903, when two events were held. These were the last for 24 years, possibly due to the closure of the summit observatory in 1904. The first was from Achintee, at the foot of the Pony Track, and finished at the summit. It was won in just over an hour by Ewen MacKenzie, the observatory roadman. The second race ran from the new Fort William post office, and MacKenzie lowered the record to 2 hrs 10 mins 6.8 secs, a record that he held for 34 years.

It is possible that there were some timed runs up Ben Nevis in between the World Wars, but no records or reports have survived. The Ben Nevis Race has been run in its current form since 1937, with no races in 1940-41 or 1945-50. The 1937 race was contested by just three runners and was won in 2 hrs 17 mins 52 secs by Charles Wilson, who at the time had the record for running Ben Lomond. Nine entered the race the next year, it again being run in June. In 1939 nine runners competed, and Daniel Mulholland, a recognised cross country expert, won in 2 hrs 3 mins 43 secs. The 1942 race had a 'Dorando Pietri' moment, when Duncan MacIntyre collapsed within sight of the finish, and because he was helped by his brother he was disqualified. The race was won by Charles Wilson in 2 hrs 25 mins 49 secs.

The race went from strength to strength in the 1950s and 1960s with a new start at King George V playing fields. There was a record for that version of the course of 1 hr 38 mins 50 secs by Peter Hall in 1964. The 1960s also saw the start of an English invasion of the event, with the record books showing many famous fell runners from south of the border, including Mike Davies of Reading AC, who was a very successful fell runner of the time, possibly with the highest profile ever from a 'southern' athlete.

The race is now usually held on the first Saturday in September. Since 1971 it has started and finished at the Claggan Park football ground which is on the outskirts of Fort William. The history of this race has been well documented. Hugh Dan MacLennan, writing in the *Journal of the British Society of Sports History*, concluded that:

It's a story of supreme athletic endeavour, from the entry of sixteen-year-old Kathleen Connachie in 1955, to the heroic achievements of Eddie Campbell who ran virtually every year for two decades uninterrupted from the 1950s; the death of John Rix in 1957, the only fatality recorded in the Race in over 100 years; Dave Cannon's five wins in six years in the 1970s; to the cancellation in 1980 as the runners gathered at the start line, and the near tragedy of a weather-induced evacuation of the mountain in 1988.

At the time of writing, the records for this course have stood unbroken since 1984. In that year Kenny Stuart and Pauline Haworth[17] of Keswick Athletic Club won the men's and the women's races with times of 1 hr 25 mins 34 secs and 1 hr 43 mins 25 secs respectively.

As well as the cancellation in 1980 there have been other controversies. In 1990 it was included in the FRA Championship roster, yet the need to impose an entry limit (which was reached five days before the advertised deadline for entries) restricted several top runners from gaining entry. The worst of it was that one of these was Colin Donnelly, whose exclusion meant he was unable to defend his title.

Different sources give different dates for the first **Burnsall Classic** race being held – varying from 1850, 1865 or a date nearer to 1870. At this time a group of villagers are reckoned to have discussed the idea in the Red Lion public house. The result of the discussion was that Tom Weston, a well-known local character, tested the course one moonlit night and ran it naked. For some reason, the local paper, the *Craven Herald*, did not report the race until 1882, in a report which neither named the winner nor the number of starters.

The Burnsall Feast Sports developed from an ancient festival held to celebrate St Wilfred, the patron saint of the village. The race itself had very small beginnings, with only three runners being noted for 1883, competing for a £2 first prize (£96), which was won by a runner named Mason. Records of these early years are not complete, but those that exist talk of runners doing the race in clogs, and for first prizes of lengths of suit material. Already fastest times were being noted though, with 19 mins 15 secs in 1903 and a new record of 17 mins 45 secs in 1906.

At this time, Tommy Metcalfe was running many of the local races. He famously used to bet people he could run 100 yards in 10 secs. Having taken bets he would then complete the run down the nearest slope, or convenient slag heap. Metcalfe's 1908 winning time at Burnsall of 14 mins 23 secs was a new record. There were doubters though, as it was so superior to the next best time, though he had set a record at Kilnsey Crag that year as well.

In *Stud marks on the summits* Bill Smith recalls a story about Tommy Metcalfe's nephew Arthur and his half-brother Bill, who crashed their motorbike on the way to the Burnsall race.

> The word was received at Burnsall that one brother was dead and the other severely injured. This news had been brought by a man who had passed shortly after the crash and had seen the bloody figures being treated on the road, though in actual fact neither one was dead, though both were badly battered. The next word to reach Burnsall was in the form of a request to postpone the start of the fell race till the Metcalfes arrived, for they still intended to run. When at last they appeared on the scene, they were given a heroes welcome.

The most famous Burnsall race occurred in 1910 when Ernest Dalzell, the legendary Lakeland runner, established his classic record of 12 mins 59.8 secs. His descent time was recorded as 2 mins 42 secs, although some doubted whether this was actually possible. Bill Smith devotes a whole page to this timekeeping dispute in *Stud marks on the summits*. He concludes with a quote from Roger Ingham stating that 'all people, except Metcalfe [the previous record holder] who witnessed the race, swore by Dalzell's record, and most said they had never seen anything like it in their life.'

The Burnsall Feast Race became an amateur event after 1931 (with the first such race being won by Pat Campbell), and a parallel professional event, organised by BOFRA, has been run over the same course a few weeks after the Feast date. In 1953 a special professional race was arranged by Burnsall Cricket Club, with an extra prize of £10 for breaking Dalzell's record. It was set up because Bill Teasdale had won at nearby Kilnsey Crag, and had suffered a bad head injury when a runner dislodged a rock onto his head at the steep chimney. Taking a wrong turn when leaving the hospital he ended up in Burnsall and decided to view the course, and thus roused local interest. Teasdale won the special race, but in a time of 14 mins 7 secs, well outside Dalzell's record.

Dalzell's time stood until 1977 when, in a special professional race for the Queen's Silver Jubilee, Fred Reeves achieved a time of 12 mins 48 secs (12 mins 47.2 secs according to some sources). A new professional race was established in 1980, won by Kenny Stuart, from Mick Hawkins, Graham Moffatt and Fred Reeves. Stuart's best time here was his 13 mins 33 secs in 1981.

As noted, an amateur race has taken place since the 1930s, although there appear to have been minor differences between the courses run. Highlights include Olympian Derek Ibbotson winning in 1953 (in 16 mins 21.4 secs), and new records of 14 mins 22 secs in 1955, and of 13 mins 56.8 secs in 1957 by David Humphries, who claimed that Dalzell's line of descent was too dangerous. In 1960 Peter Watson reduced the record to 13 mins 40 secs, and in 1970 Dave Cannon brought it down to 13 mins 29 secs and then 13 mins 20 secs two years later. Ricky Wilde apparently ran unofficially, with no number, in 13 mins 11 secs that day, a time which was officially achieved by Martin Weeks in 1973, and then beaten by him with 13 mins 1 sec in 1976.

Then in 1977, the same year that Reeves set 12 mins 47.2 secs in the professional race, Wilde ran 12 mins 50.2 secs. For some reason, he was allowed to run the direct line the professionals ran but which was normally denied the amateurs, which includes the grounds of a private property. In both cases there were still walls to be negotiated. Finally, in the amateur race John Wild also did a time of 12 mins 48 secs in 1983, and his and Reeves' times are the two fastest to be achieved in either of the races.

A race was first run at **Kilnsey Crag** in 1898, originally as part of the Kilnsey Sports. It has always been a professional event, except for 1933, where for one year it followed Burnsall by being run under AAA laws, before reverting back the next year. Due to its nature, going from the showground straight up Kilnsey Crag, it has always been a good spectator event. After being televised in 1980 it attracted an estimated crowd of 18,000 the next year. Independent TV chose a good year to record the race. Already Bill Teasdale had won the race seven times, and Fred Reeves had managed six wins, including a record time of 8 mins 3 secs in 1978. The televised race highlighted the emergence of Kenny Stuart on the professional scene. He just missed Reeves' record, winning from Mick Hawkins, Graham Moffatt, Fred Reeves and Tommy Sedgwick, a veritable who's who of the professional scene at the time. Stuart set a new record of 7 mins 46.5 secs the next year, which Hawkins reduced to 7 mins 35.8 secs a year later.

Moving into the next century, a spread of races became more evident, gradually moving from their North of England roots. The next chapter gives the background to some of the many races that were first held in the early part of the twentieth century, including the Lake District Mountain Trial, whose successful inauguration eventually was the pre-cursor to a big expansion in races in the Lake District.

CHAPTER 4

Development of a race calendar – the early 1900s

Hills are speedwork in disguise.

Frank Shorter

Northern England was still the hub of the development of races in the early 1900s, due to the greater concentration of urban areas nestled closely within surrounding fells. It should be noted that organisers in other areas were gradually setting up their own races. The following are some of the important ones that started in the first half of the century.

A race first took place up **Eccles Pike** in 1910. The current race trophy dates back to 1928, and there was an annual race until 1937. In 1969 it was revived by the local church social committee, holding the event initially in June. There was no fixed course and in some years lack of entries (for instance 1972 to 1975) meant it didn't take place. In 1977 the committee moved it to September, fixed the course at 3.5 miles, with 650 feet of ascent, and included a ladies race. It is now organised by Goyt Valley Striders and is renowned for being short, tough and demanding.

In 1934 a race up and down **Ingleborough** was held, to resolve an argument about how long it would take. The winner took 1 hr 0 mins 8 secs in that first event, a time which was reduced to 54 mins 25 secs the next year and down to 53 mins exactly by 1951. It was originally a professional race and was incorporated in the Ingleton Gala. Bill Teesdale showed his class by destroying that record the next year, finishing in a stunning 46 mins 35 secs. After a break it was revived as the amateur Ingleborough Mountain Race in 1973. The first **James Blakeley Fell Race** at Harden Moss Sheepdog trials, above Holmfirth, took place in 1937. There was a **Buckden Pike** professional race as part of the Buckden Feast in the 1940s and 50s, but it was discontinued for access reasons in around 1953, with Bill Teasdale having set the fastest time.

As well as the races noted that date from before the Second World War, several other notable races were established in the period prior to the establishment of the FRA (when the first race calendar as such was compiled). The Three Peaks was first run in 1954, Pendle in 1956, and in the mid-60s several Lakes classics were first held. Examples of the latter are Skiddaw and Fairfield in 1966, and Ennerdale in 1968.

An indication of the increasing numbers entering races is the fact that the third Skiddaw race in 1969 had 68 entrants, while ten years later it was taking more than 200 entrants, and popular races like the Three Peaks and Fairfield had entry limits. It also meant that some popular races had to change their course to accommodate larger numbers. The Three Peaks moved from a Chapel-le-Dale to a Horton start in 1974, while in 1971 the start of the Ben Nevis race moved out of the centre of Fort William. With increasing numbers, standards rose and records started tumbling, as will be seen from the record breakers summary later.

Over in Ireland, the **Slieve Donard Mountain Race** is the oldest mountain race there, having started in 1945. Initially, and for many years thereafter, the event was known as a 'go as you please'. Runners set off from the Newcastle Rural Council Office and the only checkpoint was the mountain summit. Then for several years the course went via the Bloody Bridge with a two-mile run along the road to the finish. In 1998 a decision was taken for safety reasons to go back to the original up and down route, but starting at the Newcastle Centre and returning to Donard Park. However, in 2002 a further route change took the finish back to Newcastle Centre to allow more spectators to witness the race. For some years Mike Short held the record with his 1977 run via the Bloody Bridge in 1 hr 4 mins 14 secs. The 2000 race was also a British Championship Race, and it was won by Ian Holmes in 50 mins 10 secs, the fastest ever up and down, but the finish was in Donard Park. The current course from the Newcastle Centre by any route to Donard summit and return to the centre is just under 5.5 miles in length with a climb of 850 metres. The record over this course is 54 mins 33 secs by Stephen Cunningham in 2010.

A race has been run at **Bradwell** as part of Wakes Week since 1946. The course was changed in 1981 to its current 3.75 miles with 600 feet of ascent, starting opposite the Samuel Fox Inn, Bradwell. Also in 1946 was the first **Hope Wakes Fell Race**, which is one of the oldest races in North Derbyshire. The first winner was Bob Randles, who lived in Hope. In the early days most runners were from Hope and the Hope Valley, often being only ten to twenty in total. The start was on Edale Road near the Church Shop, and the finish was on what is now Eccles Close. The race did not take place in the late 1960s and early 1970s. In 1974, local resident Martin Ashmore resurrected the event, working hard to re-establish the race. The nature of the race changed from being a locals-only race to attracting runners from further afield. In 1980, Derick Jewell took over the organisation of the race, having won the race the previous year. The course record for that variant was set in 1985 by Mike Bishop (Staffordshire Moorlands), with a time of 23 mins 46 secs. Jewell retired as organiser in 2005. No one came forward at that time to take on the mantle, so there was no race in 2006. At the start of the following year Steve Green and David Wing decided to resurrect the race. That first year they had 80 competitors. A Ladies Cup was introduced for the first time; this was named the Michael Coates Memorial Cup, in memory of the organiser of the marshals for many years. In 2009, after discussions with the competitors of the previous year, the route was changed to make it more demanding. It is now 5.9 miles with 1,483 feet of ascent.

Two other races started in the late 1940s, neither of which became more than predominantly local ones. In 1947 the **Eldwick Gala Race** was inaugurated, although it has not been held every year since then. However, it has been well established in recent years and is organised by Bingley Harriers, who say on their website[18] 'bring the family along for a great day out – burnt bangers, ice creams, spitfires, spice stalls and monkey shows etc. etc. all topped off with a lung splitting, eye bulging dash to the top of Hope Hill.' Then in 1949 the **Bamford Carnival Fell Race** was started, being won by local Sid Wilson. It remains fairly local, but it is a popular race which regularly attracts fields of over two hundred, and which includes Win Hill and its excellent views.

A keen eye will see that the main race developments were not happening in the Lake District, but elsewhere. However, in the 1950s more athletic clubs were starting to be formed in the area, such as Border Harriers in Carlisle. Along with the other athletes from running clubs in urban areas, such as Barrow, there was a move to break out into the hills and join the climbers and ramblers there. The existing guides races were often over very short courses, with steep ascents and hairy descents. Being professional, they were technically out of bounds for amateur athletic club members, not that some didn't race them anyway. With this backdrop, cyclist Harry Chapman proposed a Lake District mountain challenge over the fells. He was regional secretary of the YHA, and suggested it to celebrate his group's twenty-first anniversary. He brought the staggered start idea from cycle time-trials to his planned event.

This first event was held in September 1952; only YHA members were eligible, and they had to wear boots or walking shoes. It was based at Langdale's Old Dungeon Ghyll Hotel and was an impressive route, going via Bowfell, Esk Pike, Scafell Pike, Great Gable, Esk Hause and Rossett Gill. It attracted 21 entries and was won by Roland Moore in 3 hrs 42 mins 39 secs. Thus, the **Lake District Mountain Trial** was born. The booklet on its history records that 'a bonus above the other prizes and certificates – a barrel of cider for the winner from mine host Sid Cross – was duly shared and appreciated, with the remainder taken home aboard the winner's motor bike'. It was considered a success and was repeated in 1953, moving to May to celebrate this time the coronation of the Queen. It attracted only 15 starters, with Moore triumphing again. A shorter event for ladies attracted just four, and was won by Jane Allsebrook, who competed with her two dogs.

The event remained close to its roots for several years. This can be seen from the affiliations of the leading competitors for 1954, who were Joe Hand (Carlisle Holiday Fellowship Rambling Club), Fred Bagley (Preston Harriers – and Three Peaks race creator later that year), and George Brass (Pendle Ramblers). In that year guides racer Bill Teasdale entered unofficially, started out last and beat Hand home by 38 minutes, wearing lighter spiked fell boots. In order to expand, 1956 was the first year the event was organised by a committee not solely from YHA, and YHA membership for entrants was no longer required. The new committee was led by Harry Griffin, the noted writer and mountaineer. The event was sponsored by Griffin's employer, the *Lancashire Evening Post*, an arrangement that continued until 1964.

There was still not a smooth transition to pure fell running, with debates about the participation of 'harriers versus mountaineers' ensuing. The event was now changing venue each year. For 1956 it started from Seathwaite with the only stipulation being that competitors had to visit Pillar, Scafell and Scafell Pike (but with Broad Stand out of bounds). It was won again by Joe Hand, who wrote a piece for *Cumbria* magazine in which he described wearing:

> a hat, two long-sleeved vests, corduroy shorts, pair of scree socks, climbing stockings, and a pair of lightweight climbing boots. In the pockets were a compass, gloves, bottle of 'sustenance' and two sandwiches. All were used except the gloves and sandwiches.

Despite the kit, and his obvious speed over the terrain, he claimed to be first and foremost a fell walker.

Mention of Broad Stand above brings us to the subject of the most difficult obstacle facing fell runners on any of the standard fell race courses. Broad Stand is not traversed on any normal race, so my vote would be for the Bad Step on Crinkle Crags, which has to be descended in the Langdale race. Alfred Wainwright's *Pictorial Guide to the Lakeland Fells*[19] claims it to be the greatest potential difficulty to be found on any regular walker's path in the Lakes. Wainwright reckoned:

> Anyone descending at speed here is asking for a nasty fall. The impasse is usually avoided and the gully regained below the chockstone by an awkward descent of the rock wall to the left, which deserves the name 'The Bad Step', for it is 10 feet high and as near vertical as makes no difference.

Either way, fell runners will be seen charging like proverbial lemmings over the step in whatever way they think will work for them at the time.

In fact, the above-mentioned *Cumbria* magazine piece was a three-page letter by Joe Hand published in *A Cumbrian Letterbox,* defending himself against charges of being a 'pot hunter'. He says:

> I am not a 'pot hunter'. I deplore the whole idea of it and also the thoughtless attitude in which the label was given. Admittedly I am

a harrier in as much as I belong to the Border Harriers' Club, and on numerous occasions have run for them both on road and over country in the past two years, but I was not a harrier when I ran in the 1954 Langdale Trial, nor had I run a race of any description prior to that event. I was simply a member of the Carlisle Holiday Fellowship team.

He then goes on to give a long, but reasoned and eloquent, explanation of his 'manifesto' for the sport, which let us not forget was in its infancy. Hand's argument goes:

The act of improvising is great fun in fell-running; it is a joy to run a rocky descent; and a battle of wits develops between the runner and the mountain. Every step is a problem to be decided within a split second. No two descents are alike, and no descent is the same as it was the last time it was done … A fell runner knows that speed is already there for the plucking. To some it may go unrecognised, for it goes under another name, gravity. How to use it to best advantage needs a certain amount of skill, both physical and mental – enough, I think, to name it as a specific sport.

For the next year's mountain trial event the practice (which continues today) was established of only announcing full details of the course on the day. This decision was made in order to encourage a variety of route choices, and make navigation as important as running fitness. Gradually fields increased, with the 1958 event having Olympians John Disley and Chris Brasher as entrants. The event is now considered as having been pivotal in the development of fell running.

These early events were not without their incidents. At the 1961 event the organisers had to decide whether to disqualify an entrant who found a canoe when he came to a significant river and paddled it across, saving himself a couple of miles getting to a crossing point. They didn't – as they were pleased to get everyone home when the weather turned bad. The weather was even worse in 1962, as Harry Griffin reported in the *Lancashire Evening Post*:

On one of the most dreadful days of an appalling Lakeland summer, 29-year-old George Brass of Clitheroe was the only man to finish in yesterday's Lake District Mountain Trial. All other competitors, drenched to the skin by the incessant driving rain, buffeted and frozen by the cold gusty winds and lost half the time in thick mist, had retired.

Those retiring included Joe Hand, Eric Beard and Joss Naylor. Joss was lacking in protective gear when he cramped badly, and was reckoned to have possibly been in serious danger of exposure if several other competitors hadn't come across him and assisted him. George Brass came in to the finish carrying his left shoe, which rocks had ripped to bits throughout the event, and which had been a useless encumbrance for the last a mile or so.

The interpretation of rules affects many sports, sometimes in a not too serious way. In *Fifty Years Running* (the history of the Mountain Trial) John Disley recounts this story of the 1963 event:

> I was not having a good day and my wife had stood for some forty minutes with a glass of shandy in her hand before I appeared [it was a loop course]. I did not particularly fancy a fizzy drink, but for the sake of marital relations I took it. Harry Griffin was standing close by and witnessed this infringement of the rules. I struggled onwards and … to my shame I was passed by the Olympic 200m runner George Ellis (Keswick AC). I finally completed the course and reached the Old Dungeon Ghyll. Harry proudly informed me that I was disqualified. I asked him why he hadn't done so 2 hours before!

A major change took place in 1965 with the formation of the Lake District Mountain Trial Association (LDMTA). Harry Griffin was the first President and the aims were 'the furtherance of the sport of Fell Running in Mountain Trials, Races, Tests of Endurance and similar athletic events'. The draw that the event had is shown by the determination of Chris Brasher to compete in the 1965 race. He flew back from a commitment in Stuttgart on Saturday night and then drove up from London with a 5am start. Starting last in the staggered handicap-style start, he finished twenty-third in this toughest of events.

Vaux Breweries also came on board as main sponsor, which arrangement continued until 1982. The extra sponsorship enabled the provision of field showers by the Army. These were powered by generators, as the venues now moved from pubs to farms and other locations able to accommodate more entrants. A limit of 150 was set for 1970, which increased to 227 in 1982 (including 27 women). There was also a change in composition of the entrants. For 1966 it was estimated that about one-third were from athletic clubs, which by 1982 had become over two-thirds. When it came into existence the FRA initially classified the event as an 'A' category, but this was changed to 'O' (orienteering) category in 1979, with its course disclosure at the start and staggered interval start times.

The event's orienteering nature started attracting leading orienteers to the trial. In 1967 ten members of the British Orienteering Team entered. They were led by Gordon Pirie, who was British 'O' Champion at the time. Pirie finished third, and Chris Brasher came in ninth (aged 38). The changing status was shown by Brasher leading his club Southern Navigators to first team, the first 'southern' club to do so. Gordon Pirie was reported to have asked his team sponsor (Glaxo) to make up a special food mixture of Complan and Glucodin, packaged in toothpaste tubes. It was hard to get down without loads of water and wasn't that tasty either, and the tubes were thrown away on route. John Disley was struggling and came across some discarded, but not empty tubes. The content so revived him that he was able to finish strongly in tenth place.

The 1969 race was in Wasdale and signalled Joss Naylor's entry on what was his home ground. It also attracted Olympians-turned-orienteers Martin Hyman and John Disley, as well as Bruce Tulloh. Tulloh had just completed his run across America, and found this event even tougher, and had to retire. The year 1971 saw the start of Joss Naylor's dominance, with him winning the first of seven consecutive events, this time starting last and finishing first. The organisers were getting tougher too, rejecting six applicants on the grounds of inadequate experience. As a footnote, Bill 'Studmarks' Smith ran his best ever trial in 1974, coming twelfth and helping Clayton-le-Moors to second team place.

Joss Naylor ended up winning the event ten times in all, with Billy Bland finishing his run with his first victory in 1978, in Buttermere. This was Bland's first of nine wins in all in the trial. For the ladies Sue Parkin has been the most successful, with a record of eight wins out of nine tries. *Fifty Years Running* reported some interesting research that took place at the 1988 trial, where competitors were asked to weigh themselves before and after the event. The average weight loss was 87 ounces for men, with a range of 144 to 32; the average for women was 46 ounces, with a range of 64 to 28.

After the reigns of Joss and Billy, there was a changing of the guard in 1992 when Gavin Bland beat his uncle Billy into second by three minutes, in Borrowdale – Billy's home valley. In 1998 a Short Trial was introduced, with a distance of around ten miles and approx 3,000 feet of ascent.

After the sponsorship of the *Lancashire Evening Post* and Vaux Breweries, the mantle was taken on by the Ordnance Survey[20] from 1983 to 1993. The OS eventually stopped the sponsorship because they felt they weren't getting enough exposure for their money. John Disley and Chris Brasher had connections with Reebok and that company took over as sponsors from 1994 to 1997. At the end of this period John Disley commented that 'Reebok's sponsorship, alas, has moved on. What the company now pays Liverpool FC to provide the team clothing would enable the Mountain Trial to put a roof over most of the course'.

For one year there was no main sponsor, but several willing smaller ones, before the Climbers' Shop in Ambleside took over. After the Ordnance Survey sponsorship finished the event moved to using Harvey's Maps. Unfortunately, in 1999 the maps were wrongly printed by a contractor and the map image wore off when folded and handled in the field, causing several competitors to retire.

It was some equipment from the Climbers' Shop that I was using when I took part in the event in Eskdale in 1985. The race report records that it was 'the wettest summer for 100 years, and the fells were waterlogged'. The course was from Dalegarth, and took in Cowcove Beck, Great Knott, Rossett Pike, Round How under Broad Crag, Whin Rigg, Boat How and Blea Tarn. That year I had run 2 hrs 34 mins 53 secs in the London Marathon and was reasonably fell-fit, thus had no qualms about tackling the event when I entered. Being a relative novice I was set off very early in the staggered starts. My training diary has the following telling entry for the day:

OS Mountain Trial. Started off 7th (1 min staggered starts). Soon up into 2nd place – but proceeded to get lost before 1st checkpoint. Going OK until Rossett Pike. After that wanted to give up! Very knackered at end. Fell in stream!

Looking at the map now, this will have been Whillan Beck. I was so tired that I stumbled and went in up to my neck, map, kit and all. This wouldn't have been too bad but for the fact it was just before the finish field, and that my wife and friend were there to 'support' me and saw it all. Much amusement and a photo ensued, which I don't intend to share with readers.

Further afield, the **Goatfell Race** was held on the Isle of Arran from 1953 to 1961, and the **Cairngorm Hill Race** from 1957 to 1962, both being revived in the 1970s. Also in Scotland at this time the **North Berwick Law Hill Race** commenced in 1958 as part of a gala, but has never reached out from its local status.

More significantly, a major race was inaugurated in Yorkshire in 1954. The year 2004 was the fiftieth anniversary of **Three Peaks Race**, and the commemorative leaflet published that year contained the following:

> The very first Three Peaks Race in 1954 attracted a grand total of 6 entries. By the mid 70s, in excess of 2,000 entries were being received every year! Behind the scenes, an enormous amount happened over the years, as the race developed into the blue ribbon race it undoubtedly is. Growing popularity brought endless headaches in its wake, not least the organiser's ability to provide a competitive and adventurous event while still ensuring reasonable levels of safety. After that first race, Preston Harriers took up the baton for the second event but the next 8 were organised by Clayton-le-Moors Harriers, always a leading club in fell running. By 1963, the entry had grown from that original 6 to about 150 and this was getting to be too onerous for one club alone to support. Clayton approached other enthusiastic fell running clubs and with the support of Lancaster and Morecambe Harriers, Bingley Harriers and Leeds St. Mark's Harriers, the Three Peaks Race Association was formed with the specific remit of organising the Three Peaks Race. Its first secretary was Alf Case, who had been deeply involved in the organisation of the race on behalf of Clayton and the committee was drawn together from the representative clubs. That association continues through to the present day.

Fred Bagley of Preston Harriers was responsible for setting up the Three Peaks Race, having already competed in the Lake District Mountain Trial.

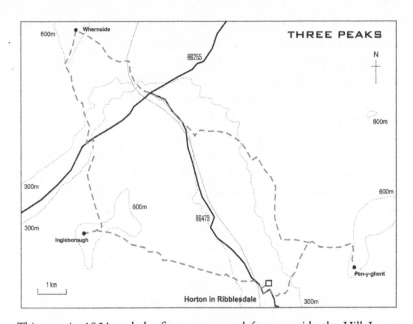

This was in 1954 and the first race started from outside the Hill Inn at Chapel-le-Dale. The start was later moved to the field behind the Inn. Bagley himself won the first race. He took 26 min 30 secs to reach a misty Ingleborough, which anyone who has been there will know can be confusing in poor visibility. He led the field off route on descending but retrieved the situation at Sulber Nick. From Horton to Pen-y-Ghent the route took a direct line over the intakes and up the fell's steep south western flank, between the crags. Stan Bradshaw (Clayton-le-Moors) reached the second peak in second place and then caught Bagley at High Birkwith, although they took different routes beyond Nether Lodge. Bagley was on the road while Bradshaw went via the fields. Bagley managed to arrive first at Ribblehead after two and a half hours running, but performed less well on the steep ascent of Whernside, which was reached via Winterscales Farm. However he pulled it back together and came down to the Hill Inn in a total time of 3 hrs 48 mins. Bradshaw took second place in 4 hrs 6 mins, after coming down from Whernside too early and coming across rough boulder fields, while fellow Clayton runner Alf Case finished third in 5 hrs 12 mins.

It took 16 years for the three-hour barrier to be beaten, by Frank Dawson of Salford Harriers. In 1970 Jeff Norman (Altrincham AC) achieved the first of his six consecutive victories. Four years later he won the Fell Runner of the Year title and became the only man to get under 2 hrs 30 secs for that version of the course, clocking 2 hrs 29 mins 53 secs in bad weather. There have been alterations over time due to erosion, artificial surfacing of bits of the Pennine Way, and to the wishes of farmers whose land the route crosses. The race was also becoming more and more popular, and a race limit of 350 runners was imposed in 1970. The need for more space and facilities precipitated a move of the start to Horton-on-Ribblesdale, with consequent minor route changes in 1975. Pen-y-Ghent thus now became the first peak, followed anti-clockwise by Whernside and then Ingleborough. Minor route changes also took effect in 1983 and 1986, the latter moving the ascent of Whernside further north.

With the route variations there were obviously new records to be set. Jeff Norman set the 1975 course variant record in the inaugural year, when he came home in 2 hrs 41 mins 37 secs. This was taken down to 2 hrs 37 mins 30 secs by John Wild in its last year of use, in perfect conditions. Kenny Stuart set the new record for the 1983 course, 2 hrs 53 mins 54 secs, in good weather but over a heavy course. This variation finished up at 2 hrs 49 mins 13 secs by Hugh Symonds in 1985. The 1986 changes made it longer still and Shaun Livesey set a new record of 2 hrs 56 mins 40 secs, which he then brought down to 2 hrs 51 mins 45 secs four years later, it being reckoned that the artificial paths had accounted for some of the time gained. Earlier Horton had been just about cut off by snow in 1981 and that year's race had to be postponed till October. The current record is Andy Peace's 2 hrs 46 mins 3 secs from 1996.

The first ladies race over the Three Peaks course took place in 1979 when Jean Lochhead (Airedale and Spen Valley), a track, cross country and cycling international, defeated an 11- strong field with a time of 3 hrs 43 mins 12 secs. This time was lowered to 3 hrs 35 mins 34 secs a year later in much better conditions by her clubmate, Sue Parkin, who was a champion orienteer. The fastest time on the 1983 route was Vanessa Brindle's 3 hrs 38 mins 10 secs in 1985. Carol Walkington set the initial record for the 1986 route with 3 hrs 49 mins 12 secs, and this she reduced in 1988 to 3 hrs 32 mins 43 secs, coming seventieth overall in a field of 410. Anna Pichtrova, from the Czech Republic, holds the current record of 3 hrs 14 mins 43 secs from 2008, when the Three Peaks hosted the World Mountain Running Championship.

A Junior race took place up Whernside from the Hill Inn between 1970 and 1974, twice being won by Dave Cannon. From 1975 to 1980 the Juniors ran from Horton to Ingleborough and back. There was no Junior race in 1981, and then from 1982 it has been Pen-y-Ghent and back, with Shaun Livesey the first winner.

Elsewhere, several fell races are run on different parts of Pendle, the so-called 'Hill of the Lancashire Witches', making its elongated summit ridge probably the most visited by fell races in Britain. Historians reckon that these 'witches' were no more than criminals who used their evil reputations to intimidate superstitious country people. Indeed it is said that the continuing prominence of such folklore is to a great extent due to romantic novels such as Robert Neill's *Mist Over Pendle*. As an aside, I do like the optimism shown by the old saying (not uniquely tied to this particular location actually), which goes 'if you can see Pendle, it's going to rain: if you can't see Pendle, it's raining'.

In the early 1900s George Coward, a local farmer and guides racer, descended from Pendle's summit to the farm at Smithfield, Downham inside 20 minutes, for a bet. In the 1990s Clayton-le-Moors revived this idea with a downhill race to the Wellsprings Hotel, with runners being asked to predict their time, but not allowed to wear watches.

The original **Pendle Race** was 6.5 miles long and started at the Bay Horse Inn at Roughlee, and it was first held in 1956. A new course was incorporated in 1974, starting from Barley, near Burnley. It is now 4.5 miles long with 1,500 feet of ascent. The original record for this course was set in that year by Harry Walker, with 30 mins 29 secs, and it held up for seven years. A ladies race over the full course was added in 1977. In 1981 John Wild was coming through in the sport and comprehensively beat the record for Pendle. His 29 mins 27 secs was the first of several records he set that year. Clayton-le-Moors Harriers started the **Pendleton Race** in 1956, it being associated with Pendleton Village Sports. There had earlier been a professional race to the summit of Wiswell Moor and back. Up to 1980 the amateur Pendleton race involved an ascent to the Devil's Apronstones on Apronfull Hill on the Pendle ridge, with the return by the same route. The race provided Ron Hill with his first fell race victory in 1958, and he won it several times subsequently. The race is now lengthened to be over five miles, with 1,500 feet of ascent. The first **Tour of Pendle** race took place in 1982, having 11 checkpoints and

4,200 feet of ascent in its 17 miles. Kenny Stuart won the first race on 2 hrs 22 mins 7 secs. For the one year in 1989 there was a **Half Tour of Pendle** on the same day over nine miles. Since 1990 the shorter race moved to a separate date.

The sequence of races based around the Pendle area show the very active race promotion work done by the local athletic clubs, but similar clubs were starting to be established elsewhere. The early ones were branching out into establishing new fell races in the Lakes and Scotland, as will be seen in the next chapter.

CHAPTER 5

Expansion of the calendar – the 1960s onwards

If the hill has its own name, then it's probably a pretty tough hill.
Marty Stern

The 1960s saw a rapid expansion in the fell race calendar, eventually leading to the publishing of a formal calendar of events when the Fell Runners Association was formed in 1970. This period saw some of the classic races established, such as Thieveley Pike and the Ennerdale Horseshoe.

Clayton-le-Moors Harriers were actively promoting new races at the beginning of the 1960s, adding **Thieveley Pike** in 1960, held from the Ram Inn. Before the Second World War there was a professional race here, in which some locals were inclined to run in clogs. The new race soon became popular, and in 1969 there had to be added a lap of the initial field in order to spread the field out. Records for this version of the course were set by Dave Cannon and Brian Robinson. The course had to be changed again in 1980 due to landowner objections, with minor alterations again in 1981. It has been quoted at distances from three miles upwards over the years and it is now a 4.5 mile course with 900 feet of ascent.

John Reade won the first running of the new version in 1981, with 26 mins 22 secs in poor conditions. Kenny Stuart reduced that to 24 mins 42 secs the next year. The story of Stuart's win over Wild to seal the British Championship in 1983 is detailed later (in Chapter 10). Suffice it to note here that it produced an exceptional new record of 22 mins 57 secs, on a

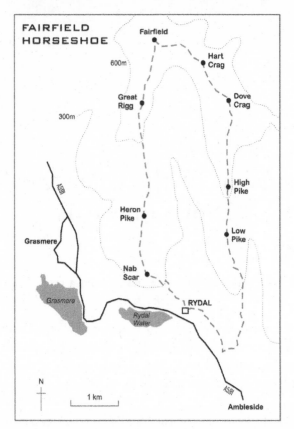

fine day with just a little mist on the summit. Stuart was pushed hard by Wild, and this also brought the next five runners inside the record. The route had to be changed again due to access issues, and now comes back on itself instead of descending to the east. The record for this new, significantly longer, version is 30 mins 44 secs by Rob Hope in 2006, with a women's record of 35 mins 41 secs by N. White from the same year.

After successfully organising the Mountain Trial, the Lake District Mountain Trial Association decided to branch out. In 1966 they organised the first **Fairfield Horseshoe Race,** which is considered to be the first of the classic Lakeland 'horseshoe' races. It started and finished in Rydal Park and took in Nab Scar, Heron Pike, Greatrigg Man on the way up to Fairfield and continued clockwise over Hart Crag, Dove Crag, High Pike and Low Pike, before returning to Rydal Park. The course has remained very similar, except for a change on Nab Scar in 1977 due to erosion, which added three-quarters of a mile to the length. Peter Hall won the first race in 1 hr 22 mins 35 secs, and this was brought down gradually to eventually be 1 hr 8 mins 30 secs by Dave Cannon in 1972, in his first season as a Senior.

When the race line on Nab Scar was changed a ladies race was introduced, being won by unattached runner Pauline Cushnie[21]. The initial record on the new course in 1977 was Mike Short's time of 1 hr 14 mins 46 secs. This was reduced by Short to 1 hr 13 mins 24 secs the next year, and then to 1 hr 11 mins 26 secs by Ricky Wilde in 1979. John Wild included the Fairfield race in his record-breaking spree in 1981, bringing it down to 1 hr 10 mins 5 secs. At that time the organisers used to create a gap in the wall just below Low Pike and you headed straight down towards the finish. Minor changes were made in 1988, and then in 1992 there was a significant route change, bringing athletes almost to Low Sweden Bridge before turning them right to join the track which goes back to Rydal Hall. The change was forced on the organisers due to runners practising the final descent, which was across 'private' land. The change increased the length of the race, with a new record of 1 hr 18 mins 53 secs being set by Craig Roberts. The course record for the longer course is now 1 hr 15 mins 11 secs by his brother Mark Roberts, from 2000. The race is now organised by Ambleside AC. It is an 'A' category nine miles with 3,000 feet of ascent.

Also inaugurated in 1966 by the LDMTA was the **Skiddaw Fell Race**, starting from Fitz Park in Keswick. It goes round the side of Latrigg before taking the main tourist track up and back down Skiddaw, before returning to the park. Keith Boyden won the first race in 1 hr 8 mins 34 secs, with Chris Fitt reducing the record to 1 hr 6 mins 7 secs the next year. Jeff Norman brought it down to 1 hr 4 mins 55 secs in 1969, and then again to 1 hr 3 mins 5 secs the next year. Dave Cannon reduced it to 1 hr 2 mins 30 secs in good conditions in 1973. The first ladies race was run in 1978, won by Jean Lochhead in 1 hr 21 mins 42 secs from Rosemary Cox[22]. The current record is one of Kenny Stuart's long-standing ones, being 1 hr 2 mins 18 secs from 1984. The women's record is held by Sarah Rowell, with her 1 hr 13 mins 29 secs from 1989.

There used to be a walker's challenge early last century around the **Ennerdale Horseshoe**. The current race was started in 1968, starting at the foot of Ennerdale Water and taking in Great Borne, Red Pike, Black Beck

Tarn, Green Gable, Kirk Fell, Pillar, Haycock, Iron Crag and Crag Fell. This was some 23 miles with 7,500 feet of ascent. It was originally organised by West Cumberland Orienteering Club, which included Joe Long, who was warden of the Ennerdale Scout Activity Centre, where it started from. It changed to be under the umbrella of the Cumberland Fell Runners Association two years later. For the inaugural race Joss Naylor entered, despite having had virtually no training. Despite that, he beat Mike Davies, who had achieved a run of four consecutive Three Peaks race wins earlier that year, winning by three minutes in four hours exactly. Joss Naylor not only dominated the early years of the race but also reckoned it to be his favourite race, claiming it had three elements that particularly appealed to him, being 'fast running in some parts, plenty of rough ground, and a lot of short, hard climbs'.

It has always been considered a tough course, especially in poor weather. Thick mist in 1973 caused even top fell runners to be completely lost for long periods. This didn't stop Joss Naylor winning by 18 minutes, just three minutes off the course record. Naylor even managed to win the race the next year, despite having been off work with a badly strained back.

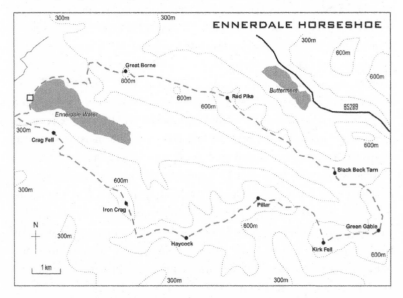

Mike Short finally broke Naylor's winning streak in 1977, just beating Billy Bland in 3 hrs 41 mins 11 secs, with Naylor coming in third, by now being a veteran. In 1978 Andy Styan came home in a new record of 3 hrs

27 mins (3 mins 40 secs faster than Naylor's 1972 record time). Styan brought that down to 3 hrs 23 mins 44 secs the next year, ahead of Joss Naylor and Billy Bland, who both set best times for the course that day. Veronique Marot applied to run in 1979 and was refused entry. She ran anyway, taking 5 hours and beating many of the male runners. Mist and rain meant that only 38 of 148 starters finished in 1980, but Billy Bland showed he had passed his apprenticeship and sailed round in a new record of 3 hrs 21 mins 4 secs, over 15 minutes ahead of Styan.

Sadly, similar conditions the next year resulted in a fatality, when Bob English went off course on the way to the last checkpoint and fell badly. He was found unconscious with serious head wounds, and died subsequently while being taken to hospital. He had entered this particular race for the first time, but was an experienced fell runner, having recently done the Bob Graham Round.

In 1985 Kenny Stuart sliced just seven exceptional long-standing marks. Women were officially allowed to run from 1980 and Pauline Haworth led the five finishers home in 4 hrs 37 mins 47 secs. Pauline set a record of 4 hrs 27 mins 52 secs in 1985, in what was her third championship winning year. The women's mark is now 4 hrs 1 min 33 secs by Janet McIver from 2008.

The **Manx Mountain Marathon** was conceived by George Broderick in 1966. His original plan was for a hill walk from Ramsey in the north of the Isle of Man to Port Erin in the south, starting and finishing at the town's two youth hostels. Initially, the idea was to complete the distance in under ten hours. In 1968 Tony Paine, from East Grinstead, arrived at Port Erin youth hostel 9 hrs 50 mins after setting out from Ramsey. Once the challenge had been proven possible, George Broderick held discussions with the various bodies to try and organise a race for the following year. Unfortunately Easter 1969 proved too much of a rush, so it was decided that Easter 1970 would be the first running of the challenge. The resulting event is a serious athletic challenge, with its 31 miles of rugged terrain taking in 11 of the Isle of Man's main peaks. May and Bill Lloyd, the wardens at Port Erin youth hostel, found an old trophy lying in a cupboard, polished it and presented it to the winner. The Lloyd Trophy is still awarded to this day.

In the inaugural race the entrants set off in appalling weather conditions. At one stage the organisers had decided to cancel the event, but the runners persuaded them to let competitors carry on. Although the event was primarily for walkers, the fell runners actually went a fair bit quicker than anticipated. This resulted in some marshals arriving at the checkpoints at the same time as the runners. An even bigger problem arose at the finish when Bob Meadowcroft arrived at the youth hostel before the timekeeper did. Fortunately the wardens were standing outside and after checking watches agreed the winner had taken 5 hrs 47 mins. Only 12 competitors out of the 74 starters made it to the finish, as the blizzard conditions forced the majority of the field to retire.

In 1971 competitors faced warm conditions, which saw Bob Meadowcroft repeat his win, improving his time to 4 hrs 48 mins, with Debra Gale being the first lady to complete the race. Alan Heaton, the second runner to complete the Bob Graham Round, finished fourth. At the time he was the Lake District 24 hours peaks record holder. In 1972 the start was moved to Ramsey's market square and the finish to Bradda Glen café, with the race being won by Joss Naylor. Stan Bradshaw, the third runner to finish the Bob Graham Round, also competed, a few months before he became the first to run the 270-mile Pennine Way. In 1973 the climbs at Fleshwick and Milner's tower were included, the route having previously gone via Surby and Bradda East. Joss Naylor won for a second time although not without some controversy, as he appeared to have not ascended the climb at Fleshwick.

For 1974 three classes with different starting times were introduced, elite for runners under 6 hours, standard 6 to 7½ hours, and walkers (although they were allowed to run) 7½ to 10½ hours. Joss Naylor won for the third time in succession and established a new course record of 4 hrs 32 mins 2 secs. One story goes that Joss flew back to Blackpool and was back on his farm in Wasdale before the last runner had finished the race. In 1975 British fell running champion Jeff Norman won, improving the course record to 4 hrs 24 mins 55 secs. Naylor won for a fourth time in 1976 improving the course record again to 4 hrs 23 mins 35 secs, achieving his victory despite now being a veteran.

Then British fell running champion Mike Short scored a hat-trick of wins improving the course record to 4 hrs 15 mins 53 secs in 1979. In 1980 future British fell running champion Colin Donnelly produced the best performance ever in the event, winning in an astonishing 4 hrs 2 mins 11 secs. Wendy Dodds won in 1979 and 1980 improving the ladies' record to

5 hrs 52 mins 58 secs. Then in 1987 Greeba summit was included instead of Beary, which increased the distance by half a mile and the three miles of road were replaced by cross country and tracks, and the descent of Fleshwick went to the beach instead of across the field. Brent Brindle set the record on the revised course of 4 hrs 28 mins 12 secs. On three occasions Brindle beat British fell running champion Jack Maitland, who never achieved that elusive win.

Wendy Dodds won the ladies race for the fourth time in 1991 shattering the record with 5 hrs 31 mins 24 secs. In 1998 the course was lengthened in the Slieu Whallian area and the finish was moved to the Cherry Orchard Hotel. This resulted in the distance increasing by a mile to 31.5 miles. Andy Hauser won for a record sixth time in 4 hrs 53 mins 13 secs and Brenda Walker won the ladies race for a second time in 5 hrs 53 mins 12 secs. In 2000 the elite and standard classes were combined and the course length was reduced slightly in the Greeba area and also in Port Erin with the new Ocean Castle Hotel finish. Colin Donnelly returned in 2002 to win for the third time, 21 years after his first two wins. His time of 4 hrs 39 mins 27 secs was a record for the new course. The current men's record is Lloyd Taggart's 4 hrs 22 mins 45 secs from 2007.

The **Carnethy Hill Race** was added to the calendar in 1971. The idea of the race came from Jimmy Jardine, of Peebles, with the intention being to commemorate the Battle of Roslin which had been fought in the area. The race programme of 1976 records that:

> in February 1302, a messenger arrived at Neidpath Tower to ask Sir Simon Fraser to meet someone at Biggar. Sir Simon Fraser rode hard, for the person he was to meet was none other than Scotland's hero – Sir William Wallace. Wallace's plan was for himself to be seen gathering together an army up north, while Sir Simon waited with the main army in the south. Sure enough the plan worked, for when the English heard that Wallace was getting ready to attack from the north, they left their winter quarters in Edinburgh heading south – Sir Simon waited.

The inaugural race started and finished in the public park in Penicuik and climbed only Carnethy, a return distance of some nine miles. From 1972 to 1980 the route was changed to climb Carnethy and Scald Law from the public park. In 1979 ladies were included for the first time, with Anne Bland winning. In 1980 due to thick fog, the road crossing onto the Pentlands was deemed too dangerous, so the race was changed to a cross country race round Penicuik, in which 26 entrants ran. However, many fell runners decided to ignore the police and organisers, and a total of 103 (including such high profile runners as Colin Donnelly, Billy Bland and Mike Short) had an unofficial race up on to the hills anyway. After that the course was changed to the current one starting in the field at Silverburn and covering five hills, which avoided any road and made it a true fell race, now being called the Carnethy Five. The current records are held by Gavin Bland and Scotland's prolific racer, Angela Mudge.

The first **Welsh 1000 Metres Race** in 1971 had 19 entrants. The fell runners class was won by Dennis Weir in 3 hrs 47 mins, two minutes outside Ted Norrish's unofficial 1970 record. In the following year Joss Naylor won in 3 hrs 37 mins, which was to be his best time. Joss won the race for five consecutive years. Mike Short broke Naylor's record by 45 seconds in 1978. In 1979 access problems required the course to be re-routed. Mike Short won the new race and was to dominate the event into the 1980s (with five consecutive victories). Since then the race has been won four times by Colin Donnelly who in 1992 set a new record for this course of 3 hrs 37 mins 56 secs. The women's record was set in 1991 by Carolyn Hunter-Rowe in a time of 4 hrs 30 mins 53 secs.

Cumberland Fell Runners Association inaugurated the **Wasdale Fell Race** in 1972. The Wasdale race is 21 miles long with 9,000 feet of ascent, and is considered one of the hardest of fell races, containing much very rough going. It is also the 'Long' category fell race with the second highest feet per mile climbing ratio. It has an average of 429 feet of ascent for each of its 21 miles, compared to Bens of Jura's 453 feet for each of its 17 miles. The Wasdale route is roughly circular, starting from the campsite at the head of Wastwater. The checkpoints are on Whin Rigg, Seatallan, Pillar, Great Gable, Esk Hause and Scafell Pike, finishing down the nose of Lingmell. Originally the descent was via Lingmell Col, Brown Tongue and Lingmell Gill, but in its second year a new checkpoint was added on Lingmell itself to give spectators a better view of the run-in down the steep fellside. The valley section from Whin Rigg to Seatallan was changed slightly in 1978, which made it marginally longer.

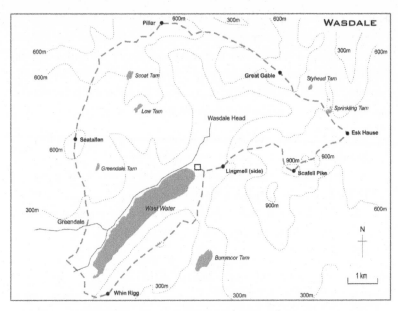

It was fully expected that Joss Naylor would win in his home valley in 1972, but he was unable to run, being injured by having an iron bar drop on his foot at work that week. In extremely warm weather only 22 of the 36 entrants finished. In a strange occurrence Jeff Norman and Harry Walker arrived at each checkpoint together, though not always taking the same line between them, and ran in as joint winners in 4 hrs 25 mins 10 secs. Naylor duly won the next year, with mist shrouding several parts of the course. This led to several competitors making navigational errors, but not Naylor as he stormed home in a much faster 3 hrs 48 mins 55 secs. The new checkpoint on Lingmell fooled many, and Harry Walker, Jeff Norman and Dave Halstead were made to return to it, still finished in third to fifth positions.

Good navigation is essential on this course in poor weather, and there have been instances of even top runners coming down into Eskdale, for instance, by mistake. Joss Naylor reduced the record to 3 hrs 41 mins 49 secs in 1975, fighting off determined challenges from Mike Short and Harry Walker. Ian Roberts set a new mark the next year, winning in 3 hrs 38 mins 35 secs, then in 1979 Andy Styan recorded 3 hrs 30 mins 51 secs in beating Billy Bland. The existing record was set by Billy Bland in 1982, with his stunning 3 hrs 25 mins 21 secs. This didn't get due recognition at the time, with the race organiser predicting that the record would not last long!

What isn't often seen by spectators at events like this, and may not even emerge from reports, is the way that things can change dramatically within the race. Eileen Jones wrote a piece for *Cumbria* magazine in 1985 entitled *England's Premier Fell race*, which noted that early on in that year's Wasdale race Billy Bland was in the lead and running effortlessly, but that:

> the full story was unfolding out of sight in the mist. At Seatallan, Bland had been in the lead; by Pillar he had dropped to 11th place, nearly 17 minutes behind Maitland. At Gable he was ninth, at Esk Hause he was third. Jack Maitland was eventually caught on Scafell Pike when Billy and Andy Ligema pulled away, but on the descent to the finish Bland ran clear to win by six minutes. That's how unpredictable it is.

In correspondence Billy Bland commented that he went the wrong way in the mist off Seatallan and ended up the wrong side of Haycock, having to go over Haycock and Scoat to get back on course, coming through after that to win.

A shorter ladies course was introduced in 1981, coming down from Pillar, but Sue Parkin chose to run with the men, finishing halfway through the field. Bridget Hogge set a record time for the full course of 5 hrs 35 mins 45 secs in 1983, bringing that down to 5 hrs 8 mins 28 secs the next year. The current record was jointly set by Jackie Lee and Janet McIver when they came in an in equal 7th overall in 4 hrs 12 mins 17 secs in 2008.

The idea for a **Bens of Jura Fell Race** also came from George Broderick. He originally thought of it as he walked the hills there. The terrain was mostly pathless and had steep scree slopes on the three Paps, suggesting a serious fell race could be devised. He thought of calling it the Bens of Jura Marathon, in a similar way to his Manx Mountain Marathon. It was felt this didn't properly describe the event, and he eventually chose 'fell race' over the more normal Scottish label of 'hill race'. The summits are delightfully called Paps, yet he chose Bens from the Gallic form Beanntan Dhiura. Originally it was to be an unofficial event, with no marshals, prizes or entry fees. This was in order to assess the viability of such an event in this fairly remote spot, with a May date in 1972 suggested. Clashing with other races meant first postponement to June and then till October, but this was eventually cancelled, despite 31 entries. The race was finally established in July 1973, with radio support and 32 competitors entering, and was won by Bobby Shields in 3 hrs 54 mins 53 secs. The next year 17 runners entered, with 13 in 1975. By the closing date in 1976 only five entries had been received and it was cancelled and postponed indefinitely.

However, runners that had competed thought it was 'the most ambitious fell race ever promoted' and in 1983 Donald Booth took up the challenge and revived the race, with much help from Broderick. The masterstroke was securing sponsorship from the Jura Distillery. They came on board and even contributed significantly to the organisation. This was despite the fact that the industry was in recession at the time, and two of the eight Islay distilleries had recently closed. A decent entry was received and the race was won by Andy Styan in 3 hrs 24 mins 37 secs. Styan's own report in the *Fellrunner* magazine describes arriving:

> coming across on the ferry is the first view you get of the Paps of Jura and you can't help but gaze in awe. They're incredible things – volcano shaped, they stand in triangular formation, looking as if they come straight out of the sea and don't intend to stop until they reach the sky. The tops are often in cloud but the clouds don't cover much – just rock. Each of the three Paps is like the worst face of Great Gable and the screes are made of football-sized lumps of granite.

The race was subsequently renamed the Isle of Jura Fell Race, and is still sponsored by the distillery. The course is 16 miles with 7,500 feet of ascent, with records of 3 hrs 6 mins 59 secs by Mark Rigby from 1994, and 3 hrs 40 mins 33 secs by Angela Mudge from 2008.

The **Ingleborough Mountain Race** is held in conjunction with the Ingleton Gala, and was first held in 1973. There was a professional race here which started in the 1930s, but it is the amateur race that has carried through to the present day. Jura winner Bobby Shields also won the inaugural race at Ingleborough in 49 mins exactly[23]. Harry Walker brought this down to 47 mins 46 secs the next year, with Mike Short recording 46 mins 55 secs in 1975. Then in 1976 Martin Weeks recorded 46 mins 18 secs, and Ian Roberts in 1978 brought it down to 45 mins 3 secs. The race is seven miles with 2,000 feet of ascent and current records stand at 44 mins 15 secs by Mark

Croasdale from 1991 and 53 mins 1 sec by Carol Greenwood from 1998.

The **Langdale Fell Race** is one of the Lakeland Classics, and was first organised by Dave Meek (and sponsored by Quiggins Mint Cake Ltd) in 1973, when the race calendar was expanding rapidly. It is 16 miles with 5,000 feet of ascent, starting and finishing at the Old Dungeon Ghyll Hotel. The route ascends Mill Gill, with checkpoints at Thunacar Knott, Eask Hause, Bowfell, Crinkle Crags, Pike O'Blisco and Blake Rigg End. There are several route choices between the checkpoints and also plenty of opportunity of navigational errors in poor visibility.

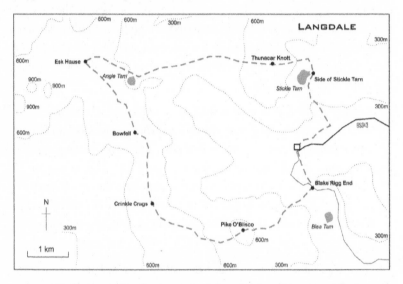

Joss Naylor won the first race in 2 hrs 8 mins 20 secs, with the mist giving several runners navigational headaches. Mike Short achieved his first ever fell race win there the next year, and came back in 1975 to set a new course record of 2 mins 5 mins 38 secs. In 1977 Andy Styan tore up the record books when winning in 1 hr 55 mins 3 secs, just pipping Billy Bland by 14 seconds. This phenomenal performance (by the two of them) has never been beaten by any subsequent runners, and is one of the longest standing records of the main races. Billy Bland's superb form of the time was shown by him winning in 1978, but also winning the Ben Nevis race and the Lake District Mountain Trial race in preceding weekends. He was the first runner to achieve this endurance treble. Due to a lack of helpers the 1982 race was not run over the usual course but only on an up-and-down route to Scafell

Pike, with Kenny Stuart winning. No race took place the next year and it was re-launched by Ambleside AC in 1984, with Billy Bland winning again.

In 1977 a ladies race up Pike O'Blisco was offered. Anne Bland (Kendal) won, with Ann Bland (Keswick) third. The next year the ladies were included in the full race with Bridget Hogge winning in 3 hrs 13 mins, preventing Ros Coats from achieving the Ben Nevis, Lake District Mountain Trial and Langdale treble, as she could only manage second after winning the other two. Ros Coats came back in 1979 to convincingly turn the tables with a new record of 2 hrs 37 mins 57 secs. Then in 1985 Angela Carson recorded 2 hrs 34 mins 28 secs in a large field, due to it being a championship race. The ladies record is now 2 hrs 23 mins 25 secs by Helene Diamantides in 1992.

When I met her, Helene Diamantides (Whitaker since her marriage) shared these memories of her record breaking Langdale run:

> I remember setting off and thinking I shouldn't be up here. I was running with Scoffer I think, and some others, saying to myself 'actually I feel OK. I'll keep ticking over and see what happens'. Going over Martcrag Moor it was really misty and I wasn't sure of the line as there was no path, like there is now. I dropped back a little, but thought I'd better hang on. Running towards Pike O'Blisco I kept thinking I could join in as the men were joking. I felt absolutely fine. It was one of those days we all train for and hope is going to happen. One of those rare occasions where everything conspired to be absolutely right. I loved it. I had a very good run out and felt fine. I had no idea what the record was. It was a bit misty and wet on the rocks, so perfect except for the rocky stuff.

Latrigg Fell Race was originally professional and part of the Keswick Sports, being held from 1891 till 1965. The amateur version that is run today was inaugurated in 1973 by Keswick AC, using predominantly the same course. From Fitz Park in Keswick it goes up Spooney Green Lane onto the steep fellside, but goes the other way round the fell from that of the guides race. The first race was won by Harry Walker in 16 mins 50 secs, from Dave Cannon and Ron Hill, with the event televised by the BBC. The next year Martin Weeks led all the way to win in a new record of 16 mins 32 secs.

In 1977 the course was lengthened, going further up the lane before turning east beside the plantation. Alan McGee was a great descender and overtook Harry Walker coming down, and took 22 seconds out of him to win in 17 mins 13 secs. The next year ladies ran, with Jean Lochhead winning in 23 mins 26 secs, and a year later Pauline Haworth delivered a 23 mins 17 secs winning time. Brian Robinson set a new record of 17 mins 1 sec in wet conditions in 1979.

New forestry fences necessitated lengthening the course again in 1981 and Billy Bland's 17 mins 46 secs from that year became the new record. Then in 1983 Hugh Symonds led six other runners inside Bland's time (including Billy in sixth place), yet Symonds still won by 33 seconds, setting a formidable new record of 16 mins 54 secs. Local man Kenny Stuart was now on the scene and in 1984 set what is now revered as an unapproachable time of 16 mins 37 secs. Kenny was running Latrigg for the first time, and carved a further 17 seconds off Symond's time. Ross Brewster reported in *Fellrunner*:

> Stuart, seeking to restore his slightly dented reputation after his Borrowdale Race defeat at the hands of Billy Bland 24 hours earlier, led the record 134 strong field a merry dance. He forged a clear lead on the climb then floated over the treacherously greasy surface on the descent to emphasise his balance and class.

The same day Pauline Haworth reduced the ladies record to 21 mins 19 secs. The ladies record has subsequently been brought down to 20 minutes exactly by Victoria Wilkinson in 2005.

Saddleworth Fell Race was also first held in 1973, originally being part of Saddleworth Sports Festival. It was held for two years from Tanner's Field, Greenfield, before moving to Tanner's Mill Yard. It is a short category 'A' event, being three miles long with 950 feet of ascent. Jeff Norman won the first race in 20 mins 56 secs. Harry Walker won the first race on the new course in 1975 in 19 mins 54 secs. The next year had good weather and Martin Weeks reduced this to 19 hrs 28 secs, with Ricky Wilde reducing it again in 1977 to 19 mins 23 seconds, after trailing Mike Short all the way round. On perfect conditions Ricky Wilde stormed round in 1978 in 18 mins 50 secs and this has not been beaten since. Ladies first ran in 1978, with the record being set at 22 mins 49 secs by Carol Greenwood in 1984.

Starting in Ambleside, the **Wansfell Race** is held around Christmas time and was first run in 1973. For three years it started behind the Salutation Hotel, giving half a mile of road at the start and finish. In 1976 this was reduced, and in 1979 the road cut out altogether as it started in a field just above town. It is now three miles, with 1,300 feet of ascent. Ricky Wilde won the first event in 22 mins 58 secs. Ladies were introduced in 1977, with Ros Coats winning in 26 mins 6 secs. Brian Robinson set the new record for the revised route in 1979 with 20 mins 21 secs, running away from Colin Donnelly on the descent. The next year this was reduced to 20 mins 19 secs by Andrew Taylor. The current record is another of Kenny Stuart's, 18 mins 56 secs from 1984, with the ladies standing to Angela Mudge with 23 mins 1 sec from 2002.

The classic **Borrowdale Fell Race** was first organised by Keswick AC in 1974, being originally intended to link the Scafell Hotel in Borrowdale with the New Dungeon Ghyll Hotel in Langdale. However, Chris Bland persuaded his co-organisers to instead go for a tough horseshoe course, with checkpoints on Bessyboot, Esk Hause, Scafell Pike, Great Gable, Honister Hause and Dale Head. It started and finished at the Scafell Hotel, and that establishment has sponsored the event ever since its inception. It is 17 miles and 7,000 feet of ascent.

Good weather greeted the runners at the first race, which was won by Dave Halstead in 3 hrs 5 mins 7 secs. In 1976 Billy Bland won in a new best of 2 hrs 53 mins 30 secs, over six minutes clear of Joss Naylor. It was Bland's first victory since reinstatement as an amateur, and in his local valley to boot. Billy's brother Stuart made his fell debut in this race, having given up football. He descended the scree from Scafell Pike to work through to third place, in a time also inside the previous record. Mike Short took on Billy Bland and Joss Naylor in 1977 and forged past Joss and into the lead ascending Dale Head, to win in a new best time of 2 hrs 49 mins 3 secs. In poor visibility Short took it down to 2 hrs 44 mins 52 secs the next year, this time out-climbing Billy Bland on Dale Head. Not to be out-done Billy Bland came back in 1979 to beat Short into second place with a stunning 2 hrs 37 mins 11 secs. In 1981 Bland won for the fourth time leading all the way, establishing a five-minute lead by Esk Hause and coming home in a new record of 2 hrs 34 mins 38 secs, which still stands. He went on to win Latrigg the next day too.

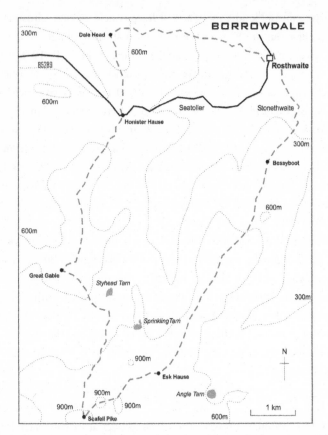

Six ladies competed in 1980, with Pauline Haworth winning in 3 hrs 50 mins 45 secs. The next year Ros Coats beat Haworth with a new record of 3 hrs 30 mins 30 secs. The 1982 event took place in low cloud, causing many problems, including the checkpoint marshals for Bessyboot not being able to find the summit. Pauline Haworth set a new ladies record of 3 hrs 26 mins 5 secs in 1984. That is now down to 3 hrs 14 mins 37 secs by Menna Angharad from 1997.

The Borrowdale Race does hold one distinction, that of once receiving Royal patronage. The 2001 fell race season was virtually wiped out due to restrictions in place because of the foot and mouth outbreak. These restrictions began to be relaxed at the end of August that year and the Borrowdale race was one of the first to be rescheduled. That it was able to go ahead at really short notice speaks volumes about the cooperation between the organisers and the National Trust and tenant farmers whose land it crossed. Miles Jessop, of the sponsors (the Scafell Hotel) learned that Prince Philip was on a visit to Honister Quarries the very same day. An exchange of faxes with the Palace ensued, and a detour was agreed. Prince Philip flew by helicopter from Clarence House, where he was attending the Queen Mother's birthday party, to Glaramara Hostel and then drove on to the Scafell Hotel, where he presented the major individual and team prizes, and chatted with runners.

Another race added to the calendar in 1974 was the **Edale Skyline Fell Race**. It was sponsored from the start by Don Morrison, the local mountain equipment supplier, and the name now appears in the race title. Taking a circular route round all the summits of Edale it is 21 miles with 4,500 feet of climbing.

Harry Walker won the first race in 2 hrs 40 mins 10 secs, after Ricky Wild had to retire after spraining his ankle while leading. Unusually for such a long race, it allowed female runners to enter and two completed the race in its first year. The next year Walker won again in 2 hrs 36 mins 3secs. From 1978 the ladies had a shorter distance race, before eventually returning to the full distance. The record for ladies is 3 hrs 9 mins 44 secs set in 2000 by S. Newman, and the men's is one of Gavin Bland's, with 2 hrs 34 mins 39 secs from 1999.

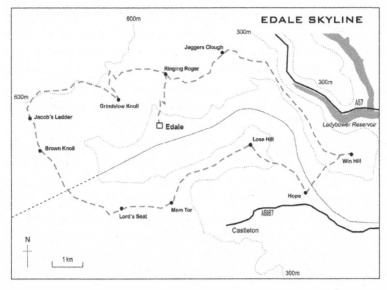

The shortish and distinctly sharp **Blisco Dash** is another of Dave Meek's inventions, which he introduced onto the scene in 1975. It goes from the Old Dungeon Ghyll Hotel, up Redacre Gill to the summit of Pike O'Blisco and back, 2.5 miles each way with 2,000 feet of climbing. Ray Rawlinson won the first race in 40 mins 23 secs, from Harry Walker. Good conditions meant that Martin Weeks slashed this to 37 mins 51 secs the next year, giving Weeks a penultimate win in his British Championship winning year. Ladies were added in 1977, with Ros Coats triumphing. Billy Bland reduced the record to 37 mins 46 secs in 1981, leading Bob Whitfield under the old time too. Then in 1983 Kenny Stuart reduced it to 36 mins 54 secs by beating John Wild, including jumping off a low crag to get a 'drop' on him. Wild's second place sealed his second win in a row in the British Championships though. In 1984 Kenny Stuart was in rollicking form and had to run even faster to see off Jack Maitland (a Leeds University student at the time), coming home in 36 mins 28 secs. Maitland came back in 1987 to narrowly beat Malcolm Patterson and set a new best of 36 mins 1 sec which is the current record.

The **Kentmere Horseshoe Race** was instigated by, organised by, and is now sponsored by, Pete Bland. It is a category 'A' race of 12 miles, with 3,400 feet of ascent, circling anti-clockwise the upper Kentmere Valley, with checkpoints on Kentmere Pike, High Street and Ill Bell. The first race, in 1975, was won by Jeff Norman in 1 hr 27 mins 52 secs. Mike Short was third that year, but came back to win the next year in a new record of 1 hr 22 mins 15 secs. Nineteen-seventy-eight saw the first ladies entering, Jean Lochhead winning in 1 hr 52 mins 26 secs. Low cloud caused many runners to get well off-course in 1981, Jeff Norman and Mike Short for instance finishing in 101st and 103rd respectively. John Wild had no such trouble though. He found his way round on his debut and reduced the record to 1 hr 25 mins 14 secs. He had reconnoitred the course the weekend beforehand, mind. Then Wild returned the next year to knock a chunk off the time, winning in 1 hr 20 mins 49 secs, with Sue Parkin setting a ladies record of 1 hr 46 mins 46 secs. There was a new start and finish for 1985 so Kenny Stuart's 1 hr 24 mins 5 secs and Pauline Haworth's 1 hr 47 mins 59 secs became *de facto* new records. The current records are by Simon Bailey with 1 hr 22 mins 36 secs from 2004, and by Tracey Brindley with 1 hr 42 mins 40 secs also from 2004.

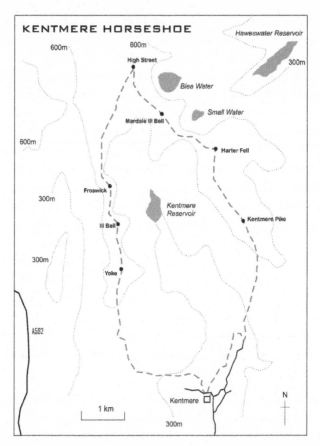

KENTMERE HORSESHOE

The first race **Snowdon Race** was held in 1976 after Ken Jones, a native of Llanberis, put forward the idea to the village's Carnival Committee. Eighty-six runners entered and it was won by Dave Francis from Bristol, who completed the course in 1 hr 12 mins 5 secs. The first race had ladies entries and it was won by Bridget Hogge in 1 hr 40 mins 15 secs. On the race website[24] Jones explains the genesis of the race:

> It was pure curiosity that sparked the idea of the Snowdon race. As a walker and runner myself I'd always wondered what was the fastest time someone could run up and down Snowdon. So we arranged to hold the race as part of the annual Carnival activities in Llanberis and the event has grown ever since with up to 450 runners taking part.

Although it is a physical challenge, being 10 miles with 3,300 feet of climbing, it does follow the wide tourist path to the summit, and rarely requires navigation skills.

In its second year there was a higher-standard field, and Ricky Wilde brought the record down to 1 hr 6 mins 7 secs, holding off Jeff Norman and Mike Short. Wilde brought that down to 1 hr 4 mins 28 secs. He was a close second to Dave Francis at the summit, but his superb descending gained him victory by three minutes. In 1977 local runner Joan Glass set a new ladies record of 1 hr 39 mins 46 secs, which she slashed to 1 hr 31 mins 24 secs the next year.

The Snowdon race encouraged international entries early on. In 1980 an Italian (Pezzoli) won, and five other Italians finished in the top 15, with the race report saying that 'a significant continental challenge in the form of a crack Italian team added spice to the 5th annual Snowdon race'. Pauline Haworth also brought the ladies' time down to 1 hr 25 mins 18 secs, and in 1981 Ros Coates reduced it again to 1 hr 24 mins 49 secs, and R. Naish further reduced it next year to 1 hr 24 mins 10 secs.

In 1984 Kenny Stuart came down to challenge the Italians and a fine battle ensued. Stuart didn't triumph though, as *Fellrunner* magazine noted in Harvey Lloyd's race report:

> the 9th annual Snowdon race attracted a record entry of 400 runners. The Italians were once again over in force with the 1980 winner Privato Pezzoli and the current Italian champion Fausto Bonzi providing a formidable challenge to the British contingent. Pezzoli and Bonzi, who incidentally hail from the same village in Italy, soon took up the challenge and were accompanied for most of the uphill by Kenny Stuart. The trio were eventually broken by Bonzi who stormed home in a new record time of 1-03-46. His feat was most remarkable considering that he is only 5'1" tall and weighs 7st 4lbs.

Pezzoli was second (1 hr 5 mins 43 secs), with Stuart third (1 hr 5 mins 52 secs). In the ladies race Pauline Haworth regained the record winning in 1 hr 24 mins 3 secs.

The scene was set for a re-match the next year, with ideal conditions and an even stronger field, which included some Gurkhas. Alan Bocking's report tells the story:

It was Robin Bryson who set the pace up the climb, once the initial burst of enthusiasm had worn off, with Kenny Stuart not far behind. There was only a 7 second gap at the summit between the two, with Fausto Bonzi being a further 30 seconds adrift. Fausto was then followed by Private Pezzoli, Colin Donnelly, Shaun Livesey and A. Amalfa, before the rest of the field began to pour through. Robin soon lost his advantage to Kenny as Fausto also quickly closed the gap. Kenny though gradually pulled clear to win by over a minute in a new record time but the main battle was for second, with Jack Maitland charging down the mountainside in a time for the descent 6 seconds faster than Kenny. Jack took Fausto on the lower slopes to finish runner-up to Kenny yet again in a championship race. Fourth went to Colin Donnelly, who matched Jack's time for the descent.

Robin Bryson's 39 mins 47 secs for the ascent is still the fastest time to the summit, and Kenny's time has rarely been approached since. Pauline Haworth also had a stormer and reduced the ladies record to 1 hr 20 mins 29 secs, a time which was eventually brought down to 1 hr 12 mins 48 secs by Carol Greenwood in 1993.

In an interview in 2010 as part of the publicity for that year's Snowdon race, with his record by then 25 years old, Kenny Stuart commented that the conditions in 1985 had been good, but that he was amazed that the record still stood. He predicted that top Kenyan runners could break the record quite easily, but that hasn't happened. As to British challengers, he thought Andi Jones and Rob Jebb had the potential to beat it, but that they were not pushed enough by the current fields which lack the depth of his era.

The **Stoodley Pike Fell Race** is short and sharp, to and from Calderdale's most famous landmark via different routes, starting and finishing at the Top Brink Inn, Todmorden. It is the longest-established fell race in the area, having started in 1976. Earlier there had been a professional race which took a direct line to the summit, but this was not practical with larger fields so the amateur race has always used a different route. The inaugural race was won by Martin Weeks in 18 minutes exactly, from Harry Walker and Ron Hill. There has been a subsequent extension in length and the record for the current course is 18 mins 10 secs by Ian Holmes from 2007.

The **Lantern Pike Fell Race** has got to be unique. It commenced in 1977, as part of the country fair named 'The Little Hayfield Show'. Ricky Wilde set a time of 29 mins 12 secs in that inaugural event, and that is still the course record. So, the event has had no change in course over that time and no one has ever beaten that time since the first year. It is also claimed as the longest-standing record in the lists, although the Eldwick and Langdale records also stem from 1977.

Wilde was also a superb cross country runner as he had earlier demonstrated in his career by finishing sixth in the 1970 National Cross Country Championships, and then sixth in the International (later World) Cross Country Championships. Second behind Wilde in that first race, yet 90 secs down at 30 mins 44 secs, was Jeff Norman whose 2 hrs 12 mins marathon time just tops Wilde's 2 hrs 14 mins. Norman's is still the ninth fastest time on the course. The first person to get inside Norman's time was Bashir Hussain in 1988, with 30 mins 33 secs. Then in 1992 John Taylor of Bingley ran in with 30 mins 27 secs to his name, ranking him fifth all-time. The next year Charles Addison of Highgate Harriers won in 30 mins 4 secs, with this time being equalled by Andi Jones in 2007.

The Lantern Pike course was designed so that it was mainly visible from the Showground. A couple of stiles have been added which would slow progress a little, but other than those the course is identical to that used when the record was set. A measure of the respect the record has is evident from this quote from Steve Vernon, who ran 30 mins 30 secs in 2008 and said afterwards[25]

> I knew to break the record would be hard, Ricky was a formidable athlete who on his day was unbeatable. He was a former World record holder at 3,000 metres indoors so that shows the quality of the record.

Holmfirth's champion fell and mountain runner Carol Haigh set the ladies record almost 30 years ago, with her 34 mins 54 secs from 1984.

Confusingly there are two **Duddon Fell Races** in the calendar. Originally they were held on consecutive days, firstly with a 20-mile race on the Saturday and then with a nine-mile orienteering-type race on the Sunday, but now they usually take place in parallel on the same day. The long fell race was started in 1978 and is now called the Duddon Long race, although the original estimate of 20 miles has been brought down to 18 miles, mainly because of GPS values of runners who have picked the 'best line'. The inaugural race was won by Billy Bland in 2 hrs 47 mins, from Joss Naylor and Billy's cousin, Anthony Bland. Organiser Ken Ledward was going against the grain by encouraging an 'open' race for amateurs and professionals both, which was 'illegal' at the time. Local guides racers Chris Hartley and Fred Reeves both entered. In 1981 Bland reduced the record to 2 hrs 43 mins 10 secs, winning from Andy Styan by over ten minutes. The record is now 2 hrs 42 mins 35 secs by Ian Holmes in 2007, with the ladies record being by Janet McIver, with her 3 hrs 11 mins 26 secs from 2008. The race is not reckoned to be as tough as the other long Lakeland rounds.

In 1979 the **Mytholmroyd Fell Race** was instigated, replacing a shorter race held as part of the Mytholmroyd Village Gala, but which had ceased ten years earlier. The first race was won by Andy Styan in 47 mins 15 secs. Minor changes in the route have taken place. The race is organised by Halifax Harriers and is now seven miles long with 1,350 feet of ascent. Also in 1979 the **Sedbergh Hills Fell Race** was inaugurated slightly further to the north, in the Howgills. This is not to be confused with the **Sedbergh Gala Fell Race**, which is organised by BOFRA and is 2.6 miles 1,200 feet of climbing up Winder and back. The Sedbergh Hills race is 14 miles and 6,000 feet of ascent. The initial race was dominated by Billy Bland, who finished in 2 hrs 14 mins 40 secs, nearly four minutes ahead of Harry Jarrett.

For the second, running conditions were appalling, including thick mist, with many runners having difficulty navigating the upper fells. This included Billy Bland and Harry Jarrett, who were unable to locate The Calf checkpoint and ran in a little after the winner, only to be disqualified for missing a checkpoint. John McGee had romped home in a new record of 2 hrs 14 mins 5 secs. Despite the conditions 12 women ran the full course for the first time, with Ros Coats winning in 3 hrs 2 mins 22 secs. In 1981 Bob Whitfield won in good conditions, breaking the record with 2 hrs 5 mins 36 secs. Pauline Haworth clocked 2 hrs 41 mins 49 secs to dramatically reduce the ladies record.

Hugh Symonds was in fine form in 1983, winning in a new best time of 2 hrs 1 min 37 secs, in what was his local race. Symonds, a resident of Sedbergh, was teaching at Sedbergh School, and in 1990 set out for what turned out to be the first continuous traverse of the mountains of Britain and Ireland[26]. Symonds had originally planned to cover Scotland, England and Wales's 3,000-plus-feet mountains but decided to carry on to Ireland as well, claiming: 'physically, I was fit to continue; emotionally I wasn't ready to finish'. His book is a fine read, detailing as it does the journey, the thoughts of his family (wife Pauline and three children were with him throughout), and the support he received from some of 'names' of distance fell running. Adrian Belton, Martin Stone, Helene Diamantides, Mike Walford, Martin Moran and Mark Rigby all paced him on at least half a dozen Munros each. In an appendix in the book Symonds makes an interesting observation on improving his navigation:

> A fifteen minute run and £15 in a professional (misnomer for races not run under AAA rules) fell race at the Moorcock Show caused me to be banned from amateur athletics in September 1986. The ban prevented me from competing on the fells and my competitive drive turned to 'the Thought Sport' ... finishing well down the field at orienteering events. The amateur athletics suspension lasted three months, and in that time I learnt more about navigation than I had in the previous ten years of regular fell running.

Robin Bergstrand, who was also a noted orienteer, was the first to get inside the two hour mark for Sedbergh Hills, winning on 1986 in 1 hr 59 mins 33 secs. In 1991 there was a fantastic tussle between the two main protagonists, with them both coming home inside the old record. John Taylor led from Keith Anderson, but Anderson showed his descending skills to take the lead off Winder. He won the race for the third time in a row setting the current record of 1 hr 57 mins 11 secs.

The **Chew Valley Skyline** fell race was initially started by East Cheshire Harriers in 1980. It takes in 13 miles of Saddleworth Moors (with 2,000 feet of ascent) and is now the responsibility of Saddleworth Runners. Mike Short won the first race in 1 hr 47 mins 39 secs, with Sue Parkin first lady home in 2 hrs 7 mins 27 secs. The 1981 race was run in very misty conditions, with snow on the tops following a recent snow fall. This resulted in many having route-finding issues. Bob Ashworth seemed to know where he was going, and Billy Bland being a stranger in these parts decided to check him out. Some classic reportage in *Fellrunner* takes up the story:

It was here that Bob made what was perhaps his only mistake of the day. When asked by Billy if he knew the way, instead of looking gormless and pretending he was on a fun run for national slimmers' week, he admitted that he did and so acquired a shadow for the rest of the race ... from here it was possible for Bland to leave a tiring Ashworth, but in recognition of his path-finding, he sportingly held back and let the Rossendale man take the honours. Meanwhile back in the melting pot of Featherbed Moss strange things were happening. The next 20 or so runners through, including Norman, Cartridge, Broxap, Short, Jarrrett, Reade and the like disappeared, who knows where, to allow a delighted group of runners who had been lying in 30th to 40th position to come through to fill 7 out of the top 10 places. Only Jarrett extricated himself in time to take 3rd place. The rest came charging through in the latter stages, passing scores of bemused runners who thought they were being lapped!

In 1983 Bob Ashworth won again and brought the record down to 1 hr 46 mins 38 secs, and R. Owen reduced it to 1 hr 45 mins 12 secs in 1985. The year 1987 again brought bad weather to this March race. In the clag the marshals couldn't even find the Featherbed checkpoint, so it was unmanned. Organiser Frank Sykes commented:

> The problem of increasing numbers is now causing us some concern. Whilst on the one hand it's nice to play the numbers game, we must consider the effect such a large entry has on the quality of the event, and the impact on the environment. Is it time to limit numbers?

Billy Bland had been heard to say that year that he wanted to win this race, and the next year he did, but marginally missed the record. Gary Devine did so in 1989, taking it right down to 1 hr 41 mins 31 secs.

Conditions were good in 1989, as that was also the year the current ladies record was set, being 2 hrs 2 mins 31 secs by Carol Haigh. The organiser's worries materialised and the race became too popular, attracting over 600 entrants in the mid 1990s. Problems with erosion and racing over private land meant it was changed to an 'O' type event. The original course was revitalised in 2010 however.

The amateur **Buckden Pike** fell race was first held in 1981 on a course which had been designed by Peter Jebb, who together with his wife Anne, organised the race for 20 years. Peter had been asked to organise a race by the Buckden Gala committee after winning the Fellsman Hike in 1981. The original race was won by Pete Irwin in 34 mins 53 secs, and in the next two years Hugh Symonds and John Wild brought the winning time down to 32 mins 48 secs and 31 mins 47 secs respectively. In 1987 the route was altered to make the race more interesting and tougher. The course has remained the same ever since and this was the course on which the current records were set. They are 30 mins 51 secs by Colin Donnelly in 1988 and 36 mins 32 secs by Carol Greenwood in 1993. Donnelly's record is an outstanding one, and the nearest anyone has got has been 30 mins 59 secs by Ian Holmes in 1995 and 30 mins 57 secs by Simon Bailey on 2004.

The current **Coniston Fell Race** was first run in 1982 and won by Billy Bland in 1 hr 12 mins 2 secs. Previously there had been various incarnations of races up Coniston, run as part of the professional circuit. This new race was instantly popular and attracted the best runners to it. In the next three years this time was reduced successively by Bob Whitfield (1 hr 9 mins 7 secs in 1983) and Kenny Stuart (1 hr 6 mins 23 secs in 1984, and 1 hr 5 mins 46 secs in 1985), who was at the peak of his powers then. In 1992 Keith Anderson was in top form and brought it down to 1 hr 5 mins 22 secs. Despite the best attempts of Billy and Gavin Bland the course record is down to Ian Holmes with 1 hr 3 mins 29 secs from 1996. Indeed, he seems to like this course, having won it again six times subsequently. A sign of the times was the following announcement from the race organiser, in the build-up to the race, via the race website (in early 2012):

> I'm scaling down the race this year as it has become too expensive to hold it at the Sports and Social club and I didn't feel it was right to pass on the cost – so the race HQ will return to the Coniston Institute.

The **Three Shires Race** was first run in 1983, being organised by Ian Stephenson of the Three Shires Inn, with help from Selwyn Wright, who is the main organiser now. The race has developed into one of the Lakeland classics, being 12.4 miles and 4,003 feet of ascent. Starting and finishing at the Three Shires Inn, it has checkpoints at Wetherlam, Swirl How, Three Shires Stone, Pike O'Blisco and Lingmoor. It features in the genesis of this book, as noted in the introduction (which refers to the second running of the race in 1984).

For the first race, misty conditions prevailed on Wetherlam and Swirl How. Billy Bland took the lead going up Blisco, winning by 19 seconds from Martin Hudson in 1 hr 56 mins 19 secs. Linda Lord was first lady in 2 hrs 43 mins 19 secs. The next year Bob Whitfield took the lead on Blisco, beating Mark Rigby by 28 seconds in a new mark of 1 hr 53 mins 8 secs, with Billy Bland in third although still inside his previous time. Kenny Stuart jogged round in twenty-sixth place, seemingly unconcerned about his elite image. Chris Brasher competed but did not finish, but he did present the prizes. Some of those he had donated, together with a reward of a free pint of beer to all finishers, which certainly went down well. Pauline Haworth smashed the ladies record with her 2 hrs 18 mins 44 secs.

Bob Whitfield beat his own record in 1987 with 1 hr 49 mins 7 secs, leading the first six inside the previous record in very wet conditions. Vanessa Brindle brought the ladies time down to 2 hrs 15 mins 5 secs, which Ruth Pickvance reduced by eight seconds in 1988 in clear weather. At the young age of 17 Mari Todd managed a 2 hrs 14 mins win in 1990. The 1993 race was run in unsettled weather but still resulted in two new course records – for Gavin Bland in 1 hr 47 mins 59 secs and Carol Greenwood in 2 hrs 13 mins 58 secs. The current records are 1 hr 45 mins 8 secs to Gavin Bland from 1997 and 2 hrs 5 mins 29 secs to Mari Todd also from 1997.

It would be possible to detail histories of many more races that have been added since the early 1980s, but it is not my intention here to be comprehensive as it would result in a massive tome. We will now look at some of the major multi-day events though.

CHAPTER 6

Multi-day events

Competitors need to be competent in the use of map and
compass in the mountains.
A mountain marathon website

As well as variety of fell races noted in the last three chapters, the racing challenge became further extended as two-day (and longer) events were established. These usually involved the competitors, often in pairs, carrying all the equipment for an overnight camp (plus food), and navigating mountain terrain. Often the actual details were only released just before the event.

The earliest of these was the **Original Mountain Marathon**[27] (OMM). Started in 1968 by Gerry Charnley (an orienteerer and a member of South Ribble Orienteering Club) the OMM was initially called the Karrimor International Mountain Marathon (KIMM), after the first sponsor. It was the first of the two-day mountain marathon events and is for teams of two, carrying all clothing, equipment, tent, sleeping bag, food for 36 hours, navigating one's own route and including an overnight camp. Interest in mountain navigation followed the interest in orienteering as a sport in the 1950s and grew with the support of people like Chris Brasher and John Disley. Teams are totally self supporting, no GPS or outside support is allowed and teams NOT arriving at the overnight camp are assumed to have camped safely somewhere. It is held in October, often in pretty remote locations. There are eight different classes, the longest being the Elite which is consecutive marathon length days, or thereabouts, and with around 2,500m of ascent over the two days.

In 1985 I competed in the KIMM with my regular mountain partner Mike Cambray. We had already that year done the 'easier' Saunders mountain marathon as a warm-up, and were keen to challenge ourselves, especially as the KIMM was to be held in the Lakes that year. We chose the 'B' Class, with 47km over the two days. The start was from Limefitt Park, in Troutbeck, with one minute staggered start times. We then ran some 700m uphill to the point where we were given our nine controls for the first day, and marked up our specially provided map accordingly. Unfortunately, I don't still have the map, and my memory of the control locations has let me down. Suffice it to say that ascending one particularly steep fell we were suddenly buzzed by a helicopter (filming the event for TV). In my haste to clean my lenses and read the writing on the side of it I managed to break my glasses. As I was going through a bad patch at the time, I didn't admit this to Mike until much later, as I thought he'd think he had a complete idiot as team-mate. I subtly let him do the navigating, and concentrated on trying to keep a reasonable pace going.

The overnight campsite was an uneven valley bottom with just an open-air toilet for company. This appeared to be very civilised. Two wooden cross members to sit on, over the inevitable pit. However, we heard later that someone had been squatting and the slats had collapsed – he was really in the ****! A short report I wrote for my athletic club's quarterly magazine gave these thoughts on finishing such a tough event:

> The last section of the day was essentially downhill – just as well judging by the state of some people. We picked off the last but one control and set off on the 4km run-in, along a farm track. Setting a cracking pace we were determined to go all the way. However, the very first uphill stretch flummoxed us and we were reduced to a walk. On the downhill we got going again and finished in fine style in just over 5 hours for the day. It was difficult to know what to do after being on the go for so long. Eventually we started relaxing, got into the tea queue and started looking for friends, and a lift back home. At this distance it all seems to have been fun – but in reality these two-day mountain marathons are a severe test of mental and physical strength, and also your ability to pick a compatible partner (how many times did we see people waiting at

the top of hills with hands on hips, awaiting their slower team-mate), and to pare down kit to a comfortable minimum.

In 1985 Helene Diamantides and Alison Wright won the 'A' Class of the Karrimor in Galloway, in what must have been atrocious conditions. As Helene recalls:

Nearly everybody else dropped out. It was one of the Galloway years! We got washed down the river under Merrick. Not good memories. Pitched our tent over a ditch, taking turns being in the ditch section, which was an awful night. Because I had come from mountaineering we had good kit, thick Goretex jackets etc. I relied on Alison to navigate. I can navigate but look up to someone like Steve Birkinshaw, and that is what we should be aiming for. I do practise.

The **SLMM** (Saunders Lakeland Mountain Marathon) has been held annually since 1978, apart from 2001, when the Lakeland fells were closed because of the foot and mouth epidemic. However, the event website[28] only has previous events listed back to 2004. Although always in the Lake District it was originally called the Saunders Mountain Marathon. It is usually less extreme than the OMM as it is held in July (thus the weather is often milder), the courses slightly shorter. I well remember competing in the SLMM in1985.

Mike and I entered the Wansfell class, roughly 30km on the Saturday and 20km on the Sunday. The start was from Askham village in the eastern Lakes, involving a 1km jog to the master maps. I made a major error in not checking the equipment. I let Mike bring the map marking pencil – unfortunately the one he had was water soluble, and rubbed off a bit when it rained. At the third checkpoint we realised we had missed one out, but we chose not to go back. The highest point of the day was the 2,179 foot summit of High Street on the line of the old Roman road. Why Romans would want to put a road in such a place I'll never know. We hit the overnight camp in Longsleddale after 6 hrs 9 mins of effort, and were in thirtieth place. In a farmer's field the organisers provided two chiropodists and a van selling cans of beer – bizarre. A brief culinary note here: if you think that stuffed pancakes, with rice and vegetable coleslaw, pre-cooked and stuffed into Tupperware and then reheated would look horrible – then you'd be right.

Fortunately, it tasted better than it looked, and the nut stuffing, rice and fresh vegetables made a balanced meal.

On the second day my much-vaunted fitness was shown in its true light towards the end of the event, when Mike revealed his superior mountain-fitness as I struggled. We gratefully accepted chocolate from a competitor who had lugged it around for two days, and now was unloading. After his generosity we had to stick with him and his partner for a bit, but burnt them off at the next hill. All we heard as we crested the hill was – 'Give them some chocolate, and they just ....'. We achieved our aim of finishing before the pubs closed. We took 5 hrs 8 mins on the Sunday. Recovery was aided by a swim in the village pool, a free lunch (M&S salads have never looked so good) and a pint. We appeared as twenty-fifth team in our class, with no mention of the missing checkpoint. However, our satisfaction was in beating the distance and conditions, rather than positions and times.

The **LAMM** (Lowe Alpine Mountain Marathon) describes itself as 'The Connoisseurs Mountain Marathon'[29] and is always held at a location in Scotland that is only revealed shortly before the event. It was started in 1994, with an Arrochar location, and is now held in June. The website lists details of all events from 1998 onwards. An impression of the event can be gleaned from a blog posting from the 2011 Elite class winner Jim Mann (who was paired with Duncan Archer). They led at the overnight camp by just 2 mins 6 secs after over six hours on the hills. Mann wrote this about the finish[30]:

> We had a small blip at CP7 when we struggled to find the lochan having come in from a bad angle but still couldn't see any other teams – a few kilometres to the finish and we would win – I think we were leading, I hoped we were leading – we just kept moving! We crossed the final beck and then it was tracks all the way. The tracks were horrible and unforgiving but we slogged it out. On the run in with only 3–400m to go we walked up a tiny hump back bridge both exhausted. Then the run in – magic! We were home but had we won? We asked an official and yes we had! WOW! Kit check – I hate that – I get really nervous even though I know we have everything – passed! We've won the LAMM – I did not see that coming – I'd dreamed of a top 5! The greatest race of my life and we've won an expenses paid trip to the Arctic for the BAMM.[31] Can't wait.

Perhaps the ultimate multi-day race is the **Dragon's Back**. It involves five days of running down the mountainous spine of Wales, racing over 200 miles over rough mountain paths, and climbing around 50,000 feet (nearly two times the height of Everest) on the way. It was first held in September 1992. The idea for the race came from John Gillham, whose book *Snowdonia to Gower* inspired endurance athlete Ian Waddell to organise a stage race for charity from north to south over the Welsh mountains. The runners competed in pairs (for safety), though there were a few brave solo competitors.

The race began at Conwy Castle on the North Wales coast and the first day took the runners over the biggest mountain ranges in Wales, the Carneddau, the Glyders and the Snowdon Range. This was the shortest day at 36.5 miles, but one of the toughest and, in the poor weather that prevailed, navigation and competence on mountain terrain was paramount. The other four days ranged from 44 to 47 miles, and on the longest days (two and five), even the winners took over eight hours, while the last competitors were out long after dark. The winners were Martin Stone and Helene Diamantides, who had navigated through foul weather and fought back to win after losing the lead on the final day. They completed the five stages in a total time of 38 hrs 38 mins. The fastest solo competitor was John Redmayne in 42 hrs 59 mins, and the quickest female pairing were Sue Walsh and Wendy Dodds in 54 hrs 6 mins. The slowest finishers over the full course took over 68 hours, and only 16 of the 32 pairs who started made it to the finish. Helene Diamantides and Martin Stone had run together quite a lot and knew they ran well together. Helene adds:

> Actually Martin was a last minute partner. My original partner fell through and I had asked Martin to be on standby. I had done a reconnoitre over the whole course. Everybody was racing flat out. Different days suited different people in different ways. Sometimes we may have pushed too hard and suffered, so others tried to take advantage and then suffered too. It wasn't just us that were pushing. Mike Walford was there, Mike Cudahy, it was hard racing.

That original race was not repeated, and lived on only in running legend and lore. Then, in 2012, Shane Ohly decided to organise a second event. When asked why he wanted to revive the race he said: 'Conceptually, the Dragon's Back Race is close to my heart as a pure mountain running experience, as I believe that there is no 'real' adventure without risk and that there is no 'real' satisfaction without effort'. He added: 'I want to run the whole route myself during the planning stages, both for my own satisfaction and so that I can look every competitor in the eye ... and dismiss any of their moans about the enormity of the challenge!'

This time the competition was for solo entrants. Thirty-two of the 82 entrants completed the race. The winner was Steve Birkinshaw in 43 hrs 25 mins 30 secs. Remarkably Helene Diamantides/Whitaker came back after 20 years and finished first lady, in fourth place overall. The event website[32] has some interesting reports on the 1992 race, and also some very short YouTube videos of each day of the 2012 event. Provisionally, the third Dragon's Back Race is being planned for 2015. Jim Mann finished sixth in the 2012 event and he gave me these thoughts on his effort:

> I finally confirmed for the Dragon's Back race on the Tuesday less than a week before the start on the following Monday – I'd been injured and wanted to ensure I could get through a 7-hour outing without too much pain, which I did the weekend before. It was with some apprehension that I travelled to Conwy for the start, as it was my first stage race. Day 1 was a long run out and then all the Welsh 3000's – that is a huge day and dropped about 2/3 of the field, but I got though it OK – I was out for around 12 hours. I had a good day on Day 2 and a chasing group started to form which made things a lot easier as we looked after each other and carried each other along through the low points (which we all had!). By Day 3 it was apparent that this was more about us versus nature than a race anymore – this was by far the hardest day for me – Steve Birkenshaw had a commanding lead and was running well, as did Helene Whitaker in the ladies (running with the same group as me). For me once day 3 was over it got easier as I was sure I would now finish – I just hoped to get through injury free. Day 5 was the best – with clear sky, warm sun, Red Kites gliding overhead, nice underfoot conditions and not a care in the world. I am looking forward to 2015 already.

These are the premier events of this type. There are links to similar events, such as the Mourne Mountain Marathon and the Highlander Mountain Marathon, on the Durham Fell Runners website[33].

It is now time to look at some of the great racers who competed in the early events in the sport's history. As we move on to consider some of the early greats of fell running let us note a slightly alternative comment on finishing a race. It comes from Ronald Turnbull's *Long Days in Lakeland* and records his thoughts from the end of a Kentmere race:

> afterwards we sit around in a damp village hall enjoying the fatigue poisons. It's a straightforward pharmacology: morphine and heroin are laboratory copies of this stuff. Such is our drug-induced stupor that we actually enjoy the orange squash in plastic cups and the waiting for the prize giving. Anyway it is the traditional entertainment, the fell runners' equivalent of purple lampshades, joss-sticks and the Velvet Underground. Fellrunners are not consumers, except of our own bodies. We don't discuss the latest expensive gear; we discuss our leg injuries. Then we get into our cars and drive home.

A *conversation with*: Helene Whitaker (nee Diamantides)

We are sitting in her lounge under the watchful eyes of the two magnificent dragon trophies she has won in the two Dragon's Back races that have taken place. As well as winning Dragon's Back Helene Whitaker has competed at the highest level across a whole range of events in athletics, particularly on the fells. Just now she should probably be packing for a family skiing holiday which they are setting off on the next day, but she has kindly agreed to discuss her career and explain what motivates her – over an excellent cafetiere. She agrees she still has ambitions over the fells, but coyly declines to be specific.

'*I didn't realise at the time that it was the fastest female time when I completed.*'

There are often contrasting backgrounds in the athletic prowess of athletes, and Helene's gene pool is no different. '*My mum could have been a very good runner, she is still quite nippy. My uncle on my mother's side was quite good. I have seen some of his medals from running when he was in the army. My mother's side are incredibly long lived and have always done manual jobs like boatbuilding. My father's side were as inactive as it was possible to be.'*

Helene started off with a traditional young athlete's track career, also doing cross country, being brought up in Greece. *"I'd always done lots of different sports and was good at a multitude of things. It tended to be individual sports though. At the time we did pentathlon not heptathlon. I tried to carry on at heptathlon training when I was at Durham Uni. I went up to Gateshead for a while, but the travelling put me off. In all honesty I wasn't that good at it."*

She was in Greece, which is the home of the marathon. And, strangely she did a marathon at the age of 16. *'The school used to have a school marathon over the original course, and kids and staff used to do it. I wanted to do it at 15 but my parents rightly said no. They said if you train you can do it next year. I trained with my PE teacher and did it with her. It was miserable. I can still remember how awful it felt.'*

I wondered if there any off-road options that she could have taken up. *'I didn't really know you could even walk mountains. The only look-in I had to mountaineering was what was on TV – Chris Bonington, Doug Scott, Everest etc. Mountains required oxygen. I thought off-road was cross country.'*

Fell running came on to Helene's radar when she went to Durham New College on a teacher training course. She went to the university and joined their fell running club at Alison Wright's instigation. *'I was now 18 and we trained for a marathon together, but did lots of other things together including fell running, and had a good Sheffield Marathon. As a student you go wherever they go. The orienteering club was very strong, but I wasn't that good at it. I joined the mountaineering club as they went to nice places, and made good friends there.'*

Helene's introduction to fell racing was through some of the standard fell races. *'Kentmere was my first race. Alison and I went orienteering in the morning and she wanted to do the race so persuaded me to do it as well. I thought it was really quite good. I think I did Buttermere Sailbeck next. Then Alison persuaded me to do Three Peaks, which you had to have experience to do. Alison did have, I probably didn't have enough.'*

Helene claims to have had no interested in the fell championships, and just enjoyed the running. '*I wasn't really at that standard. I joined Dark Peak at the time, and was thrilled to be third counter for the club once and we won a prize. Just fabulous and unexpected.*'

As to inspirations, Helene cites Ros Coats, mostly for the way she broke down boundaries and her attitude. She would have liked to meet her, as Ros had just finished when she started. Helene also admits to being desperately competitive. '*I am glad I found a sport where that is OK in females. Anyone in front of me I would have a go at. The pleasure is being out there, if I can win so much the better. If I do my best, that is better than winning. One of my favourite races was when I came second to Jackie Lee at Wasdale, and we were both under the record. That was such a good run. I got so much out of it and worked so hard that I enjoyed being second and having a good go, even more so than some I had won*'

She admires people like Angela Mudge and Wendy Dodds, who have won everything but still find huge enjoyment from the sport. '*People come and go, and race for different reasons. You see people who train inappropriately, and others that don't last. I don't mind being beaten, I'd rather be out there doing the thing I love than sitting in the house worrying about being beaten.*'

Helene is not a great one for remembering her own times and records, but I asked her which other performances impressed her. '*Angela Mudge's statistics impress me. She is so far under any other women's percentage off the men's records, which is absolutely outstanding. Also probably Billy Bland's BGR record. No one has got anywhere near it. Jon Broxap's Munros round is just absolutely brilliant. Stephen Pyke had a good go at beating it, but he had awful weather on his attempt. I think that people sometimes forget how good and fast those guys were.*'

When it came to training Helene was mainly self-coached. Until she joined Ambleside AC it wasn't very structured, she just ran. She reckoned the people at Ambleside were very good for her. '*They showed you could have fun, train hard and get good outcomes as a result. I got back to track sessions in order to get faster on the fells. By the time I went up to Glasgow I realised I needed to do structured training. I also had a very memorable conversation with Ann Buckley in the early 90s, over a pint after the Borrowdale. She was saying "these fell runners don't know how to train, and until they do I will always be beating them on short stuff". I thought she was right.*'

At the time Helene was trying to get into the hill running teams to represent her country, and finding she couldn't make it. She was even taken aside by someone who said 'you are more of a carthorse than a racehorse'. *'I thought I will show you. What do I have to do to get better? These people were representing my sport, some were seeing it as an easy vest, track runners for instance who could run up a hill. I spent a lot of time training more seriously. I ended up running for Scotland for nearly ten years, mostly on the fells, but also at cross country, would you believe. I won the West District race. I needed to make what I did count as I was studying at University and short of time. No time for junk mileage, and I had found I cannot train doing high mileage.'*

Then Jack Maitland was an early influence (in the 80s he showed Helene his diary) – a big influence. *'I remember being in the Sahara desert doing a five-day stage race and he was writing something. He was keeping a training diary, with intensity, HR, how much sleep he was having. I thought maybe I should be doing that. Better notes helped me know what worked for me.'*

Then she met Martin Hyman, who she thinks is one of the most unorthodox people she knows. Instead of looking at things and saying you had to do it this way, he would question her on why she was doing what she did, recoveries for instance. *'He would suggest HR monitor sessions I could do on my own. He was a major force in changing what I did and how I did it. He was really understanding on things like me wanting to do things differently. I wanted to do the World Hill Running Championships and the World 100k Road Championships a week apart. That meant in my mind doing the selection for one, and doing a 35-mile road race two weeks before the World Hill Running Championships, which wouldn't be acceptable now. He thought it would work for me and it did, as it was my best results in the World Cup. I think I was 20th in both events. If I hadn't had him as a mentor to give me confidence that I was right, I wouldn't have achieved nearly as much.'*

Later, when building up to the Dragon's Back she worked with Pete Shields, a coach from Ilkley. She likes to know what is coming up and train properly. *'I did 14 months of training with Pete's advice. I think it is invaluable in having someone who is objective going "no that is not good" and saying why. I have had success and know what works for me. You can't do what you have always done – your body changes and time constraints change. I think I got it about right.'*

Helene reckons that her ability to run uphill and downhill has changed over time as well. She was definitely a downhill demon. She used to love hammering down the hills, and could catch most people, men included. Now she counts on being able to climb past people. *'After you've broken a couple of bits, and your knees ache and your back jars, it is just uncomfortable. It was partly watching Jack Maitland that made me think my style was OK. I watched him, all arms and angles hammering off Mt Cameroon. Phenomenal speed, nobody told him to change.'*

My inquisitiveness about physical attributes brought us to VO2 max testing. When Helene was funded as a Scottish athlete they did lactate threshold testing and also VO2 max. They did it a couple of times because they couldn't believe it was so low. She says she can't remember the numbers. *'It was also part of the 100k team testing, as part of enhancing performance. I had the lowest VO2 max on the 100k squad. They gave me threshold sessions but I couldn't do them. I became sick and jelly-legged. What I was able to do, which they thought was quite unusual, was to sustain a high level of performance, close to the threshold for very long periods of time. I was just incredibly efficient. I use a HR monitor now to keep close to maximum but not go over it, to get the best out of myself.'*

In 1987 Helene went to Kathmandu. The Crane brothers had done the run from Kathmandu westwards and completed the Himalayan Chain. *'Alison Wright and I decided to go eastwards. You realise it is Sikkim, Bhutan, Mongolia. Permission-wise you are not going to be allowed to do that. We noticed though that the Cranes had also done the Everest Base Camp run and beaten the previous record, and thought that sounded interesting. We used the time we thought we were going to run the Himalayas as training for the Everest base camp run.'*

When Helene completed the Big 3 Rounds in 1989 she had already done the BGR. She did a slow BGR after about a year of fell running, because that was what people did. She didn't realise that was an unusual thing to do. *'Then I did a solo unsupported round because no woman had got round in under 24 hrs on their own, which I thought was unforgivable. I didn't realise at the time that it was the fastest female time when I completed. I was pretty tired and uncomfortable on it. Going from the training to the BGR, yes you are going to beat yourself up, but you have the muscle memory and the systems are used to doing it. My knees weren't great at the end of these events.'*

The build-up to Dragon's Back in 1992 included some fell race records by Helene. She equalled the Borrowdale record and beat the Lairaig Ghru, and also set a new record for Langdale which still stands. *'Langdale is in September so was after the three Big Rounds. Every year I expect it to go when it is sunny conditions. I am quite proud of it really, as there have been a couple of championship races over the course too.'*

At the end of 100k races she says it used to take her five weeks to bend right down properly. She had never run very far on roads and went to South Africa at the end of her degree for a holiday with her sister. She tied it in with doing the Comrades Marathon (the uphill version), and had a good run, beating Hilary Walker. *'I didn't even know who she was. I was asked if I fancied running for GB in the World 100k Championships in three months. The possibility of a GB vest was of interest, but really I thought I could do it and also do it well. I did back-to-back marathons for training and pace judgement. I was running for Fife AC at the time, who were absolutely brilliant. On the Sunday runs half the runners would come for the first couple of hours with me and we would meet the other half at my house who would do a couple more hours. I fed them all afterwards.'*

Helene has good memories of doing a five-day stage race in Algeria. *'It was through rocky mountainous areas, very little sand, but some beautiful scenery, spectacular. It ended in Tamanrasset on the salt route. It was only run a few times.'*

Although she competed in a good few KIMMs, it was not a main focus for the year. It was interesting at the time, and a challenge to see how well she could do, and seen more as a good way of training. She had all sorts of different running partners, which she feels was part of the fun. *'I think if you know the person you can anticipate whether it will work. I have really enjoyed running with Angela Mudge. We do race well together. I am not as fast as her, but we complement each other. She has different strengths. The way I navigate is fairly coarse, but I might have been better at choosing the best overall line. She is much better at the last km sq finding the re-entrant for instance. Also Jon Broxap, it was really good running with him as well. In those days there was a 12-hour first day for the Elite, and Jon and I finished in daylight. Now it is sometimes 12 hours altogether. Once my team were out for 14 hours on the first day at Ffestiniog, and still won the women's event. The map was huge, which we used as a sleeping mat.'*

Dragon's Back for 2012 was announced more than a year in advance. Helene asked her husband John what he thought about her doing it again. He said she should do it. Her worry was the commitment before the race, when the hard work has to be done and the greatest time and effort committed. *'We then sat down and worked out how to best get fit and planned the races up to it. I reconnoitred the mountain sections. You need to fix the pattern of the event. I had to get a new set of maps as they were 20 years out of date.'*

Helene pointed out that the bits in between the mountains depended on permissions. Even the original course sometimes changed while the event was underway. *'I was far more scared doing it as an individual, yet happier, if that makes sense. If it all goes horribly wrong I am not letting anyone else down. If I do get injured, which there was a chance of, I'd rather drop out and know I could carry on running for another 10 years than feel I have to keep going and get completely knackered for someone else's sake. Trying to tie in with someone else for training wasn't going to be easy either.'*

When it came to future ambitions Helene said sure, but she wasn't about to admit what they might be. *'One I have had a go at but been unsuccessful at and I will probably come back to. I used to love climbing and was fine with heights. When we came to Crib Goch on the Dragon's Back I had the wobbles. I said I can't do it. I had done it in winter with my hands in my pocket practically. This lovely guy was there and he said you'll be fine. Just step there, go round the corner and you'll be right. I was gripped. I seem to have lost my head for heights since having a family. Any ambition doesn't involve rock climbing that is for sure!'*

Finally, I asked Helene to nominate her greatest achievement(s). She thought for a while before deciding it was different things for different reasons. *'Dragon's Back certainly is what I am built for, physiologically as well as psychologically. The strategy of trying to get yourself from A to B in good nick day after day, that suits me, I enjoy it. It doesn't really matter what other people do. I really enjoyed my solo unsupported Bob Graham Round. It was probably the best day out in the hills I ever had. I was running at my pace, I didn't feel pushed really, I could eat when I wanted to not when the pacers wanted.'*

Then interestingly: *'Getting a Scottish vest at cross country was a real honour. I am old- fashioned in that I put on a vest I will kill myself as it is such an honour to be selected. Even getting selected for Yorkshire at the age of 47 was a real thrill.'*

What does she think the future holds? *'I just want to keep doing what I enjoy really. I'd love it if in about 10 years time if one of my girls asked me to do the Karrimor with them and I was able to say "yes" because my knees are OK, not "I'd love to but I am so crocked because of what I used to do". I must say I don't like some things I see in Junior athletics – pushy aggressive parents for instance. So, we do a lot of orienteering with our girls, and fun running.'*

CHAPTER 7

Some early giants

*If I have seen further than others, it is by standing upon the
shoulders of giants*
Isaac Newton

Several athletes left a huge mark on the sport in the early days. It is important
to acknowledge our debt to these individuals. The exploits that followed
them are all built on their achievements, some of which still appear remarkable
many years on.

One of the earliest athletes to leave a significant mark on the sport was
Ernest Dalzell, and mostly because of one race record really. As already noted
in Chapter 3, the Burnsall Feast week included a fell race from the
mid-nineteenth century. The year 2010 marked the hundredth anniversary
of the record-breaking run by Dalzell, who was from the Lake District, and
who completed the Burnsall course in a staggering (literally) 12 mins and
59.8 secs.

Unusually, two fell races were staged in Burnsall in 1910, a month apart.
The first took place during the normal feast sports in August and was won
by Accrington runner R. Thomas. The weather conditions were awful and
only three runners managed to finish the course and the winning time of 16
mins 5 secs was well outside the record of the time – 14 mins and 13.5 secs.
So, the landlord of the Red Lion, and Robert Smith, the local postmaster,
decided to put up the prize money for a re-run of the race in September. It

was then that Dalzell broke the record, with Thomas finishing runner-up. The *Craven Herald* reported:

> Thomas was first to the summit, but it is impossible to describe the terrific pace at which Dalzell flung himself down. He passed Thomas like a flash. It was so thrilling that some people lowered their field glasses; others felt theirs to be fixed as by some magnetic impulse and they could not have taken them away if they had wanted.

Some questioned Dalzell's descent time of 2 mins 42 secs, which seemed incredible. The then vicar of St Wilfrid's, the Reverend Stavert, insisted that Dalzell had descended in 3 mins 42 secs. However, those who witnessed the race swore by Dalzell's record, saying that they had never seen anything like it.

There is a footnote to this record run. Tommy Metcalfe, Dalzell's rival from Hawes in Wensleydale, had completed a hat-trick of victories at Burnsall in 1909, but his time of 14 mins 23 secs the previous year had been 1 min 4 secs faster than his other two, giving rise to doubts about its authenticity. That year had been Metcalfe's outstanding season, however, and he had twice defeated Dalzell in Lakeland events and finished second to him at Grasmere, after winning the Mile there. The second Burnsall race (reported above) attracted eight entrants, including four from the Lake District, with conditions on the day being perfect. Metcalfe was running more track races than fell races that year, but was still anxious to see his record survive. He therefore made sure that his rivals were aware that he knew the best routes up and down the fell, hoping they would follow him. He took the lead going up, and deliberately went off-course into rougher terrain. However, Dalzell had decided to follow Thomas, who reached the cairn in 10 mins 15.5 secs, two seconds ahead. Dalzell, a noted downhill specialist, then embarked on a typically suicidal descent and swept to the record.

Ernest Dalzell was of slender build and was born at Sheep Fold, Skelwith Bridge in 1884. He worked as a gamekeeper at Ormathwaite, near Keswick. Throughout his racing career he was noted for fearless breakneck descents. W.C. Skelton wrote of him[34]: 'He could leap down a fell with the speed of a Helvellyn fox and the surefootedness of a Martindale deer.' According to the *Craven Herald,* Sir Percy Hope, Master of the Blencathra foxhounds, was quoted as saying: 'Dalzell was the best runner down a fell I ever knew.

To see him take a flying leap over a stone wall and roll over in the bracken, his feet on the other side, was unforgettable.' E. Mortimer Batten, who was a spectator at the 1910 Dalzell record run, wrote in the 1949 Burnsall sports programme:

> Dalzell's descent was hair-raising in the extreme. Never would one have credited that legs other than those of a deer could perform the terrible leaps and bounds over hollows and boulders which carried Dalzell to victory.

Ernest Dalzell subsequently dominated the sport for many years. He was 21 when he achieved his first victory at Grasmere in 1905. He won this race seven times, setting new records on four occasions, but he is most certainly best remembered for his legendary run at Burnsall. Dalzell's victory there brought him the first prize of £5 (£285) plus £1 (£57) for breaking the record. Some of the times put up by the old timers, like Dalzell, are even more remarkable when it is remembered that they wore much heavier boots and more restrictive clothing than today's athletes. Lighter spiked shoes only came in later. Sadly, Dalzell was killed in the First World War.

For a brief period in the 1920s Langdale's George Woolcock was the dominant guides racer. He won 22 of the 24 fell races he entered in 1922. The record he set at Coniston Gullies of 14 mins 57 secs was not beaten until 1988. He earned the title of 'The Flying Devil', and in an article on daredevil descenders in *Up and Down* magazine his wife is quoted as saying:

> There was nothing my husband liked better than pitting his surefootedness and balance against a scree bed, particularly the one at Coniston.

Dalzell's Burnsall record stood for 67 years – until the Jubilee Challenge fell race for professionals on 18 June 1977 when Fred Reeves crossed the line in a time of 12 mins 47.2 secs (12 mins 48 secs in some accounts). It may be considered appropriate that a runner who dominated his branch of the sport for ten years in succession up to 1979 should be the one to achieve this momentous feat. The *Craven Herald* said at the time:

> His reception from spectators sensing 'it was on' was rapturous. As he unwound at the finish, threshing arms moved upwards in salute

of a mighty victory. Reeves' scorching run up and down Burnsall Fell had shattered a 67-year-old record set by legendary Dalzell. Since that epic pre-World War One run, Dalzell's record has been shrouded in doubt and controversy. Many deemed that time not humanly possible and that it would stand for ever. It stood the test of time and the challenge of thousands of athletes, both professional and amateur, until Reeves came, saw and conquered.

The *Craven Herald* reported that Reeves had led from almost the start, reaching the top of Burnsall Fell in 9 mins 5 secs – 18 secs behind the fastest ever ascent. He had not played all his cards yet.

He threaded his way downhill, conceding vital seconds when he careered off-course. But he picked his way smartly through the heather and boulders to rejoin the rough sheep track lower down the fell. From then on he looked a record-breaker all the way.

Speaking after his victory, Reeves said: 'I pushed myself going up, but had not got the lead I would have liked. Once I knew the record was won, I went for it.'

Similarly to Dalzell, **Bill Teasdale** was a very consistent racer on the professional circuit. He won Grasmere 11 times, and also 13 times at Croglin, ten times in succession at Keswick, eight times at Alva and seven times at Kilnsey Crag, to name but a few. He is regarded as one of the greatest short-distance fellrunners of all time, setting a Grasmere record of 13 mins 5 secs in 1965, at the age of 40. He had a go at the Dalzell record at another special race in 1953. At the turn he led from Sid Woof and John Bell, and his time of 14 mins 7 secs made him second fastest for Burnsall at the time. The *Craven Herald* described him as:

making a lightning getaway from the cairn, bounding and sprinting over knee-high heather, huge boulders and high walls with the agility and surefootedness of a mountain goat.

The special race created a huge amount of publicity and he claimed to have been harangued by the press before the race and consequently did not have time for a decent warm-up.

The professional/amateur divide was evident in Teasdale's time. In 1952 he set a record for the Ingleborough Mountain Race. The previous record of 53 mins was slashed to 46 mins 35 secs. In the same year he knocked 22 secs off the Grasmere record. However, he wanted to do some longer races so applied to enter the Lake District Mountain Trial, which in the 1950s was run over a 16-mile course in Langdale, from the Old Dungeon Ghyll. In 1954 Teasdale was allowed to compete unofficially, running without a number. He was last to start and beat the existing record by half-an-hour.

Bill Teasdale was born in 1925. He was known as 'the Caldbeck Shepherd' and was ahead of his time in some ways. For instance, he had a trainer in Bobby Thirwell who earned his living as a window cleaner in Keswick. Despite having a trainer, by all accounts Teasdale did hardly any training. He really was just a superbly fit person, with fantastic natural physiological gifts. He was a mere 5ft 3ins tall, and weighed under nine stone at his racing peak. In *Grasmere Sports – The First 150 Years*, he is quoted as saying:

> I never did any training – a lot of walking with the sheep yes, but getting to 2 or 3 races a week by motor bike kept me fit enough … Being a big fellow is not an advantage in fell racing because of the higher centre of gravity. I'm fairly short so had no problem. Walking the fells and handling sheep all day keeps your muscles active.

Richard Askwith, in *Feet in the Clouds*, records tests that were done on him at the age of 62 when a television documentary was made of him at the Grasmere sports of that year. He had:

> a resting pulse rate of forty-one beats a minute and superb power-to-weight ratio (he weighed just 8 stone 7 pounds at his peak). His oxygen uptake … was according to former British Olympic coach Tom McNab, 'comparable to an exceptionally fit twenty-year-old – his VO^2 max was pushing seventy'. We can only guess what such tests would have recorded in his prime.

Teasdale did acknowledge that he used to train at times on the grass track in Fitz Park in Keswick. It was here in 1955 that Michael Glen ran the world's fastest mile on a grass track, with 4 mins 7 secs. At the time the four-minute mile had only been achieved by five runners. Gordon Pirie had a crack at this grass record, but could only manage 4 mins 7.5 secs. Teasdale showed fantastic longevity, winning Grasmere aged 41, and coming third in the British Fell Championships at the age of 47. He was also awarded the MBE for services to sport in 1970.

Teasdale must have been a phenomenal athlete. Harry Griffin, writing in *Inside the Real Lakeland* (published in 1961) commented that he didn't just win races by daring descents:

> In some seasons Teasdale won every one of his races and he has broken records at almost every local sports meeting. Teasdale's lung power, even at 35 (his age in 1960), is quite remarkable, and it is probably true to say that nobody has ever been able to run up a fell like this little chap. This is where he tears the heart out of his opponents – on the way up the fell – and he can often afford to take things relatively easy on the way down, although he can be as nimble and fast on the descent as anybody, if necessary. And he generally reaches the finishing tape no worse than slightly out of breath. He does very little training, believing that his daily shepherding keeps his leg muscles in perfect condition.

Teasdale became so dominant that the betting that took place at the time would not be on whether he would win or not, but on how much he would win by. At the long Ingleborough race he once bet on himself being able to beat the existing record by six minutes, and proceeded to beat it by seven minutes.

While setting no significant race records **Stan Bradshaw** is revered in fell running circles. He was once described by Joss Naylor as 'the greatest sportsman ever'. High praise indeed.

Bradshaw turned to athletics in the late 1920s, after his football career with Padiham FC had been cut short by injury (cartilage). He was from a footballing family, being named after Accrington Stanley, the club his father Ernest played for. Two of his brothers also played league football, with Harold playing for Burnley, and William playing for Blackburn and winning four England caps between 1910 and 1913. In his early days Bradshaw was a reasonably successful sprinter. He joined Bury AC to run road, track and cross country races. Unlike his contemporaries, who might train twice a week, he tried to run every evening, after working long hours in the family tripe business. In the late 1950s he employed a manager in the works to give himself more training time, often recording 30-mile training runs at this time.

Bradshaw ran his first race at Rivington Pike in 1930. At this time there were few amateur fell races in England, so he regularly competed at Rivington Pike and at Burnsall, coming second in both in 1939. After serving in the forces in the war, he helped to re-form Clayton-le-Moors Harriers. He was club president from 1959 to 1980, and also served on the FRA Committee for six years in the 1970s. Bradshaw finished second in the first Three Peaks Race in 1954. Three of the six starters completed the 22-mile race, which started then at the Hill Inn. Fred Bagley won, with Bradshaw second and Alf Case third. It is believed that he was the last survivor from that first race. In all he took part 24 times and went back as a spectator in 2008, when the race also incorporated the World Long Distance Mountain Running Championship. Bradshaw reckoned newcomers to the Peaks race were always told to follow a Clayton-le-Moors runner, as there were so many of them it was assumed they knew where they were going.

As well as the Three Peaks, Bradshaw often did the Lake District Mountain Trial, despite not knowing these fells well, and often having to tag on with someone else. In the early days you were set off at one-minute intervals by the first letter of your surname. In his first attempt, also in 1954, he was off first in this way and was soon lost, eventually having to retire. Bradshaw will also always be associated with the Bob Graham Round. He was the second man to break 24 hours in 1960, following club-mate Alan Heaton. Seventeen years later made another successful attempt at the age of 65. This record stood for 21 years, when it was beaten by another Clayton man, 66-year-old Brian Leathley.

In 1965 Bradshaw was the winner of the inaugural Lakeland 3000s event, and he was Vets winner at Ben Nevis six times. He first ran the Ben in 1956 at the age of 44, and ran it for 12 years in a row. Similarly, he medalled at the Vets National Cross Country Championships, returning to his first love in athletics. Like Joss Naylor, he set some notable individual challenge marks. In 1968 he completed the Lakeland 2500s in one round and the Six Northern County Tops in a 73-hour round trip, without sleep. He was probably the second person to run the Pennine Way[35], which he completed in 6 days 9 hrs and 50 mins in 1972, walking and jogging for 12 hours a day.

Stan Bradshaw passed away in 2010, a month short of his ninety-eighth birthday. A new race in memory of him (replacing the Half Tour of Pendle) was instigated by his club Clayton-le-Moors in March 2011.

A little later **Tommy Sedgwick** arrived on the scene. He was born in 1950 into a farming family in New Hutton in Cumbria. He did a little running at school, showing some talent at cross country. Aged 14 he ran his first junior fell race, winning at Sedbergh. He had been sixth at the summit but showed his future descending prowess by storming down to take victory. He seemed to just fall into running as a professional, mainly as it was in the fell races at Lakeland sports meets that he wanted to run, and they offered prize money.

His dashing style did gain him spectacular wins, but unfortunately also more than his fair share of injuries. Even in that first season he fell badly at Grasmere and was out for the rest of the season, a pattern that would continue and see him often having incomplete seasons. Tommy played this down a little when we spoke, saying:

> I have done my ankles, thigh and hamstring in – nothing too
> dramatic in all fairness. My knees are now a bit iffy. The last time
> I ran at Alva my wife said you have some black marks on your
> shoulder. They were gorse prickles in my shoulder from tumbling.

In 1965 he won the Grasmere Juvenile Guides race, but he wasn't really dominant as a junior. He became a Senior in 1968 winning seven races, but not yet Grasmere, where he was eighth – carrying an ankle injury.

In 1969 a decade-long series of tussles with Fred Reeves commenced. At Grasmere Sedgwick and Reeves were to take first and second positions for those ten years, though the order of finishing varied. After losing out again in 1970 and 1971 Sedgwick finally beat Reeves at Grasmere in 1972, repeating the victory in 1973, taking home a £20 winner's bounty. The next year Sedgwick ran approximately the same time, but Reeves had an outstanding run, beating Bill Teasdale's record for the course by eight seconds. Then in 1975 he lost to Reeves again, who knocked seven seconds off his own record. Sedgwick had been running five years longer than Reeves, yet was five years younger than the later starter, so maybe he felt that this age differential would eventually give him the advantage.

Sedgwick had no trainer, but trained on the steep local fells around his home in New Hutton, often with other fell runners. Thus, he came back in 1976 and watched by an estimated 1,100 spectators turned Reeves over, knocking a magnificent 25.9 seconds off the Grasmere record. This brought it down to 12 mins 24.8 secs. Remarkably, it was achieved in an unseasonal heatwave, which overwhelmed many of the spectators and some of the younger show dogs. The dry conditions allowed the supremely fit Sedgwick to do the unheard of – actually overtaking Reeves just prior to the summit, before swooping to victory and the new record. Sedgwick claimed he usually tried to stick too closely to Reeves when ascending, but this time it paid off for him as he closed on him near the summit, and:

> I was first to the top. The other two times I beat Fred he'd turned the second flag and was coming down the steep section, which we used to mow out, and I was fairly confident he was mine.

The comment above refers to the fact that sometimes these athletes would be on the fells the week beforehand to clear the bracken with a bill hook – Sedgwick usually on the descent and Reeves on the ascent – to make their intended paths for the race as clear as possible.

Despite his nemesis Reeves, Sedgwick was very successful on the steepest courses. At Alva, in Scotland, Sedgwick won 12 times in all, each time giving him the grandiose title of British Hill Running Champion. His twelfth and last win came in 1980, where his fearless descending allowed him to overtake Graham Moffatt and the upcoming Kenny Stuart to seal his win. Kenny took the record there the next year. Tommy feels that probably for everyone but him Grasmere was special, but for him it was Alva. As Tommy recalls:

> I was never beaten there. I won it eleven times in a row. I was ill once and missed it. I went back and won a twelfth time. I wasn't good when I finished that day. I was in a mess but won and I said 'that is it'. It was straight up, no quarter, and straight back. We all linked hands as we went round the top, Kenny, Moff and me. No-one cared about the £5 for first to the top. We leap-frogged each other all the way to the top. I came down like a dream from top to middle. After that I just rolled and rolled. I got onto the golf

course at the bottom and looked back. It was only 600-700 yards
to the finish. I just needed to keep going although it was quite a
steep path. Then I fell on the track and Fred Reeves was there
shouting at me to get up. I did manage it but thought it was time
to call it a day.

Despite all this training, racing and travelling Sedgwick worked very hard
to earn his living. At one time he had a milk round in Kendal, worked
on his father's farm and fattened rainbow trout for sale to local hotels.
Although he claimed his motivation was his love of competing, and
wanting to develop his natural ability to negotiate the fells where he had
always resided, he did suffer serious bouts of nerves in a similar vein to
several other top fell runners. This is shown by the quote from Rex
Woods' *Grasmere Giants of Today*, which refers to his first Grasmere
triumph over Fred Reeves:

Arrived early, as usual. Watched the Juniors, and then retreated to
the changing-rooms, to look miserable and feel terrible, like the rest
of the lads in there. The atmosphere is terrific; you could cut it
with a knife – guess it means as much to all of us to do well I
go out on to the track, try to relax and loosen up, but it seems in
vain. My legs feel dead, my nerves tight. I feel like doing anything
but run. When they call you to the line, nerves reach a peak. The
gun goes off and nerves go instantly, oblivious to everything but
the race.

Sedgwick based his whole year round the Grasmere Guides Race. It was the
one race that mattered to him. When profiled in *Cumbria* magazine in 2005
he speculated on why today's runners weren't beating the Grasmere record
that Reeves set back in the 1970s.

I think it is because today's top runners like Rob Jebb and Ian
Holmes run Grasmere 'cold'. To them it's yet another fixture on the
fell racing calendar. But to Fred and me we knew Butter Crag
intimately. I can honestly say I knew every stone that could help
me so that I could use them on the descent to 'brake' my
speed.

In the same interview he also explained that he:

> would drive to Grasmere after work to practise running uphill faster
> in short sprint sessions. Whilst I was doing this I knew full well that
> Fred would have probably been on the fellside before me because he
> finished work earlier, also making a beeline for Grasmere, to try to
> improve what he saw as his weakest point – running downhill fast.

Tommy had a break in 1981 for a few months and he thought 'that is it,
I've done it long enough'. He had a big milk round and had extended their
cottage, and had a fish farm at the time – he was working very hard. As he
explained to me:

> Age was moving on, although they are defying age now. I came
> back in 1982 and won Grasmere for the last time (aged 32). Fred
> had been reinstated and Kenny too. I had had a break but I missed
> it. I enjoyed the break, no miles, no training. I couldn't watch races
> at that time though. I used to watch from a distance. It used to get
> to me. Then I started training again, and you have a do, whatever.
> I ran Grasmere when I was 60. I won the Vets when I was 40 in
> 1990. Wherever you are in the pack you still have your own group
> you race against. You miss that to a point.

Tommy likened training to a wheel you can't get off. He suggested that you
should listen to everyone, and sift through it all the ideas, and work out
what is right for you. He summed up training and racing thus to me:

> There was this Scottish lad, one of the Stewarts I think, running at
> the same time as Bedford. He started lifting his mileage and the
> wheels fell off his wagon. I only lasted a week doing three sessions
> a day. It takes a while to work it out. Some years you don't get it
> right. Other years it will. I was always nervous and pumped up.
> Sometimes nerves spoil your race. I remember one of the youngsters
> got nervous and should have won Grasmere in 1982. I responded
> well to the nerves.

Tommy still occasionally runs with the kids, but says he can't stand the
knocks and needs to listen to his head now. He acknowledged the tremendous
support his wife Jennifer had given him throughout his career.

Although born five years before Tommy Sedgwick, **Fred Reeves** came later to fell running. Born in Birmingham in 1945, he moved with his family to Barrow four years later, as his father's work as an engineer in the Post Office took him there. He was a good standard cross country runner at school. He trained as a ship draughtsman – at Vickers, one of Barrow's big employers at the time. Working there for eight years he joined Barrow Amateur Athletic Club and ran for the County of Lancashire at both track and cross country. Later he worked as a draughtsman at Burlington Slate, a firm which backed his running.

Bored with track running, at the age of 22 he turned to professional racing, initially in flat races. He enjoyed the camaraderie and, when he became successful, the remuneration. Initially he ran in the short handicap races, like the one mile at Hawick, which he won at his first attempt. After winning the Ambleside handicap he started being noticed and his handicap adjusted, so that at Grasmere he was scratch in the two-mile handicap, which he still managed to win. In 1969 he won the British Two-mile Professional Championship at Glenrothes, and also a double in the one and two-mile races at Alva. Subsequently, he still included track work when he was at his peak as a fell runner.

Handicappers became tougher on Reeves and he took his previous cross country fitness on to the fells. In his first race he showed his inexperience though. This was Sedbergh in May 1969, where he led at the summit but found running in his spikes a disadvantage and fell several times as he slid, literally, down to third place. However, he did win a local race a month later, and managed to win Grasmere at his first attempt. He won his first of ten Guides Races at Ambleside after being taken round the course in advance by Pete Bland, who was a previous winner. He then began to be seen as a leading runner on all but the steepest fells. In 1970 Reeves won Grasmere again on very wet going. He exchanged leads with Tommy Sedgwick a couple of times on the descent, and despite the conditions was only 30 seconds off Teasdale's record. The following year in dryer weather he beat Sedgwick again at Grasmere, being this time 14 seconds off the record.

The Grasmere reversals against Sedgwick have previously been noted, although Reeves was dominant elsewhere. Reeves realised that he needed to improve his descending if he was to hold off Sedgwick. By now he had moved to Coniston and he trained on the fells nearby. He also decided to gain even more familiarity with the Grasmere course by training there. He trained by walking up and practising running down, often with three such runs in a session, which he repeated 20 times during this period of training. This dedication paid off, as in both 1974 and 1975 he beat Sedgwick again, setting new records each time.

Then in 1978 Reeves set the Grasmere Guides Race record of 12 mins 21.6 secs over the Butter Crag course, taking it back from Sedgwick's 1976 time. Sedgwick was quoted in the *Cumberland News* afterwards:

> There was no keeping up with Fred in this present form. He led right from the first wall, and even though I came in second, there was no catching up on his 500-yard lead.

The friendship and rivalry between Reeves and Sedgwick is very evident. Miller and Bland's Grasmere book includes a long reflective piece by Reeves on regaining the record, in which he describes his feelings throughout the race and concludes with:

> was it worth it? Yes it was – it's always worth it. I even felt like that in the years when Tommy ran me into the ground. I got almost as much pleasure from seeing Tommy celebrate his wins with his family as I did with mine ... where Tommy and I are together, we are always smiling. He's a great friend to have. People refer to 'my' record, but I like to think of it as 'our' record. Without the other runners and Tommy in particular, pushing me to the limit, I don't think the record would have been broken that day.

It was the Queen's Silver Jubilee Year in 1977 and a special fell race for professionals was run at Burnsall. It had originally been a professional race but since 1932 was an amateur race. The acknowledged record was Dalzell's 12 mins 59.8 secs from 1910. In this special event 25 professionals started and Reeves won in 12 mins 47.2 secs, despite the heavy underfoot conditions. He had reached the cairn in 8 mins 55 secs. After the questions about the timekeeping for Dalzell's record there were now some bizarre objections to the Reeves record, because the professionals chose a different way to the top than amateurs normally did, which they are at liberty to do in fell racing. There were also suggestions that his time was made possible by having walls dismantled, but these seem to be unfounded. Tommy Sedgwick's recollection of the race (in which he was second) was that it was:

over a slightly modified course. They invited us to run, and allowed us through this garden. Yorkshire TV were doing a piece on it. They said for the sake of some of the filming look as if you are racing – just for the cameras. In the actual race I couldn't live with Fred, there was too much flat on it. I could hold my own on the climb, and make ground coming down. If someone gets away there you won't get them back.

The year was a good one for Reeves as he won Ambleside for the eighth successive year, breaking the record for the third time, with 13 mins 4.8 secs. He beat Sedgwick again at Grasmere and won 23 of his 26 fell races, while also running 14 track races as well. A feel for the professional scene of the time can be gained from the races Reeves won that year, which included Helme, Malham, Kendal Gathering, Aboyne, Loweswater, Levens, Embsay, Innerleithen and Crosby Ravensworth. Reeves is reckoned to have won only about £300 in that very successful year.

Reeves immediately began working with coach Dennis Beavins when he turned professional. He helped strike the right balance, ensuring that flat speedwork continued, particularly to complement the tough downhill training. In Roy Lomas's *Grasmere Sports: The First 150 Years* Reeves notes that Beavins said he could coach him to win Grasmere.

My training consisted of running over 70 miles per week, mainly on hills and trails around Coniston, plus 2 speed sessions per week with Dennis and the other runners during the race season. Grasmere was always difficult for me – quite steep and fairly rough, but it was always the one to win, and there was always a lot of hype, press coverage and big crowds to add to the tension. I had no special diet – I even enjoyed a few cream cakes during training, which once resulted in a headline from one desperate reporter 'Cream Cake Fred sprints to victory'. I always ate cheese and honey sandwiches one and a half hours before a race.

Beavins may have said he could coach Reeves to win Grasmere, but this coaching relation seems a world away from that propounded by the Greek Stoic philosopher Epictetus, whose take on coaches was:

You say you want to be an Olympic champion. But wait. Think about what is involved … You will have to hand your body over

to your coach just as you would to a doctor. You will have to obey
every instruction.

Come to think of it, I know a couple of coaches who subscribe to a version
of that philosophy. My underlying philosophy as a coach is to work towards
making myself redundant, and the athlete as self-reliant as possible.

Reeves had no real issues with injury, despite a tendency to want to
over-race. Imagine this race schedule. After setting the record at Grasmere
in 1975 on a Thursday, he set out on a run of six daily races from the next
Saturday to Thursday. He won five of them, only failing at Ennerdale on the
Wednesday, arriving late and missing it due to being held up in traffic.

When asked, Reeves stated that he just enjoyed running. His motivation
was being fit, appreciating success that came his way, and just enjoying the
environment. You get a feel for the man from this quote noted by Rex Woods,
from after his record-breaking Grasmere run of 1974:

> It's all over now, so into the changing-room, a quick rub-down
> from my trainer, a lovely shower and perhaps thirty minutes of
> re-running the race over and over again with the lads. No malice,
> no hard feelings; just delights and disappointments, but still great
> friends.

When Kenny Stuart came on the pro scene in 1980 Fred Reeves found he
was no longer the main man. He commented when interviewed in *Fellrunner*
that Stuart was the most talented fell runner he had ever seen:

> he went through us like a dose of salts. You'd be flogging yourself
> uphill and he'd be trotting along in front and looking behind, not
> even flat out. When you see that it just deflates you. He can come
> down too.

Reeves got fed up with running the same courses and challenged himself by
being reinstated as an amateur in 1982, but his best days were behind him
by then. Regarding his training, he admitted in the interview noted above
to normally averaging 60-65 miles a week, twice a day with mostly short
stuff, with a long run on the fells once a month. Later on he moved on to
road training more and ran 2 hrs 35 mins at the Coventry Marathon, and
after that planned to run the New York Marathon, but it fell through. He

also admitted to a time of 50 mins dead in the Chas. Kendall ten-miler, and also gaining a seventh place in the Ben Nevis race at the age of 19.

In a profile of him in *Our Traditional Lakeland Sports* Reeves adds this further comment on Kenny Stuart ending his dominance.

> I recall my young son Phillip asking why I let him beat me. I recollect words to the effect 'I didn't have much choice in the matter!'

He also gives a moving tribute to his own father, who was his greatest supporter:

> never missing a race, always there for me. I always knew that my running was his hobby and that was a nice feeling. When he passed away, our family's wish was that his ashes be scattered on the summit of the [Ambleside] Guides Race so it was with sadness but pride that Phillip and I made that last run to the top. In every trip back to the Lake District a visit to the sports field is always included. To sit for a while and remember Dad with his binoculars doing his own little commentary.

Once again there is the imponderable question of whether Reeves could have been a top class marathoner if he had moved to the event earlier and trained more specifically for it. He is 5ft 10ins tall, and weighed 9st 7lbs in his peak years. Richard Askwith reported on tests done on Reeves at Leeds University in 1981, which prompted the national marathon coach to suggest he still had potential at the marathon, being 36 years old at the time.

> Reeves was recorded as having a body-fat ratio of just 6.64 per cent, a resting pulse rate of 42 beats per minute, and a VO2 max of 79 millilitres/minute/kilogram.

Tommy Sedgwick's take on this was that a sports professor contacted himself, Billy Bland and Fred Reeves to test them and find out how they trained. He added that:

> Fred was more technical than me, and was coached by Dennis Beavins. I tried to explain to the professor what training I did, by writing it down for him. I have the greatest respect for Billy Bland, but he is rumoured to have responded 'I go out the back door, run

on the fells till I'm knackered and then come home'. No technical
stuff with him, but his stamina was tremendous.

Reeves retired, went on to become secretary of Ambleside Sports, and
eventually emigrated to the USA, taking up coaching track and cross country
at his local High School.

All these runners were competing in the professional/amateur era, but
sport was changing rapidly, as will be seen when we look at the administration
of fell running (and other sports) next. Eventually an open sport emerged,
but it certainly wasn't a smooth process.

A *conversation with:* Tommy Sedgwick

*As I pulled up outside Tommy Sedgwick's house I noticed what
a fabulous view of Ingleborough he had. Mentioning it to him as
we introduced ourselves he pointed out that 'out the back' he
could see some of the Lake District peaks as well. A mighty fine
spot to be living in. Tommy had come away from his farming
work to speak with me about his career and fell running from his
era. He had his scrapbook and photos out ready, and shared some
fascinating stories of his and other's exploits. The afternoon
finished with his wife Jennifer kindly letting me use their scanner
to copy some of his personal photos for possible inclusion in this
volume.*

'*I knew Fred was training three times a day, so I tried that.*'

We started talking about Tommy's family upbringing, which he reckoned
had been hard. '*My father was brought up in a tight financial environment.
He had a talent for running but it wasn't a consideration in that age. He
was born and bred in the Sedbergh area, and went to the local school. Locals
were allowed to run the Wilson Run, which is a big public school run. He
got into trouble in the year he was eligible to run, so he was banned. He
set off in farm work, then agricultural contracting. He built a very successful
business, then bought a farm outside Kendal.*'

Tommy was brought up in a valley and used to have to go for their own milk at a farm up the hill. As kids they used to freewheel the downhills, letting themselves go. Tommy started out at 14, running at school over cross country and also on the fells. *'I believe that set the seeds to why I could run well downhill. As a lad Kenny Stuart limited his training, and then he was doing it at a different level just before he was reinstated, more intensive than we were. Pete Bland set me off, training three times a week. Dave Bedford was getting publicity for running 200 miles a week, and we all started thinking differently. We got up to 7 days a week, and the results and times showed. I wasn't doing 200 miles a week, but 7 days a week, even at 17 years old.'*

Tommy ran for Kendal AC till he was 16, along with Dave Cannon. Kendal AC won the mid-Lancs League with Cannon and Willie Reid. He helped set up the winter league, which was run originally by BOFRA. *'It is quite a big event now. The season went from May to October. We all trained through the winter. We used to go to the track at Longlands Boys School, which I went to. In my early 20s the farm I used to work for gave me access to a flattish field. It wasn't 400m but we marked it out for repetitions. I don't know the exact distance but it was the same each time. I did a mile warm-up, then a 400m repetition, jogged 100m, walked 200m, jogged 100m, and then hit the 400m rep again. This was all done on my own. You knew your times. I used to like to do them consistently, but the last rep always had to be the quickest. Then a mile warm-down. I was doing track for leg speed.'*

By the time he was 23 he had gone from seven days a week, to training twice a day for the first half of the week. From March he used to do a three-mile run in the morning, with no pace, no effort. In May that was increased to five miles. On Sundays he sometimes did a long run. *'From Monday to Wednesday we would do the 5 mile run in the morning. Thursday would be a light run only, with Friday just a stretch. Then we were set-up in our minds for a race Saturday – all short races. Mind you, I did do the Three Peaks Race three times. It was a nightmare the first time. We were used to running 15-30 minutes. I hit the wall going up the last peak. We started at the Hill Inn that year. The second and third times we started at Horton. This was before all the pro/am controversy. I started off at the back to not impede anybody. At the finish I branched out half a mile from the end, and at checkpoints I branched off and shouted "non-competitor".'*

At this time Tommy worked for his father, then he took a milk round which he did before work. Then they bought two more milk rounds in Kendal. At that time he was starting work at 4.20am and finishing at 8am, getting home at 9am. *'Then I trained sometime between then and 12 noon, doing track work for Grasmere. Then we worked three or four hours in the afternoons and I'd train in the evening. I knew Fred was training three times a day, so I tried that. I was fencing, knocking posts in and I was shattered. Twice a day was fine, but three times was too many. It took several years before you got a training regime that suited you.'*

His ascending was improved by the track work. He also trained on the Grasmere course, doing handicaps. This was with quick youngsters like Steve Carr, and Graham Moffatt (who still holds the under 17 record at Grasmere). They used to adjust it from day to day. *'If I caught them by racing down we would adjust the next time. We might do this once a week. My father used to take times at the first wall, where we split from the under 17s, and where we came into sight between the two flags. If I went up too quick I blew up. If I could get to the first wall in reasonable shape and still be running at my pace I could usually be confident of coping with it.'*

I asked Tommy to compare himself and Fred Reeves. He reckoned Fred's weakness was downhill, and that he used to do repetitions at Grasmere to improve it. *'He'd jog uphill and come down as hard as he could and repeat it. I did the exact opposite. Although we were competitive we were good friends. There was no quarter given. My best times were when I did a lot of track work. I was never going to be a track runner though, I was too slow. I was doing 400s and 800s – not in races. My weakness was I couldn't hang on till the fell. Once I got on the steep stuff I could hold my own.'*

Then Kenny Stuart came along and he could really run uphill. Tommy said it would have been good to have seen Kenny and Fred race when they were both at their prime. *'Before he was reinstated I ran against Kenny at Wasdale in a short Kirk Fell race. It was steep. I thought he can't run up there. If I could have got him to walk I'd have walked as quick as him. I remember looking up and he was going away. I don't see how anyone could do his level of training and keep doing a manual job.'*

I asked Tommy about the guys that had preceded him, like Bill Teasdale, and what it was like when he came into the sport. He reckoned it was a quieter time in the sport. *'Fred and I had the advantage of being stronger and older. But some younger ones were coming through. Bob Morton and Peter Hall were also running. Reg Harrison had done very well, being an old rival of Teasdale. He put on a lot of weight. They said he lived on Complan for a long while to get weight off. He was a hard man. Bill Teasdale was a bit too old by then really when I ran against him. The first time I beat him, at Sedbergh, I hit him under the ear. I tripped as I passed him. He was first at the top, Pete Bland was second and I was third. I passed Pete and caught Bill on a steep section. I stumbled and my arms flailed and I caught him under the ear. He always ragged me about it.'*

I wondered whether Tommy had ever run against Joss Naylor, and what he thought about him and his achievements. He replied that he had raced once with Joss on the Kentmere Horseshoe. *'We went up Kentmere Pike before Nan Bield Pass. I was as near as you to Joss. I had heard about his reputation. Don't take this out of context but at that time neither Joss or Billy Bland had won it. I thought he looks nothing special. But I wasn't with him by the time we were on High Street. I was out the back door, and he was just warming up. Joss is rightly to be considered the top man, without doubt. Kenny Stuart for speed though. We used to watch Kenny run when he was reinstated. I remember on one of the Howgill races – it was a loop and he didn't know the course, just the finish. He just sat there and then it was "right lads thank you very much".'*

When asked who else he thought were the demon descenders, Tommy gave a slightly oblique answer, although it says a lot about his approach to racing. It was a story about having an 'awful tussle' with Billy Bland before he got reinstated. It was at Mungrisdale, but not on the normal course. *'I wouldn't say I won it, but I was first on to the road. We were pretty much together at the top. Coming down I passed him and he passed me, and then I fell, and we passed each other. We got to this plain wire fence above a banking before the road. We were neck and neck and I thought "I'll dive through there"'. So I dived through and rolled on to the road. I did beat him, but I wouldn't say I was quicker than him.'*

We didn't spend much time on betting and 'fixing', as Tommy hadn't really any knowledge of it. As noted elsewhere, the rivalries were too great for them to be sullied by any of that sort of thing. *'I heard rumours, not long before us, of runners being told not to win a race. I never bet on a race I have run in. My father wouldn't either.'*

Tommy pointed out that his boy, Ian, had run as a youngster for one season, and that his two girls Judith and Helen are runners, keen at different levels. Helen won the Three Peaks race in 2006, running for Ilkley Harriers. *'It was her last race before she got married. Judith joined the army and also did the Three Peaks, but not at the same level. Her son is an absolute flyer. He has won at Craven. We will see if he remains motivated, he is just 10 at the moment.'*

Tommy keeps an eye on the sport still. He watched a race two weeks ago - the Wray Fair, just a local race. *'I will probably go to the Sedbergh Gala race. Many of our races were attached to galas or shows. They weren't run under AAA rules and it created really silly problems. They were stopping children running at school because they had run in races. Is it not crazy! Surely encouraging children to do sport was a good thing. A small minority created the problem.'*

His response when asked to nominate his best personal achievement was twofold. *'It would be Grasmere '76 for a one off race, and the Alva wins were special. I have some brilliant memories. Fred beat me to the top of Alva one year, and even Duncan Gillies was ahead of me. I took them out pretty quickly though. You swing under a flag, round the back, everyone went over and then down, into like a gulley. As we climbed out I thought it had gone. I'd won it about 6/7 times by then. I came off the summit and couldn't see them at first. I had a good run that day though.'*

Finally, Tommy commented that there was a closeness amongst the runners that hasn't been matched since. *'There were some quick guys: Fred Reeves, Kenny Stuart, Mick Hawkins. Mick Hawkins ran in the Commonwealth Games at steeplechase. He had a real turn of speed. I used to have to hang on. Fred's Grasmere record stands from 1978. I had it in 1976. Fred took a second a half of it in 1978 and it has stood ever since. We had a get together in 2012. Fred was over from the States, plus Kenny, Pete Bland, Graham Moffatt, Steve Carr, William Reid and Roger Gibson. We ran some miles – in the lounge. A great craic.'*

CHAPTER 8

Administering the sport

Our greatest glory is not in never falling, but in rising every time
we fall.
Confucius

To understand the developments outlined herein it is necessary to have some
understanding of the social changes that were taking place; also to appreciate
the developments in similar and allied sports that were taking place as fell
running developed, as the participants tried to retain control over their own
sport's destiny. Social conditions have greatly influenced the development of
sport in the UK. There have been many changes over the centuries.

In Medieval times people had little time or energy for recreational activities,
which were really confined to feast days, and were often very local in nature.
Occasionally the government would ban these activities in favour of archery
training. Traditional folk games and activities flourished in Tudor times,
although Puritanism greatly reduced the opportunities to play and the types
of activity. Throughout the 1700s increasing industrialisation forced workers
into regular (and longer) work patterns. However, there was soon pressure for
Sunday to be a day of rest. Then regular and organised sport on a national
scale began to emerge. In the early 1880s the church criticised the populace
for their idleness, drunkenness and slack morality. The commercialisation of
sport started, especially in horse racing, cricket and prize fighting.

Throughout the Victorian era the ethos became that sport developed one's
character and morality. Competition had to be fair and rule-governed, with

similar conditions for all players. Sport should be played, not for reward, but for its own sake. For the masses, having Saturday afternoon free from work was the turning point, enabling people to both play and to spectate. Furthermore, amateur and professional sport became increasingly separated. Edwardian sport increasingly came to be played separately by the different classes of society. Public school athleticism dominated sport, and working-class women were pretty much excluded from sporting involvement. Since the Second World War improved standards of living have enabled greater participation in sport for most social groups. The concept of amateurism for competition was replaced by that of eligibility, and professional sports people began a long battle to be given fair rewards in some sports.

The rise of amateur sport in the Victorian era, and the formation of the Amateur Athletic Association in 1880 brought changes to athletic sports that would eventually create the modern sport of Fell Running. Note that prior to the establishment of the Amateur Athletic Association other popular and allied sports had already been regulated.

Mainstream athletics began being formalised in the 1850s, initially with the establishment of the first athletic clubs. There is some dispute among the main players as to who was first. The history of the Oxford University Athletic Club, as noted on its website[36], records that it started in 1850 when a race or two on the flat were suggested. 'Again the party agreed. The conditions were drawn up, stakes named, officials appointed, and the first meeting for Athletics Sports inaugurated' – so more gambling there then. Cambridge University Athletic Club was founded in 1857, and Thames Hare and Hounds in 1868. Thames Hare and Hounds stake a claim to be the oldest cross country club.

There is some similarity to fell running in the sport of climbing, particularly when you look at some of the endurance feats. Skye's Cuillin Ridge for example includes some unavoidable 'climbing' in it. The first formal climbing club that was founded was the Alpine Club in 1857, with the Scottish Mountaineering Club (SMC) following in 1889. Hugh Munro was a founding member of the SMC. He listed the mountains in Scotland over 3,000ft, which were subsequently called Munros after him. Hugh Munro never climbed all those on his own list though. Of his original list he failed to climb one mountain in the Cairngorms (Carn Cloich-Mhuillin), which he was saving to be his last. At the time of his death he had just produced a revised version of the list, adding Carn an Fhidhleir, which he had not climbed. The Fell and Rock Climbing Club of the English Lake District (in everyday parlance the Fell and Rock Club or FRCC) is the senior climbing club in the Lake District, founded in 1906/07. The club had been originally suggested by John Wilson Robinson around 1887, about the time that rock climbing began as a sport in England. He is commemorated by Robinson's cairn on the side of Pillar.

The popular sport, both for players and spectators, of football became formalised by the setting up of the Football Association in 1863, with the Football Association Cup being first held in 1871, and the Football League following a little later in 1888, just after the AAA.

In his book *Man walks into a pub,* Pete Brown quotes the chief constable of Liverpool as saying, in 1898:

> the passion for games like football and athletics which has been so
> remarkably stimulated in the last quarter of a century, has served
> as a powerful rival to boozing, which at one time was the only
> excitement open to working men.

Sports were seen to be taking people out of the pub, and pub landlords were working hard to find any way they could create associations with sport. The first cross country club, Thames Hare and Hounds, was formed after a paper hunt from the King's Head pub in Roehampton. A paper hunt or chase involved 'hares' starting ahead of the main pack, marking their route with a paper trail – in a similar way to today's hound trailing, where an aniseed trail is used. With the paper hunt the pack would follow the trail, with the first to catch the hares being the victor. A year earlier still, the Thames Rowing Club had organised a steeplechase from the Red Lion, Putney.

Walkers were a little later in forming a national association. The radical British Works Sports Federation organised the mass trespass on Kinder Scout in 1932. Many walking clubs had been formed well before then (e.g. the Association for the Protection of Ancient Footpaths in the Vicinity of York from 1824). The national Ramblers Association was formed in 1935 (now the Ramblers), although it was preceded in 1931 by the National Council of Ramblers Federations.

There are many stories about the origins of the sport of cyclo-cross. One is that, in the early 1900s, European bicycle road racers would race each other to the next town. They were allowed to cut through farmers' fields, over fences or take any other shortcuts in order to make it to the next town first. This was sometimes called a 'steeple chase' as the only visible landmark in the next town was often the church steeple. This was really a way for the cyclists to stay in shape during the winter months and provided an alternative to road racing. Not only that, but riding off road over more difficult conditions than smooth roads increased the intensity at which the cyclists were riding and also improved their on-the-road bike handling abilities. Forced running sections, or portage, were incorporated to help deliver warm blood to the feet and toes, as well as to exercise other groups of muscles. Daniel Gousseau of France is credited as having inspired the first cyclo-cross races and he organised the first French National Championship in 1902. Géo Lefèvre, the originator of the idea for the Tour de France, also played a key role in the early days of the sport. Cyclo-cross is now governed in Britain by British Cycling (formerly the British Cycling Federation).

The formation of the British Cycling Federation in 1959 brought to an end an era of cycle racing in this country which was overshadowed by some remarkable schisms within the sport (sound familiar?). These reflect as much on the society of the time, as they do on cycling itself. To understand the events which led to the formation of the British Cycling Federation, it is necessary to go back almost 70 years. This was a time when cycling faced a very uncertain future and when the governing body of the time took a most unusual decision, one which was to have a profound effect on cycle racing until well after the Second World War. The first governing body of the sport in the UK, the National Cyclists' Union (NCU), was the originator of a ban on racing on the open roads in 1890 which was to persist into the 1950s.

That ban, which to modern eyes seems all the more bizarre in that it was the work of a governing body. With cycling rapidly taking off in the second half of the nineteenth century, racing was soon becoming a popular pastime. However, the bicycle was, on the whole, seen as a machine of working classes and a strong resistance to racing rapidly emerged from the wealthy ruling classes. There are some who believe that we came close to a total ban on cycling in this country as the upper classes railed against the mobility it gave the 'common' man and the resultant incursions into their beloved countryside. It was against this background, which seems so unreal today, that the NCU banned cycle racing on the highways and insisted that all racing must take place at velodromes and later on closed circuits. The British League of Racing Cyclists was set up in 1942 by the rank and file to try to overthrow the governing body. This whole saga is entertainingly revealed in a quirky book written by Tim Hilton[37]. Eventually NCU and BLRC did merge to form the British Cycling Federation. All cycling – track, road, BMX, cyclo-cross, etc – is now administered by BCF's successor, British Cycling.

So, some time after many other sports, the Amateur Athletic Association came into being in 1880. Fell running went its own merry way for many years, with its diverse professional and amateur activities.

Finally though, the Fell Runners Association came into being at a meeting held after the Pendle race on Saturday 4 April 1970. That meeting was chaired by Gerry Charnley, the then organiser of the Karrimor Mountain Marathon. Its aim was 'to serve the interests of the sport of fell running in the UK'. The annual fee was 25p which entitled members to the typescript newsletter, which first came out in 1971. In the newsletter was a statement that

> one of the primary objects of the Association is to be able to provide information to members, particularly on events. To further this object a file is kept on every event in the calendar and all information is recorded as it becomes available.

There was already a provisional calendar of events published for 1970 (dated February 1970), which was reproduced in *Athletics Weekly* in March of that year. This obviously anticipated the forming of the Association, but it carried the names of Charnley and Eddie Leal on it, and had details, at variable levels of completeness, of 39 races. It included such entries as races at Ingleborough ('Universities/Colleges only'), Ben Lomond ('YHA and SYHA members only') and Pendleton ('not so far under AAAs laws – efforts being made to this end for 1970').

Strangely, another body calling itself the FRA had emerged four months beforehand in Cumberland, headed up by race organisers Frank Travis and Joe Long. It was formed to promote the Ennerdale fell race, which they had started in 1968. They happily changed to become the Cumberland Fell Runners Association (CFRA) and went on to organise several other races, such as Wasdale and Kinniside. There had also been two false starts. In

August 1966 an editorial in *The Climber* magazine proposed the formation of a national fell running body. It didn't happen, perhaps because people were expecting the newly formed British Orienteering Federation (BOF) to encompass fell running. Then in 1969 the AGM of the LDMTA discussed that organisation covering fell running nationally, but that came to nothing either.

Initially, the Fell Runners Association seemed keen to keep the sport's profile fairly low, thinking it unique enough to be well separated from mainstream athletics. However, towards the end of the 1970s it was felt within FRA that discussions with other organisations were necessary, because the growth in the sport was causing worries in the environmental bodies and in the AAA (Amateur Athletic Association) (because of runners competing across the athletic spectrum). It was particularly felt that fell runners needed to manage their own sport to protect their interests for the best.

In 1978 the FRA Committee formed a sub-committee 'charged with the task of negotiation over rules of competition with the A.A.A.s' – which met on more than one occasion that year. By the end of the year the sub-committee had submitted its 'points for discussion with A.A.A., W.A.A.A. and Scottish A.A.A.' The full committee commended 'the detailed and thorough review of the Laws and Rules for competition of the A.A.A.'s and their relevance to fell running', and concluded that they hoped 'discussion with the amateur athletics bodies will soon take place'[38].

The 1979 FRA AGM reported that the FRA Development Sub-Committee had 'a long meeting conducted in general, in a helpful and friendly atmosphere'. Four options emerged for further discussion:

1. Affiliation to AAAs under existing rules
2. As 1) but with some amended rules
3. Affiliation but with a measure of Authority delegated to the FRA
4. Go independent

Of these options the sub-committee recommended option 3, which was approved by the AGM. Chris Brasher was the Secretary of the sub-committee and was mandated to try to organise a meeting with the AAA to pursue these ideas.

Fell running had always been fiercely independent. The options outlined above were seen to possibly result in the FRA not being the controlling body, having no authority but acting merely as advisor to the AAA. The sub-committee had, over the two years of deliberation, come to the conclusion that they should seek to affiliate as an organisation to whomever the AAA would delegate a measure of control of the sport (similar to the Race Walkers Association). This view that was confirmed by the FRA AGMs of 1979 and 1980. However, it transpired that the AAA were happy to recognise the FRA 'as the specialist body best able to represent the interests of fell runners', but it saw them as a specialist club like the Road Runners Club. The AAA would concede a voting seat on their General Committee, but not delegated control of the sport. Thus a motion was passed at the 1980 FRA AGM, the full text of which was:

> The FRA should continue negotiations with the AAA provided that the AAA have indicated that they have agreed that the affiliation be on the same basis as of the Tug of War Association, RWA [Race Walking Association] and ECCU [English Cross Country Union] by April 26th 1980 (one week after the next general Committee Meeting of the AAA). This AGM realises that if this affiliation comes about it may be necessary for the FRA to take steps to enforce its rules and the laws and rules of the AAA. AGM also empowers the negotiating committee to institute discussions with any other relevant governing body of athletics in the UK and to affiliate on the same basis as with the AAA provided always that if these negotiations fail it may be necessary to withdraw our affiliation with the AAA and take steps to become the independent governing body of fell running.

The FRA was invited to a AAA General Committee meeting on 19 April 1980 to put their case and answer questions. Peter Knott and Peter Walkington attended, with Chris Brasher as invited additional delegate, and they reported a lot of sympathy for the case and some antagonism. The case was accepted by 11 votes to eight, with the proviso of approval at the AAA AGM in November, plus the provision of a suitable constitution, and rules for competition. Chris Brasher was co-opted on to the FRA Committee and they decided to concentrate on resolving the English situation first, before moving on to bring the Women and Scottish members into the arrangement, followed by the Northern Irish. This phase was bookended with a message in *Fellrunner* magazine to 'spend as much time as we can afford running on the fells with a minimum of rules and regulations commensurate with safety and fair competition'. FRA reported:

> The AAAs tabled a motion to their own AGM on 8 November 1980 but it was withdrawn at a late stage, resulting in a distinct chilling in the relationship between the two organisations. FRA tried to correct what they saw as some misunderstandings and also to improve relations, with a view to the original motion being placed before the AAAs as soon as possible.

The AAA was requested to re-present the FRA proposal, and accept that the objections raised prior to the AGM had been addressed, including work on the constitution and discussions with NCAAA. The AAA committee discussed this request in April (*after* the FRA AGM) and replied that their committee was 'against giving FRA the status similar to the ECCU under clause 9'. The reason given was that FRA was based on individual membership, and not club membership, as were AAA and their affiliates. At this point the FRA Committee agreed to consider an alternative approach and called an emergency general meeting for that November to discuss it with the membership.

At the FRA EGM it was noted that Keswick AC had put a motion to the AAA AGM (held a week earlier, on 7 November) that the FRA should affiliate to the AAA under clause 9 to become the formal governing body of fell running. The AAA meeting was attended by Peter Knott, Peter Walkington, Jon Broxap and John Blair-Fish, who saw the motion supported, but the lack of a two-thirds majority meant that the motion was not passed. An invited rep from the Women's Cross Country Association told the EGM that FRA was welcome to affiliate to the WCAA, thus becoming the governing body of fell running for women in England. The meeting voted to continue negotiating with AAA, and to continue to insist on individual membership.

In early 1982 the FRA committee decided to approach the Scottish AAA about possible affiliation, and attempted to hold a referendum of members on the AAA situation. Finally on 6 November 1982 a motion from Keswick AC to the AAA AGM that FRA should affiliate to the AAA under clause 9 to become the governing body of fell running was passed on a card vote of 216 for and 86 against. The AAA Handbook for 1983/84 contained the following:

9(d) Fell Running – The Management of Fell Running is delegated to the Fell Runners Association. The FRA has the power to draw up regulations for the management of Fell Running, subject to the approval of General Committee, but no such regulation is valid which contravenes a law or rule of the Association. An appeal shall be from any decision of the FRA to the General committee whose decision is final. The FRA has jurisdiction to enforce any by-laws or regulations it may make from time to time.

The FRA Committee then had to consider the implications of the new status, and had to submit a revised constitution to the AAA, which was duly accepted.

What it did mean (after about five years of negotiations) was that FRA had formal responsibility for the sport – but as yet only for England and Wales, and only for men, and that this responsibility (development, safety, etc) must be carried out within the framework of the AAA laws. However, the constitution made it clear that it was not necessary to belong to a club affiliated to the AAA to be an individual member of the FRA, nor was it necessary to be a member of the FRA to compete in fell races – although most competitors were both. FRA were granted one voting representative on the General Committee of the AAA and one on the Northern Counties sub-committee on fell running.

The Scottish Hill Runners Association (SHRA) was established in February 1983. There was an informal meeting 'in the back of a car' after a road race in Glasgow in January 1983. Those present were the founding members – Roger Boswell, Colin Donnelly, Dick Wall and Robin Morris – so quite a big back seat then. The first formal meeting took place following the Carnethy Five Hill Race at Penicuik in February 1983. The aims were to organise a separate Scottish championship and to produce a calendar of Scottish races. They immediately hit trouble when, during the first championship, SHRA received a letter of complaint from the Scottish AAAs saying that they did not have the right to organise a championship, or indeed call it that.

In 1984 contact was made between FRA, SAAA and SHRA to address hill running in Scotland, and with a view to eventually SHRA becoming a branch of FRA, with governing body status granted by SAAA. Unfortunately, nationalistic views impeded any progress on the Scottish front. Contact was also made with the Women's AAA regarding governing body status. Meanwhile discussions were ongoing in athletics on setting up UKAAA (UK Amateur Athletic Association) / BAAB (British Amateur Athletic Board). During 1985 these negotiations seemed to just go nowhere, with no new agreements reached. BAAB seemed to want to have one place for fell running, but it would be an internal UK Fell Running Board consisting of representatives from England, Wales, Scotland and N. Ireland – with FRA being squeezed out.

In January 1986 SHRA noted that SAA had offered an amnesty for a period of three months to the end of March. For the sum of £15 a professional in Scotland would be reinstated as an amateur. It was suggested that FRA should consider a similar initiative with the AAAs. This request was made and turned down by the AAA. A dangerous confrontation loomed, but attempts were made to continue negotiating. Meanwhile, the first official SHRA newsletter appeared in February 1987, along with an 'alternative view', memorably entitled 'Booze 'n Trouble'.

Meanwhile there was administrative disarray in mainstream athletics. In late 1988 the British Athletics Federation arose out of the ashes of the national athletic associations. In January 1989 good progress was made with BAF. The FRA Committee records note that:

> for the first time ever representatives of fell runners throughout the UK sat down together to discuss the future of the sport. A Fell and Hill Running Commission (FHRC) will be directly represented on BAF rather than as at present being responsible to a national Athletic Association. England will have three representatives on the Commission, Scotland two, and Wales and Northern Ireland one each.

BAF and the Commission came into operation in March 1992, and the FHRC took over running the British Championships, as FRA was not deemed to be a British body. One advantage of the BAF arrangement was that money was available to support coaching developments in fell running.

Championships

The first British Championships (Fell Runner of Year as it was called at the time) were set up in 1972 and won by Dave Cannon. The scoring was devised by Mike Davies, with ALL races of any category included, but with varying points levels for A, B and C category races (first places were worth 22, 16 and 4pts respectively)[39]. In 1976 this was changed to the runner's best 10 of all 'A' category races of any distance.

The format for the British Championships was changed from 1981. It was to be scored from 15 elite events (five in each category of short, medium and long), with an individual's best ten to count (with three having to be in each category, and the final one in any category). Some races in each category would rotate each year. The races were chosen to be: all category 'A' races; geographically spread; and not bunched together in the calendar. For this first year the races were: short – Butter Crag, Burnsall, Melantee, Blisco Dash, Pendle; medium – Ben Nevis, Kentmere, Fairfield, Snowdon and Ben Lomond; long – Ennerdale, Wasdale, Welsh 1000s, Borrowdale and Moffat Chase. This pattern continued, with minor variations in venues for several years.

For the 1986 season an English Championships was added and the British Championships drastically reduced. The British Championships became four from six races, of which two races were in each category (and athletes needed one in each category, plus one other). The races were: short – Eildon Two Hills, Gategill; medium – Moel Elio, Ben Nevis; long – Wasdale and Llanbedr to Blaenavon. The English Championships were to be seven from nine, of which three races were in each category (and athlete must have two in each category). The races were different from the British Championships, except for Wasdale, which appeared in both lists. To me, this was going to be better than the 15 races option, although the choice of races meant that some of the classics might be lessened by their exclusion. However, there were soon comments surfacing to the effect that the extra championship was dissipating the athletes' efforts and might not be such a good idea.

From 1993 the British Championships became the responsibility of the BAF Fell and Hill Running Commission, although they retained the same format. It now included Seniors, Vet 40s, Vet 50s and teams, plus Ladies,

Lady Vets and Ladies Team. The English Championships was the same as previously, but with even more Vets age groups.

Ireland, Scotland and Wales

The Northern Ireland Fell Runners Association (NIMRA) was founded in January 1979 and in 1980 inaugurated the first ever fell running champs of Northern Ireland. The Championship consisted of eight events, comprising two short, three medium and three long races. Several races had been in existence for a while, and some were incorporated especially for the championships.

In 1980 the Irish Hill Runners Association was formed as the sport was developing south of the border. Scotland had its first separate championships with the formation of the Scottish Hill Running Association in 1984, but not without some posturing by individuals and regions. Wales also had its own championships in 1984, over nine events, and co-ordinated by Ken Jones, the Snowdon race organiser. An Isle of Man Championship had been inaugurated in 1980, there being enough events on the island to base the result on the individual's best performances in two short, two medium and two long races, plus one other of any distance.

So, some semblance of order came to the sport of fell running. It was one of many sports that was male-dominated early on, but this was beginning to change, as we will see in the next chapter, where the unofficial, and then formal, gradual involvement of females is documented.

CHAPTER 9

Ladies

Pain is nature's way of telling you that you are still alive

Anon

At the Olympics now there is complete equality of events in athletics, but it has been a long time coming. Any sense of equality of opportunity (and reward) certainly took a long time to arrive in the sport of fell running. Some of the pioneers in trying to achieve this change are highlighted below.

After the formation of the Fell Runners Association in 1970, the first magazine of the FRA was dated September 1971. It listed the members of the Association, which at the time consisted of the 117 who had paid up their 25p subs. There was a footnote at the bottom of one page that said: 'At least one enquiry has been received from a lady re membership! How about lady members? Our constitution doesn't specify sex!'

Women had been agitating earlier than this. There had been some solo female runs up Ben Nevis, but not in an official race. Unofficially, local girl Kathleen Connochie (who was just 16 at the time) completed the Ben Nevis race in 1955, by dint of setting off one minute after the official start. The Lake District Mountain Trail had actually added ladies races in 1953 and 1954, but attracted few entrants and it wasn't a success. In the next decade the Fellsman Hike and the Lake District Four 3,000 Foot Peaks Marathon also accepted a very small number of female entrants.

Eventually, in 1974, three years after the suggestion of allowing female membership of the FRA, the Edale Skyline race was first established, and the first ladies race to be held (nominally) under AAA laws was included. It wasn't a separate race, and the three female entrants ran over the same 22-mile course as the males, with two of them finishing respectably in fifty-fifth and seventy-first places. There were a hundred finishers altogether, and the third female and 28 males were forced to retire.

It should be noted that the furthest that female athletes could run at the Olympic Games at this time was 1,500m, and that it would be the Los Angeles Olympics in 1984 that first allowed women to run as far as the Edale Skyline course (and that on the flat!). To complete the comparison with women unofficially running fell races consider this about the inaugural Olympics in 1896, from a web guide to marathons[40].

> In March of 1896, Stamatis Rovithi became the first woman to run a marathon when she covered the proposed Olympic course from Marathon to Athens. The following month, a woman named Melpomene presented herself as an entrant in the Olympic Marathon. Race organisers denied her the opportunity to compete. Undiscouraged, Melpomene warmed up for the race out of sight. When the starter's gun sounded, she began to run along the side of the course. Eventually she fell behind the men, but as she continued on, stopping at Pikermi for a glass of water, she passed runners who dropped out of the race in exhaustion. She arrived at the stadium about an hour and a half after Spiridon Louis won the race. Barred from entry into the now empty stadium, she ran her final lap around the outside of the building, finishing in approximately four and a half hours. One Greek newspaper wrote that the Olympic organisers were discourteous to disallow Melpomene's entry into the race, but nonetheless it would be nearly a century before another woman would run the Olympic Marathon.

In the mid 1970s some organisers were more co-operative, allowing women to run, but recording their initials and surname in the results with no indication of gender to avoid any repercussions from the draconian WAAA. Others required ladies to set off 10–15 minutes earlier than the main start, which meant that they were then hounded down by the men. One leading fell runner summed it up with these words:

Sooner or later someone is going to take certain organisers to the sex discrimination board! I suppose it's a bit like the fight to allow women to run marathons, yet look at the number of men Grete Waitz can beat. I don't see any reason why women can't run any fell race, and start in the same race as the men.

Of course Grete Waitz went on to win the third London Marathon in 1983 in a new world best of 2 hrs 25 mins 29 secs.

Things then moved on fairly quickly. The official Edale ladies race was inaugurated in 1978, and it took the form of the earlier ones by being over a shorter course than the men's. Nineteen seventy-seven had seen shorter races for ladies set up in parallel with some of the long classic Lakes races like Wasdale, Borrowdale and Ennerdale. Langdale also had a shorter race for ladies, up Pike O'Blisco, although this soon changed to have all entrants traversing the full course. Earlier, on 2 April 1977, the Pendle Fell race had held the first official ladies race under AAA laws. It was won by Kath Binns (Sale) who was just 19 at the time, and later became a prominent cross country runner.

Relatively, women seemed to excel over the longer courses, getting nearer to the men's times in percentage terms. Indeed, later in 1977, Jean Dawes was inducted as the first female in the Bob Graham Club, achieving her round in 23 hrs 27 mins, being the sixty-ninth to complete the round.

The deeds and words of the female athletes were starting to be noticed. In 1978 the FRA committee discussed a possible Ladies Fell Runner of the Year competition, with an outcome:

that Carol Walkington would like to hold a brief meeting with as many ladies as possible one hour before the 1979 AGM ... to discuss the scheme ... with a view to establishing a 1979 competition (if this is generally favoured).

A meeting was held after the 1979 Pendle race and a plan was hatched. The first championship featured ten races, three long, three medium, three short, plus one other. Initially there weren't enough long races for women, thus races like the Kentmere, a medium men's race, became designated as a long race for the women.

Cross country skier and British Orienteering Squad member **Ros Coats** won the inaugural championship in 1979. Coats had come to orienteering from a mountaineering background. She entered the 1977 Karrimor and her running partner, Anne Salisbury, suggested they ran the Moffat Chase as practice. Salisbury then couldn't make the race but Coats ran anyway, managed to win and was hooked. She tended to compete in the various mountain marathons, very successfully, including those abroad. In 1979 she also completed the Bob Graham Round in 20 hrs 31 mins, which was the fastest ladies round at the time.

The Three Peaks Race Association decided to introduce a Ladies race in the 1979 event covering the full 23.5 miles, with a common start time but separate result list and prizes. Race organisers were not universally accepting of ladies and the 23-mile Ennerdale Horseshoe organiser reported in 1979 that 'one lady completed the Ennerdale course unofficially, though expressly requested not to do so'. That lady was Veronique Marot, who ran on the fells a lot early in her career, and who went on to reach great heights at the marathon. In 1989 she won the London Marathon in a British Record time of 2 hrs 25 mins 56 secs.

Even when organisers did accept entries from women it still didn't go smoothly. The 1979 Ben Nevis ladies race was, according to the organisers, run:

> without the official sanction of the SWAA [Southern Women's Athletic Association]. Though the Ben Nevis Race Association (BNRA) sent off an application for a permit, no reply was received. Presumably for this reason, the BNRA felt unable to offer any prizes in the ladies race; though they did accept the £2.50 entry fee. Further, they insisted that the ladies should start 2 minutes after the men.

During the 1980s more women came into the sport wanting to race, rather than just run. The backgrounds of these athletes were varied, coming as they did from many other sports. As noted, Ros Coats was a former national orienteering champion, who also represented Britain at Nordic skiing at the 1984 Olympics. Jean Lochhead came from a cycling and athletics background, representing Wales at the Commonwealth Games. But, despite increasing numbers, and steadily improving performances, women were still not taken seriously in many ways.

Despite women being invited to compete in the World Cup from early on they really struggled to get financial support to attend the event. Angela

Carson had to take out a bank loan to participate when she was selected, and Carol Haigh was able to attend one World Cup event thanks to an anonymous donation, after her situation was highlighted in the local press. She duly went on to win the race.

Slightly later even more diverse backgrounds became evident from females coming into the sport. Wendy Dodds was a junior international swimmer, championship level orienteer, skier and triathlete. Tricia Calder, who won the British Championships in 1990 and 1991, was a jockey, actually riding in the first ever flat race under Jockey Club rules. Helene Diamantides was Greek pentathlon champion, also excelling at 400m hurdles and cross country. Sarah Rowell was British record holder for the marathon, holding the record prior to Veronique Marot.

The first female to stake a significant claim to greatness was **Pauline Haworth/ Stuart**, who become the British Fell Running Champion in 1980 (winning ten out of the twelve races), after Ros Coats won the inaugural championships the year before. She is not a Lakelander, having being born in Northampton. After spending time as a nurse in Liverpool, she moved to Threlkeld, in the Lakes, in 1980. She dabbled in fell running from 1977, having come from a fell walking background. Then she entered the first official ladies race at the Fairfield Horseshoe race, and won. On moving to the Lake District she joined Keswick AC. Unfortunately, she suffered from a heel spur and also had a bunion operated on in 1981. These both meant that her training was limited, never managing more than 50 miles in a week, and she more usually ran between 35 and 40 miles a week.

In 1984 she upped the training and won the British Championship again, repeating the win the next year too. In 1984 she also set the current record for Ben Nevis of 1 hrs 43 mins 25 secs, the only record she still holds. Interestingly, Kenny Stuart's Ben Nevis record is from that same race. He was in the process of claiming his second British title that year, and Pauline and he were to be married at the end of 1985. They swept all before them in these two years, winning many doubles at races, and uniquely it is the only occasion that male and female British championships were BOTH retained in successive seasons.

Pauline Stuart represented England once in the World Mountain Trophy, finishing ninth. In an interview published in NIMRA's *Northern Exposure* magazine she claimed that she 'was pregnant and suffering from morning sickness! I thought it was nerves!' In the same interview she assessed her own abilities:

> I guess I was good at climbing and descending, especially steep craggy fells, but not so good on the flat bits in between or the run out to the fell and back again. I didn't do any specific training but I suppose I raced a lot more than other people. My advice would be to be confident – if you are hesitant you fall!

Like husband Kenny, she tried road running but didn't take to it. She completed the Barnsley Marathon in just over three hours, and had PBs of 1 hr 24 mins for the half marathon, and 1 hr 2 mins for ten miles. She obviously had great powers of recovery, as in the 1984 season when she won the 17-mile Borrowdale race on a Saturday, and then the Latrigg three mile race the next day, in a new course record. Her career may have reasonably short, but she dominated the sport when at her peak. In the championship winning season of 1984 she ran 28 races of distances varying from 23 miles down to 1.5 miles, and won 24 of them, setting 14 course records in the process.

The next few years saw the women's side of the sport developing in both numbers and standards. Although she never won the British Championship, **Carol Greenwood** won the English Championship twice and set an amazing number of records in a ten-year spell at the top of the sport. Eleven of these course records are still current, a higher total than anyone else – either female or male. Greenwood first won the English title (as Carol Haigh) in 1986 and repeated it seven years later. She was prolific in many branches of athletics, running for England at cross country (1984 World Cross), and Ekiden road relay (1986), as well as the inaugural World Cup Mountain Race (1986). In this race, over a distance of 7,500m, she pushed the pace hard from the start and concentrated really hard on the two climbs. She established a significant lead and duly won, despite sustaining a badly sprained ankle when she went over on it in the latter part of the race.

Greenwood had some success as a teenager and young senior on the track, and then moved to cross country and to the fells. As well as winning the World Cup in 1986, Carol set 12 course records and also won the 16-mile

Langdale Horseshoe race that year. At her peak she was doing around 80 miles per week training and was self coached. She did a fair amount of cycling, including time trialling, and swam several times a week. She also trained regularly on the track, using grass, cinders or tartan, depending on where she was. In the middle of her career she suffered badly from sciatica, but came back well in the early 1990s. In 1986 she beat Pauline Stuart's Snowdon record by nearly five minutes, with a time of 1 hr 14 mins 36 secs.

On getting over the injury and coming back to form in 1992, she won the Three Peaks and in 1993 had a remarkable run of 38 consecutive wins, 23 of which set new record times. In that year she was selected to run for England at Snowdon in the 'International' race. She won the race in a new record of 1 hr 12 mins 48 secs. This was despite saying of the descent 'I could feel the soles of my feet getting hotter on the steep shale track after crossing under the mountain railway, and I felt my heels begin to blister. As I hit the steep road section at the bottom, my left heel seemed to pop!' The skin on her left heel had come away, leaving two inches or so raw and exposed.

An indication of Greenwood's range is the fact that her still extant records include the classic Burnsall short race, where her time of 16 mins 34 secs from 1983 still stands, as well as the 1 hr 12 mins 48 secs from the ten-mile Snowdon fell race from 1993. Perhaps significantly though, her 11 records which are recorded in this book's appendix don't include any FRA 'long' category races.

At around the same time as Carol Greenwood's career was finishing **Sarah Rowell's** was starting, although they did overlap for a couple of years. Rowell was in born in Germany, as her father was stationed in the army there. In 1983 she won the World Student Games marathon in Canada in 2 hrs 47 mins 37 secs. The next year she was selected for the Los Angeles Olympics, finishing fourteenth in 2 hrs 34 mins 8 secs. Then in 1985 she finished second in the London Marathon in 2 hrs 28 mins 6 secs (the British Record at the time). She also won the 1986 Severn Sisters Marathon outright – an off-road event with 3,000 feet of ascent.

As a youngster Rowell was a great all-rounder, reaching county standard at hockey, lacrosse, cross country and track (being Suffolk schools 100m champion). In the late 1980s she moved from marathons to fell running and between 1989 and 1996 she ran the World Mountain Running Trophy five times, coming second in 1992. That same year she came fifteenth overall in the Three Peaks, her time of 3 hrs 19 mins 11 secs being over 24 minutes ahead of second-placed Carolyn Hunter-Rowe. She was British and English Fell Running Champion in both 1995 and 1996. She has had many race wins, including Burnsall, Ben Nevis, Three Peaks, Borrowdale, Wasdale, Coniston, Fairfield, Fellsman, Duddon and Struc a Choin. She still holds the course records for Skiddaw from 1989 and Dale Head from 1995. Latterly she has been competing in mountain marathons, and has written a book on off-road running, and more recently co-authored one on trail and mountain running.

After Sarah Rowell's two championship years **Angela Mudge** dominated, winning the title for the next four years. She also came back eight years later to win the British Championship in 2008. Mudge was born in Devon and had a difficult start in life. Both of her feet and one of her twin sister Janice's were twisted awkwardly. For the first few years of their lives both of them needed to have their legs in braces to rectify this. As a teenager, Angela raced on the track, and sometimes found cross country courses to be insufficiently challenging. After graduating, she moved to Scotland to study for her Master's, became interested in hill running and joined Carnethy Hill Running Club, and chose to represent Scotland.

Mudge has had great success both locally and internationally. She secured fourth place in the 1997 European Mountain Running Trophy, and also won the Scottish Hill Running Championships in 1997 and 1998, and the Scottish Cross Country Championship in 1999. She also showed rapid progress on the international stage, placing forty-sixth in the eleventh World Mountain Running Trophy when it was held in Scotland in 1995, five years prior to winning the event in 2000.

She continued this trend in 1999, breaking the course record for the prestigious 13,500ft Mount Kinabalu Climbathon in Sabah, Malaysia. Mudge also triumphed in similar record-breaking style in the 2001 Cinq 4,000s in Sierre-Zinal, Switzerland, becoming the first woman to achieve a sub-three-hour time on the 19-mile course. She also won the women's World Mountain Running Trophy in Bergen, Germany, despite it being an uphill only race. Further abroad she set a course record for the Pikes Peak Marathon in 2003.

Following her World Mountain Running Trophy win, she was one of only five Britons nominated at the 2001 Laureus World Sports Awards, alongside David Beckham, Steve Redgrave, Jonathan Edwards and Lennox Lewis. However, she was unable to attend the ceremony as she had a holiday already booked and, she claimed, she 'didn't possess a little black dress, and would only have wandered around collecting autographs.'

Knee injury struck in 2005 yet, although missing most of the summer, she recovered sufficiently quickly to win the fifth World Masters Mountain Running Championship in Keswick that September. For a while she spent nine months of each year working to fund her sporting interests, and spent the remaining three months training and competing in Europe, sleeping in a tent, cycling between race venues. Commenting in her club newsletter[41] on her dedicated and committed approach Angela says:

> Each year I target races I want to peak for and use these as my motivation to do the hard stuff. The only time I really get fed up is when I've over-trained/raced (which happens every year!) and my body seems to be screaming for a rest. I think I need a mental break more than a physical one.

In 2006 she entered the Buff Skyrunner World Series (more naked mountain running?) and was World Champion that year and again in 2007. That year Mudge won the twelfth Everest Marathon, the world's highest marathon that starts only two hours from Everest Base Camp, at an altitude of 17,100ft. Finishing eighth overall, she was the first woman and the second person from the West out of the 80 participants, setting a course record of 5 hrs 3 mins and taking 13 minutes off the previous record. Although predominantly competing internationally she also won the Ben Nevis race in 2008. She still holds course records for Wansfell and Carnethy (from 2002), Creag Dubh (2006), Slieve Donard (2007) and Bens of Jura (2008) – the last three set as a veteran.

Janet McIver became British Champion in 2007 and won the English title as well that year. McIver jointly set the record for Wasdale in 2008 when she dead-heated with Jackie Lee in 4 hrs 12 mins 17 secs. McIver also set records in 2008 at Duddon, Ennerdale and Fairfield, and won the 2008 Lakeland Classics Trophy. **Jackie Lee** won the Lakeland Classics Trophy in

2004 and 2005, but has not won either the British or English Championships. She has set new courses records at both the Coniston Fair and the Manx Mountain Marathon, both in 2007. Recently, however, there has not really been any one woman who has dominated, and it is a vacancy waiting to be filled.

There is a long and broad history of champions and record breakers on the men's side of the sport, and the next chapter details the male champions and record breakers, and some of the stories behind those feats.

A conversation with: **Pauline Stuart,** Keswick AC

I am sitting in the lounge of their modest house in a village in the Northern Lakes, and Kenny and Pauline Stuart are making me feel very much at home, while trying to keep Molly the dog off me. I was fortunate to be invited to talk with them both. I spoke to Pauline after talking to Kenny. She had been listening attentively to Kenny's conversation, and interjected with her own comments now and again. A picture emerged of a really together couple, who are content with their place in life, and who were really happy to share their experiences of fell running. Pauline also kindly agreed for some of their photos to be reproduced in this book.

'My greatest achievement is most probably the Ben time.'

Pauline could identify nothing in particular in her family background that might have suggested a high-profile running career. '*I started running when I was 17 while working as an assistant warden at Wasdale Youth Hostel. I was a keen fellwalker spending most weekends travelling up to the Lakes from Southport before starting work at Wasdale. I saw Joss Naylor, who lived just up the valley, rounding up his sheep and he was running. I thought that looks really good. Whenever I walked I would run back to the hostel. I got further and further away and in order to be back for 5pm I got faster and faster. That was my start if you like. Joss inspired me to run. I was reasonable at it, and was good going downhill, and got quite fit.*'

There were so few females running then that there was no one to inspire her really. '*In fact the first race I entered was Fairfield in 1977, and I won it, and thought this is alright. It was the first official ladies race in the Lakes. There were people from a cross country background coming up, Brenda Robinson for instance. I didn't do much, there was only half a dozen of us, it was a bit of a jolly really. Nearly every race I entered I won.*'

For the long races you were only allowed to run shorter courses, for instance, at Wasdale ladies ran the Burnmoor Chase. '*In 1979 Veronique Marot entered Ennerdale unofficially, and they were horrified. The following year they allowed ladies to run and I won and thoroughly enjoyed it. Veronique later won marathons, including winning Houston when Ken won there. She was a hard lass.*' Kenny interjected here: '*I was easing off for Houston and Veronique was running ten miles with a couple of days to go to the race.*'

Pauline used to run to work and back. She had no advisor, and never did any specialised training. '*I didn't know about speedwork, and didn't know about distances. I just ran when I felt like it, and had a lot of spare time. I got fit by racing. In 1980 you had to do a lot of races. You had to do twelve for the champs. I think I did 26 races that year and won 25 of them.*'

That is how she got fit. She says she wasn't a natural by any means. '*I won the British champs again in 1984 and 1985 and ran the World Championships in 1985, when I was eight weeks pregnant. I didn't feel very well when I ran. I came about eighth or ninth in the Worlds, but I was throwing up before the start, felt really dreadful in the race, but was very cussed. I didn't know I was pregnant, thought I had a stomach bug.*'

She also did the Barnsley Marathon, doing 3 hrs 12 mins in the snow. '*I wasn't a really fast runner to be honest. I found it really boring. I was good over very rough ground. I think that was why the Ben Nevis time is good. I was quite fearless coming down hill. I was equally strong going up and down on steep ground. Similar to Ros Coats really. I think she has done the second fastest time on the Ben. She was fearless and tough.*'

In 1984 she claimed that she didn't know what the Ben Nevis record was, although she had done the race twice. '*I knew the course suited me. The main reason I was inspired to do it was because I overheard this well-known coach talking at the start. "Ros Coats is here, Pauline isn't going to have it her own way. She never tries hard enough, she always looks as if she is out for a breeze." I thought damn you, I'll make sure I win this. I got really annoyed, and it fired me up. I was absolutely determined, which is why it was a good time, and I beat the coach as well, much to his disgust. I showed them I could run really hard.'*

She admitted that she didn't always push herself that hard, as she didn't need to. There weren't enough women running, and she just found herself winning. *'On the Ben, as soon as I heard this chap, who trained a lot of people, I tried really hard. It was greasy day, misty on top. I fell a couple of times. I know I've got pictures with blood all over the place. I thought Ros was just behind me. I remember going hard up and with her close behind me. When I turned round I saw her coming to the summit and just went for it. I thought I am not going to be beaten. When I could see the bloke in front who had made the comments, I thought I'll have him as well.'*

Like Kenny, Pauline Stuart had a mightily impressive racing range. *'Latrigg is dead short and was the day after Borrowdale, I think I was pretty knackered. I had broken the Borrowdale record the day before, which is over 17 miles. Most people just do the Latrigg. I think Victoria Wilkinson only did the Latrigg when she took the record.'*

There weren't too many women running on the fells in the 1980s, the ladies raced against the men as much as possible. Some races made ladies set off at separate times, Skiddaw and Fairfield for instance. *'Often then I would be running on my own, like a time trial. Not like a race, which is why that guy may have thought I wasn't trying. I would have liked more competitive running. A few more women started running in 1984/85.'*

She ranged from Ennerdale (23 miles) to Latrigg (1.5 miles), often racing against a group of men who were the same standard. *'My greatest achievement is most probably the Ben time. I felt so dreadful on that last mile run in, which seems uphill. I thought I might have missed the record as I took an awfully long time to run that mile, I was practically on my knees. I always enjoyed Fairfield, Ennerdale, and I loved the Borrowdale. I enjoyed racing really.'*

Pauline reckons that despite smallish numbers it was much more competitive in the 1980s. She and Kenny kept in touch with the sport until quite recently. *'We used to follow races when our kids were running. Angela Mudge was an excellent runner and Sarah Rowell was brilliant, a 2 hrs 26 mins marathoner. Carol Haigh came after me and beat me at Saddleworth, and she won the Worlds the year after I retired. She was a brilliant runner. I don't really know the current ladies that well.'*

Pauline also questioned the approach taken by some of today's runners. *'It is far too scientific. Timing everything. They have their heart rate monitors and they do their certain bits in the gym. Rather than just going out like Ken did. They were all manual workers then, and just went out and ran. They didn't time everything. You look at our marathon runners now. It is all about going in oxygen chambers and training at altitude. None of them in our day did any of this. Something is going wrong.'*

CHAPTER 10

Record breakers and champions

My whole feeling in terms of racing is that you have to be very
bold. You sometimes have to be aggressive and gamble
Bill Rogers

This chapter covers some of the male fell champions and the records they
set. Mind you, analysing fastest times for fell races is a somewhat tricky
area, as there is so much that can change, not least the conditions that an
event is run in. Even more important is the fact that courses necessarily have
to change, often because of access issues, or changes in start points due to
facilities/parking etc.

Over time there have been a range of record breakers. Three of them
have been Billy Bland, John Wild and Kenny Stuart. In 1980 Billy Bland
won his only British title and had a record-breaking spree. He was followed
by the next two champions over the next five years – John Wild and Kenny
Stuart, who hold ten records between them still, with Bland holding two.

However, these three record breakers have quite different racing profiles.
Bland's two records are both categorised as long and are both in the Lakes
– Borrowdale at 17 miles and Wasdale at 21. Wild's three are all short and
in Northern England – Wrekin (5.5 miles), Rivington Pike (3.25 miles) and
Burnsall (1.5 miles). Stuart by contrast has seven records, or which three are
short, three are medium and one is long, and they are in Wales, Scotland
and the Lakes. They are Wansfell (2.5 miles), Latrigg (3 miles), Eildon 2
Hills (3.5 miles), Skiddaw (9 miles), Snowdon and Ben Nevis (both 10 miles)
and Ennerdale (23 miles).

Obviously records get beaten; those above are ones that have held up. An interesting comparison is given by figures produced by Andy Walmsley in 1989. He counted the number of course records held *at that time* for all races in that year's FRA calendar. The results are pretty startling. For the men, Colin Donnelly, who was in his triple British title winning spree at the time, had 16, to Kenny Stuart's 12 and John Wild's nine. For the women, Carol Haigh, who never actually won the British title, had a staggering 43, to Angela Carson's 17 and Vanessa Brindle's 11[42].

However, many of the major races, for example Wasdale and Fairfield, have had significant changes to their courses. Sadly, when change like this happens the holders of the records for a previous course are down-graded when a new record is subsequently set on a shorter or longer course. Who is to say that in some cases they wouldn't still be the record holder if the change hadn't happened? Having said that, there is a certain fascination in knowing who has set the fastest time for a course and in which year. The list of men's records for the 'classic' courses (see Appendix 3) shows three that have lasted from 1977 – Langdale, Lantern Pike and Eldwick. For the women the oldest are four that date from 1984 – Ben Nevis, Pendelton, Saddleworth and Lantern Pike.

In the September/October 1990 issue of *Up and Down* magazine, Neil Shuttleworth speculated on improving standards in an article entitled 'The Record Has Stood …'. He noted that fell runners have only a once-a-year opportunity to break records, unlike track and marathon runners (when comparing records for the distance, not the particular marathon). Shuttleworth concluded that race conditions were probably the most important factor to consider, that is to say both the weather and the underfoot conditions. Popularity of events also has an effect, in that a more popular event will attract more, and better, runners and possibly increase the likelihood of records. Shuttleworth also felt that neither improved footwear nor better diet were likely to have a significant effect, but that competition (i.e. intense rivalry between top athletes) was likely to be a big factor.

There are many instances where it can be shown that records were broken due to close rivalries, both in individual races and throughout seasons. One of the examples noted above is the Langdale record from 1977. It is held by Andy Styan and when asked by Shuttleworth about it (in the article just quoted), he reckoned it was so fast for two reasons: good conditions and a very strong field. Styan commented:

Billy Bland, Alan McGee, Mike Short and myself pulled clear off
Thunacar Knott, and the four of us pushed each other all the way.
Billy and I got away on the descents, and Alan and Mike would
pull us back on the climbs until we got away off the Crinkles and
held it over Blisco. I left Billy by the cattle grid and that was that.

Even so, these four all finished between 1 hr 55 mins 3 secs and 1 hr 56
mins 8 secs, and it was the first time four runners had finished inside two
hours for the course.

Similarly, John Wild set a record of 12 mins 48 secs (by two seconds)
for the Burnsall Classic in August 1983. Kenny Stuart was first to the top
but was overtaken by a speedily descending Wild, who in Kenny's view was
'taking risks he just wasn't prepared to take, including leapfrogging the wall'.
Two weeks later at Ben Nevis they met again, and faced strong challenges
from Shaun Livesey and Jack Maitland. Strong winds and mist made for a
difficult race. Maitland led Stuart to the summit, with Wild and Livesey close
behind. Somehow Wild took the lead on the way down to the burn in heavy
mist and had a lead of 20 seconds there, holding Stuart off by 17 seconds
at the end. Despite the foul weather these two, and third-placed Livesey, beat
Dave Cannon's 1976 record, with Wild taking 1 min 20 secs off it. John
Wild credited the record to Maitland's pushing so hard on the ascent against
such a known climber as Stuart.

Stuart beat Wild by five points in the British Fell Running championships,
and the two of them were the dominant racers that year. In the 15
championship races Stuart had seven wins and six seconds, and missed just
two events. Wild had five wins, and four seconds, and missed four events
– the same two as Stuart plus two others. However, where they did both
choose to run no one else got a look-in. In the ten races they both ran they
took the first two places in nine of them, with Stuart winning four and Wild
winning six – quite remarkable season long form from both of them really.
You certainly had to race hard to win the championship in those days, as
the table of championship race positions for the two of them shows:

	Kenny	John
Blisco	1	-
Buckden Pike	2	1
Melantee	1	2
Burnsall	2	1
Thieveley Pike	1	2
Kentmere	-	-
Ben Lomond	2	1
Fairfield	2	1
Kinniside	1	2
Ben Nevis	2	1
Three Peaks	1	-
Northern Counties	1	4
Welsh 1000's	2	1
Wasdale	-	-
Borrowdale	1	2

In the 1984 British Championship Kenny Stuart won the title convincingly. He took victory in nine of the ten championship events he contested. He was beaten at Borrowdale, where a semi-retired Billy Bland beat him over his local course. Showing remarkable powers of recovery Kenny Stuart tackled Latrigg (A, three miles, 900ft) the very next day, and stormed up and down to knock 17 seconds off the record that had been held by Hugh Symonds. Not only that, but one month later he raced to a new record at Ben Nevis on another cloudy day. This time Hugh Symonds took the pace uphill to claim the summit prize, but Stuart descended imperiously to clip John Wild's record from the year before by a mere one second.

Kenny Stuart went on to win the Snowdon race in July 1985, with the ideal weather suggesting that a tilt at Fausto Bonzi's record of 1 hr 3 mins 46 secs from the year beforehand might be on the cards. Robin Bryson led Stuart to the summit, with Bonzi thirty secs down. Bonzi initially closed a little on the descent but eventually Jack Maitland took him for second, after coming down in a time faster than Stuart by six secs. However by then Kenny was away and strode in to a fabulous new record time of 1 hr 2 mins 29 secs.

Looking back over the years, the winners of the Fell Running Championship are obviously some of the most consistent competitors, but often with runners only having one 'peak' year. When the Fell Runner of the Year title was instigated in 1972 it was won by Dave Cannon in that first year, and then by a different runner in the next five years: Harry Walker, Jeff Norman, Mike Short, Martin Weeks and Alan McGee. In 1978 Mike Short was the first to win the title twice, before Andy Styan took it the next year. Of these champions only Andy Styan still holds any course records, that being the Langdale one from 1977. Styan was another of the 'daredevil descenders' noted by *Up and Down* magazine, who recorded this comment when in 1974 his fourth fell race (at the Burnsall Classic) provided his first victory:

> I believed before the race that I could win – a totally naïve belief, except that I knew that I was fast downhill – and when I hit the top in 6th position, I just took off on the descent like I was in a dream. It never occurred to me there was any danger and I felt that my body had taken over completely and I was just an exhilarated 'passenger'. I did actually fall – or rather bounce! – several times but never felt any pain until later when I found I had a badly sprained ankle.

Styan also reckoned that he would sometimes fall into a slide and overtake people on his backside. However, he claimed to have had no major injuries from these antics.

After Styan, **Billy Bland** won the British title in 1980, and he is profiled later, as one of the true greats (in Chapter 12). However, he was not able to retain his British Fell Runner title, which was taken in 1981 and 1982 by a newcomer on the scene, **John Wild**. Wild was a relative latecomer to fell running, being 28 at the time, and was teaching flight systems in the RAF. He had success in athletics prior to concentrating on the fells, including winning the Inter-Counties Cross Country in both 1974 and 1980, and reaching the final of the 1978 Commonwealth Games steeplechase event.

His track background showed in his training regime, which included speed sessions (such as 300m repetitions), and circuit and weights sessions. He advocated conditioning work, arguing that a lot of runners would not get injured so much if they did more of it. He experimented with 100-mile training weeks, but settled on 65–70 miles a week as best for him. He is 5ft 8ins tall, and at his peak weighed 9st and had a resting pulse of 44bpm.

Having earlier run Stoodley Pike (coming second to Ricky Wilde in 1977), he decided to have a concentrated year on the fells for 1981 and was immediately successful, setting a new course record in the first championship event at Pendle. He next took the Kentmere record, the Ben Lomond and Fairfield records, and swept to the championship title. In the 1982 Championship Wild entered 11 out of the 15 counting races, winning seven of them, including four of the medium length counters. Of the races he didn't win, Kenny Stuart beat him in three of the short races, and Billy Bland won Wasdale in a new course record with Wild languishing in twentieth place.

Then **Kenny Stuart** emerged from the professional scene, and dominated fell running for a while, winning the British Championship for three years from 1983 to 1985. His exploits and many records are detailed in Chapter 12.

After the reign of Kenny Stuart, **Jack Maitland** won the championship in 1986. He was born in Aboyne in Aberdeenshire, and dabbled at several sports at school. He began to concentrate on orienteering, being selected for the Scottish junior and then the Great Britain junior squads as a 17-year old. When he went to university he also took up fell running, introduced to the sport by Colin Donnelly. He also joined the university swimming, orienteering and volleyball clubs. In 1982 he won the elite class at the Karrimor Mountain Marathon with John Baston. After missing out on qualifying for the senior orienteering world championships in 1985, Maitland began to really focus on running in the hills. Within a year he was at the top of the sport.

Perhaps his greatest individual success was to go out to Switzerland and win the Sierre-Zinal in his first year of serious fell running in 1985, despite falling quite badly twice. A confirmed racer, he competed over a hundred times in the year (not all on the fells), yet still had the energy to take the British fell title. In his early career Maitland thought nothing of running the Cumbria Lakes Marathon (in 2 hrs 23 mins 27 secs) then turning out at the Butter Crag fell race the day afterwards, and coming third. Maitland still holds the course records for Pendle from 1984, and the Blisco Dash from 1987. He later moved to triathlon competition, gaining 12 Great Britain caps in various world and European Championships. He is now a leading triathlon coach, working with the Brownlee brothers amongst others.

After Maitland, **Colin Donnelly** secured a hat-trick of championship wins between 1987 and 1989. Born in Scotland, Donnelly did the usual dabbling with sports at school. He found individual sports like running and cycling to his liking rather than any team games. His father used to take him walking, and when he went to Aberdeen University he competed at cross country and on the road, but by then preferred hill running. In 1979, while at university, he won Ben Nevis on his debut, the first Scotsman to win there for twelve years. He tried competing in the British Championship events but when in 1981 the system was changed to the best ten from 15 specified races he became disillusioned. He felt it was heavily biased towards English races/ racers. For a while he just concentrated on local races and long-distance challenges – setting a new record for the Bob Baxter Round in the process. He also set fast times for other rounds such as the Grey Corries Twelve 3,000 footers and the 16 Mamore 3,000 footers, which have never achieved the same status as the Bob Baxter for instance.

Joining the RAF in 1984 and being posted to RAF Valley in North Wales brought Donnelly back to championship racing. Increased fitness, and more importantly better tactics and a better psychological approach, enabled him to secure the three British Championship wins. He then raised his horizons to the international scene, even competing in the Mount Cameroon race, which he said was 'the toughest and most dangerous race I've yet done. After looking at the course I half-hoped to catch a disease or something, just to have an excuse not to compete!' Although he set other course records, including the Manx Mountain Marathon and Cader Idris (1 hr 21 mins 18 secs in 1996), the only one still on the list is Buckden Pike from 1988.

In the same year Donnelly set the record of 4 hrs 19 mins for the Welsh 3000s Challenge, which still stands. Interviewed in the July/August 1990 issue of *Up and Down* magazine he commented:

> I admire Billy Bland. He's an excellent ambassador for our sport. He incorporates high principles and sportsmanship with athletic brilliance, a typical fell/mountain runner. Kenny Stuart and Bob Whitfield are chips off the same block.

In the early 1990s there wasn't really a dominant fell runner in Britain. The championship was won by Gary Devine, Keith Anderson (who claimed he was never beaten in a descent), Steve Hawkins, Mark Croasdale, and Mark Kinch (twice) in this period. However, four of these athletes still hold course records for classic fell races. They are Gary Devine for Chew Valley (from 1989), Keith Anderson for Sedbergh (1991), Mark Croasdale for Ingleborough (1991) and Mark Kinch for Dale Head (1995).

Then **Ian Holmes** took over as the top runner in the British Championship, winning in 1996, 1997 (uniquely, tying with Mark Roberts), 1998 and 2000. He was an early starter, with his first race being in 1976 when he competed in the under-12 fell race at Malham Show and finished third. His first race win was at Scafell Pike in 1989. He has been remarkably consistent and is regarded as one of the best descenders in fell running history, if not the best. He has also moved into the international racing scene, selected to run in the World Mountain Running Championships three times, and also three times in the European equivalent. He also won Kinabalu three times in succession from 1997 to 1999. Domestically his wins in major races have included the Three Peaks once (in 1997) and favourites like Ben Nevis and Bens of Jura an impressive six times each. He holds course records for Coniston (1996), Otley Chevin (2001), Stoodley Pike and Duddon (both 2007).

Gavin Bland interrupted Ian Holmes's run of championship wins by taking the title in 1999. Gavin was the next most successful of the Bland clan, after his uncle Billy. Born in 1971, he is the son of Billy's brother David. Gavin was brought up in Rosthwaite, before moving to Thirlmere, where he was a shepherd in the Dunmail area. He competed for a while in the junior guides races, before joining Keswick AC on being reinstated as an amateur. In 1989 he ran his first Senior race, at Loughrigg, finishing tenth. The nine miles was further than he had ever run before, but he seemed comfortable with the distance after the pace of the short pro junior races.

In 1990 Gavin Bland started to make his mark, winning the Langdale and Gategill events. He also had a fantastic result in the junior race at the World Cup in Austria, finishing second. In 1991 he started winning races, including the Blisco Dash, Three Shires and Borrowdale. That year he finished second in the British Championships to Keith Anderson, and won the English

Championships without actually planning to, or even concentrate on it, preferring to focus on World Cup races. 1992 included a host of wins, including classics like Borrowdale, Duddon and Ben Nevis.

Gavin Bland is 5ft 11ins tall, and weighed 10st at his racing peak. He admits to not being a brilliant climber, nor indeed navigator. He also says he has not got an especially good sprint finish, although he is bracketed with some of the great descenders. He is a self-acknowledged lazy trainer, doing no speed work, and being unable to train at all at lambing time. He was not a great one for training over courses used in races, but he did sometimes reconnoitre them in the early days, particularly long 'A' category courses. His stated preference is for steep, rough courses and he does better in longer races, giving Borrowdale and Ben Nevis as favourites. In 1993 Bland became the youngest ever winner of the Three Peaks in appalling conditions, a feat which was recorded in a television programme of the race made for Yorkshire Television.

Despite several near misses it was several years before Gavin Bland was able to secure a British championship title win. In the early days he claimed he wanted to run roads later, and wanted to beat Billy's Bob Graham Round record, but his careeer took a different path. In 1997 he set the present course record of 1 hr 45 mins 8 secs for the Three Shires race. Then in 1999 it all came good. Setting records that still stand at Carnethy and Edale Skyline he finally achieved his ambition of being crowned as the best fell runner in Britain.

After Ian Holmes the most successful fell runners have been Bingley's **Rob Jebb**, winner in 2003 and 2006, who is profiled later for his cross-sport successes (in Chapter 18), and **Rob Hope**, from the Pudsey and Bramley club, who was British Champion three times, in 2007, 2008 and 2009. Hope's longevity (and attitude) is perhaps best summed up by a quote from an interview with Hope conducted by Boff Whalley for their club magazine:

> I never tire of winning. Anyway, there's always a different race to win, and you can always strive to run faster or try to beat a different field of runners ... I don't want to become a boring, single-minded runner. My running's only an hour or so a day on average. Still got 23 to play with!

The athletes covered in this chapter are all great champions, but I have been mulling over those that I consider the greatest, and why. We now look at those I consider to have been the three greatest ever fell runners, the first of whom was never actually crowned British Fell Champion.

CHAPTER 11

The greatest – Joss Naylor

Someone may beat me today, but they're gonna have to bleed to
do it
Steve Prefontaine

In my view there are three fell runners who have to be considered as the greatest of the modern era, for different reasons. Firstly, Joss Naylor, who is noted for his longevity in the sport and his immense endurance records. He bestrides the sport, and is still performing magnificently in his eighth decade.

Joss Naylor has quite possibly had more written about him than anyone else in the sport of fell running. This includes an in-depth profile in Keith Richardson's book *Joss: The life and times of the legendary Lake District fell runner and shepherd*, and even TV documentaries. In some ways his achievements have transcended the sport, and his will be one name that folk on the street may have heard of. Oddly, his activities as an amateur fell runner may have reduced his early profile somewhat, as he didn't appear at such popular gatherings as Ambleside or Grasmere Sports with their professional events and large crowds, but instead showed his prowess at events like the amateur Wasdale race or the Lake District Mountain Trial.

Although looking a somewhat ungainly figure as he lopes over the fellsides, Naylor had two natural advantages for succeeding as a fell runner. Firstly, his slight frame weighed only nine stone at peak fitness, and secondly he was brought up in a natural training arena for the sport. He was born in

1936 at Middle Row Farm, Wasdale Head, with Yewbarrow rising behind and Pillar, Kirk Fell, Great Gable and the Scafells all there for training over.

The Lake Poet Samuel Taylor Coleridge, one of the first recreational fell-walkers, paused in Wasdale in the summer of 1802 and gasped, 'Oh my God, what enormous mountains these are behind me!'. Statistically, Wasdale scores at both ends of the scale. As well as the highest mountain in England (Scafell Pike), it has the deepest lake in England (Wastwater) and also what is claimed to be the smallest church in the country (St Olaf's).

Joss Naylor was the youngest of four children. His three brothers were all subsequently farmers, with Joss later farming at Bowderdale (as a tenant), just along the Wasdale valley from his birthplace. He was helping on the family farm from a very early age, before and after his school day down at Gosforth at the entrance to the Wasdale valley. As a youngster he played a little football, and took up Cumberland and Westmorland style wrestling, but a serious injury to his back put paid to that. He gave evasive answers for years to the question of how this original injury occurred. Joss admitted in an emotional interview for Keith Richardson's eponymous book that he was actually messing about at the age of nine when his mother kicked out at him and caught him badly, and that this was in fact the root cause of all his later problems.

He left school at 15 to work at home on the farm, claiming not to have missed a day's work with the injury, which was constantly troubling him. In his early twenties he had an operation to remove two discs from his back. That proved successful, but he had to wear a corset for a while. At the age of 24 he threw away the corset and perversely took up the tough sport of fell running. Things didn't come easy in the early years but he showed his legendary determination by training for the longer events, which he realised were to be his forte eventually. In his mid twenties he had a bad fall jumping a fence, which aggravated his back even further.

Initially, he had been just dabbling in the sport. Then the Lake District Mountain Trial came to Wasdale in 1960. Joss entered and ran in his working boots, leading for the first two hills before suffering with cramp and struggling home in fourteenth place. The next year he remained in front all the way and finished 15 minutes in front of the next man. Unfortunately, he had got lost after the third checkpoint, and thus didn't win as he had missed a checkpoint. He claimed that his sheep didn't range that far. At the relatively late age of 30, in 1966, Joss gained his first victory in the Lake District Mountain Trail, this time over a nominally 17-mile course in Eskdale.

During this period he won the Karrimor International Mountain Marathon in 1970 and 1971. He also won the Lake District Mountain Trial again in 1969 and in 1971, starting a run of wins through to 1977 (with one more win in 1979). He might have won in 1970 too as well as he was going well when he was kicked by a cow, and was forced to slow, dropping back to second place.

Joss Naylor was a class apart in two-day events like the KIMM. This is an event for pairs, which takes place in a different area of Britain each year, and involves navigation over 20 miles each day and camping overnight, having carried all your kit and food for the two days. Joss, and his partner, Alan Walker, had won the event in 1971 by such a margin that the sponsors invited over some top Scandinavian orienteers for the next year, when it was held at Tibbie Shiels, in the Scottish Borders. After two days, over 53 miles and 13,200 feet of ascent Naylor and Walker were beaten, mostly by better navigation by the orienteers as it happens, by 32 minutes, yet with the next pair 1 hr and 25 mins behind them.

In his formative years Joss had some favourite courses and built his season round them. These included in season order: the Edale Skyline, the Three Peaks, and the Ennerdale Horseshoe, which Joss won for the first nine years of its existence, only being denied a tenth win by an ankle injury in 1977. He set the record of 3 hrs 30 mins 40 secs for the Ennerdale race at the time. This is now 3 hrs 20 mins 57 secs set by, who else but, Kenny Stuart. The second half of the season would include his local race, the Wasdale Horseshoe, plus Ben Nevis and the Lake District Mountain Trail.

In 1971 Joss was the sixth person to complete the Bob Graham Round. After Graham himself, the next four were Alan Heaton, Stan Bradshaw, Ken Heaton and Eric Beard, so Joss was already in good company. In fact, he was in good company on his own round as the Heaton brothers and Bradshaw all paced Naylor on various sections of the run. Moreover, it was not long before Joss was expanding his horizons, literally, to further endurance challenges. Meanwhile, he dropped a railway sleeper on his foot in 1972, but this did not stop him coming second in the KIMM, and winning the Mountain Trial, the Manx Mountain Marathon and the Welsh 1000s race that year.

The International Three Peaks challenge was an early target for Joss, and he took it on in 1971. With Ken Ledward driving, in a Ford Corsair, they admitted to hitting speeds of 120 mph at times when travelling between the highest mountains in Scotland, England and Wales. At least they did the job properly, starting by touching water in the loch at Fort William and finishing by touching water again alongside Caernarvon castle.

When my athletic clubmate and I did it a few years ago we did it car park to car park. We started at the break of dawn from the car park by Glen Nevis Visitor Centre, having slept in the car, and finished at the car park at Pen y Pass. We had completed the peaks well within daylight hours, although way slower than Joss, but WITHOUT breaking the speed limit. We also had an unplanned highlight moment, when we were so hot running off Scafell in the middle of a boiling summer's day that we 'took 5' at Stockley Bridge. The skinny dip in a plunge pool just by the bridge to cool off was just so refreshing it gained us more than five minutes back in renewed enthusiasm for the task in hand.

Joss was obviously in good nick and went well on his own Three Peaks effort. He chose to ascend Scafell Pike via the Corridor Route from Seathwaite, and descend via Langdale, whence Ledward had driven meanwhile. Nowadays the speed that you attain on the M6 if you do an out-and-back via Borrowdale and drive out via Keswick makes it not really a worthwhile option, in my opinion, to descend via Langdale. An indication of Joss's strength is that the weather came in for the Snowdon leg and he changed his route from the Pen y Pass option to start from Llanberis instead, giving himself considerably more height to gain. He probably started from either Victoria Terrace, or at the Victoria Hotel, and thus his route will have been slightly shorter than that for the Snowdon race, which starts at Padarn Park. Having said that, at the end of a long day, much of it spent cramped in a sports car, he still did the return trip to the Snowdon summit and back in 1 hr 5 mins, just three minutes longer than Kenny Stuart's course record in the race. Coast to coast the Three Peaks took them just 11 hrs and 54 mins. The next day Naylor helped pace a Bob Graham Round effort for a fellow runner.

In 1974 he ran the Pennine Way, from north to south, in just over three days, leaving him thinking that under three days was possible[43]. Joss Naylor was also a pioneer of racing abroad, being invited to compete in the famous Sierre-Zinal race in Switzerland in 1974, travelling out in advance to train and acclimatise, and finished a creditable sixth in a field of 1,600. The following year he travelled to the USA to run the Pike's Peak Marathon, an event described in Chapter 17. Meanwhile, the first of his multi-peak endurance runs took place in 1975, when he scaled 72 peaks in the Lake District in 23 hours.

In 1976 he ran the 'Coast to Coast' (made famous by Alfred Wainwright's book[44]) from Robin Hood's Bay to St Bees Head from 4am Saturday to 9pm on Sunday night. At St Bees he ran into the sea and when he removed his socks, the soles of his feet and some toenails came off with them. His wife Mary reckons she 'has to agree when people say Joss is not like a human. He has iron control and a fantastic will. He can shut out pain.' As an aside, I sometimes wonder if he has some form of congenital analgesia.

All this racing, and the training for it, took place while Joss managed his farm at Bowderdale, taking over the tenancy there when he got married in 1962. It must have been a tough existence, which was fully supported by wife Mary. She is an outcomer, hailing from Newcastle. Electricity only reached Wasdale in 1977, thanks to a cable running up under the lake in order to keep this scenic dale free from overhead wires.

Much later the Naylors starting taking in B&B guests in the summer to boost their income, but it was always a simple life. In *A Walk Around the Lakes* Hunter Davies paints a stark picture of the daily shepherding life for Joss (this at the tail end of the 1970s):

> He never eats anything during the day. All he takes with him is a Mars bar. If he gets hungry, he might have a few mouthfuls of spring water on the fells. Hunger soon passes if you drink. When he comes down from the fells, he has a scrub down in the beck. In the summer, he gets up to his waist but in the winter he just takes his boots and socks off and freshens his legs.

At some point while researching this book I was reading Adharanand Finn's *Running with the Kenyans*, in which the author theorises about the amazingly successful Kenyan distance runners. He is told: 'They all come from a poor, rural family. We have not had a good runner from a city.' He finds that from a young age the Kenyans have to work hard, herding goats or digging in the fields, and they run or walk everywhere. Just for a moment I am tempted to see a parallel with the Kenyans in the lifestyles of folk like Joss Naylor and Gavin Bland (shepherds both), but decide this is too simplistic to have any real merit, so drop it.

Joss now lives at Low Greendale, and the Bowderdale farm is run by his son Paul and his family. The farm is still delightfully old-fashioned and yet superbly welcoming to visitors, with its fantastic views over the vale. Having had a night's stay there two summers ago I have a good feel for the life that Joss must have had there. As we drove up the rough unmade track to the farmhouse we saw the piles of stones in the lower fields where they had been collected by hand to aid managing the fields in this tough environment. Two of them have been sculpted by Joss into monument-like structures, which stand guard imperiously.

For a short while in their teens Joss's two daughters, Gillian and Susan, were keen fell runners, as was their younger brother Paul. Now Paul's son Craig is a leading exponent of Cumberland- and Westmorland- style wrestling, having achieved international honours as a junior.

Joss and his family have always been involved in activities in the community. There are many examples of Joss 'putting something back' by helping organise events, and especially helping pace others on endurance rounds. For many years he used to lay what were acknowledged as the finest hound trails, always with spectators in mind, at the Wasdale Head Show and Sports. This is held each October, and it seems somehow appropriate to note that it is the traditional show that is the last in the calendar year, located as it is out in this remote valley.

Joss had to take four weeks off work in 1977 as four discs in his back had deteriorated and were hindering him very badly. He was told that he would be wheelchair bound for the rest of his life if he didn't give up farming. He considered his options, and later that year paced his friend Ken Ledward to his Bob Graham Round, which was the fifty-sixth recorded. He went all the way round with him eventually, and Ledward remarked: 'He'd race ahead and he'd look at the views and he'd run back and then he'd start away again. So I was on my own for an awful long time!'

So, in 1979 Naylor took a second job, training apprentices and doing shift work at Sellafield, the nuclear reprocessing plant on the western edge of the Lake District. He sold his cows, but kept a thousand sheep, so it really was a second job as they still had to be looked after in his spare hours. He always reckoned the boundary between his work and his training was indistinct, as he was out on the fells so long with his flock. Having said that, he would often set out on very long training runs. These were sometimes up to eight or nine hours in length, much to wife Mary's dismay.

Unorthodox training certainly, but the effect is shown by the results, which were awesome, by anyone's standards. Rex Bellamy, in his book *The Four Peaks*, quotes Chris Brasher – who had run with Naylor occasionally, and run against and witnessed the Olympic greats – on Naylor:

> at his best, in the 1970s, Joss was superior to any other long-distance runner I have known. As a fell runner he burnt them all off. They couldn't hold him.

Brasher compared him to athletes like Emil Zatopek or Vladimir Kuts:

> We often talked about that – and we rejected them all. Joss was better than Zatopek, Kuts, Coe, Ovett … There was only one man in his class and that was 'Wilson' of the Wizard. You had to go into fiction. What Joss did was unbelievable, but you knew it had happened because you were there.

A totally unscientific comparison, not even of like against like, but I hope you get the point. Brasher also thought that Naylor could have performed well at road marathons and long-distance track events. He never tried a road marathon but, as we will see, his dally with long-distance track racing wasn't exactly world-shattering.

The rigours of fell running have produced a fair amount of injuries, but Naylor doesn't ever let that affect him or lessen his personal drive to push himself to further limits. For a while he ran with steel supports in his shoes. He also seems to have a phenomenal pain threshold. It is possible that the back issue has forced him to make do, and that the lack of sleep he got on many of his endurance events lasting more than a day was bearable as he had learnt to go without much sleep anyway because of the pain. When asked by Rex Woods in his *Lakeland profiles* for his motives for undergoing all this pain and strain his reply was simply that he

> likes being out among the fells; likes running over them; likes being fit; and likes competing, both against fellow running enthusiasts and above all himself.

He also used to drink cod liver oil to lubricate his joints. When asked how many teaspoons he took, his reply was that he took it 'from the bottle, like whisky'.

One of the most bizarre challenges Naylor ever set himself was in 1977. After a busy fell season he entered a 24-hour track race at Crystal Palace, aiming for the world record of 161 miles 545 yards, held by Tipton's Ron Bentley. Joss and Boyd Millen (also of Kendal AC) started along with ten 'track' runners. The race was run on a tartan track and Joss finished fourth having covered 132 miles, finding it very hard on his feet. Perhaps he should have looked for a cinder track for his attempt. Naylor had felt his knee 'go' a fortnight before the event, and boldly claimed that he could have done 170 miles 'nee bother' otherwise. The fact of the matter was that he had had knee trouble for years. His right knee had all the cartilage removed by the time he was 18. This wasn't particularly successful, and he has had a knee joint which doesn't work properly ever since, although physiotherapy has improved things in later years. In fact, he was deemed unfit for National Service in earlier days.

Some of Naylor's lasting legacies are his endurance runs. When he found that the Lake District 24-hour record was at 60 peaks he subsequently raised this to 61, then 63 and finally 72. Details of some of these are in the chapter on fell challenges (Chapter 16). In an interview in *Climber and Rambler* in 1983 Andy Hyslop asked Joss what training he did for the 72 peaks effort. He replied:

> A lot of miles, especially during the winter months. I was out most days running 10 or 15 miles on the fell and Sundays I'd do a 30 or 40 miler. I did the eleven highest peaks in the Lakes a fortnight before with no backup and the week before I did the 4 three thousanders in 7 hrs 29 mins. I should have broken 7 hrs really but the weather was terrible.

In the same interview Joss also gave an intriguing insight into two challenges he considered, but never actually took on. He claimed that he had thought of running up and down Kilimanjaro from the road head, and then run up and down Mt Kenya. He thought he needed altitude training for that and someone to set up ropes on the climbing difficulties on Mt Kenya. When asked about taking on Eric Beard's Cuillin Ridge time (just over four hrs at the time), he commented:

Well I don't know now, but a few years ago I was meaning to have
a go if the ropes had been set up on the climbing sections. You
would certainly need a lot of running in your legs for it and your
reflexes would have to be very sharp on such rough ground.

At the same time that people were extending the Lakes 24-hour peaks total,
Alan Heaton had completed a challenge to visit all the lakes, meres and
waters in the Lake District. These number 27 and the trip is about 105 miles,
including several high passes/peaks to get from valley to valley. Heaton had
completed it in 26 hrs 30 mins. Naylor repeated the round in 1983, taking
a 'mere' 19 hrs 20 mins 14 secs. He was paced on the Ennerdale to Wastwater
section by clubmate John Wild, who left him at Wasdale to nip off and win
the Blake Fell race.

A measure of Naylor's status in the area is that a complete stranger saw
him coming from their cottage near Brotherswater and ran him a bath, which
he gratefully took to refresh himself. Joss also shows his softer side when
commenting on his feelings at Kentmere Reservoir on this epic:

It was really beautiful at the reservoir there. I laid down for about
10 minutes just to tek it all in. You're looking up at Ill Bell and
the sun is shining in. I was on this green-cropped part of the dam
and it was just like lying on a good bed. I thowt I was in heaven
and I had to give missel a shek and git on wid it. I jumped up and
went over the top to Blea Water and Small Water.

Having trod that very ground recently I concur on the beauty of the upper
Kentmere valley, but I did feel it went on for ever, as we came home after
a long (by my current standards) day walking on the fells. On another
occasion, way back in time, I was once mistaken for 'a noted fell runner'
while out running on my own in upper Kentmere. It is kind of cool that
someone could think I was going well enough to have actually been such
an exalted person. Mind you, that was not as bizarre as being mistaken for
climber Doug Scott once in the Old Nags Head in Edale. Having already
'taken a drink', for some reason I said that I was indeed him when questioned
by a fellow drinker. To my embarrassment (well now anyway, perhaps not
at the time) this resulted in me being plied with free drinks for the whole
of the evening.

Plate 1. John Greenop, winner of the Grasmere Guides Race 1876-1881

Plate 2. A group of Grasmere Guides racers in 1876

Plate 3. John Grizedale, Grasmere winner in 1888 and 1890

Plate 4. J Pepper (1st) and W Barnes (2nd) after the 1893 Grasmere Guides Race

Plate 5. Rivington Pike 1991. Mark Croasdale, Colin Donnelly, Paul Dugdale, Keith Anderson and Craig Roberts

Plate 6. 1958 LDMT winner Joe Hand (Border Harriers)

Plate 7. The start of the 1957 LDMT from the Old Dungeon Ghyll,
John Nettleton leads

Plate 8. Joss Naylor running in the Mountain Trial 1987

Plate 9. The leaders on Red Pike in the Ennerdale race in 1985

Plate 10. Helene Whitaker training above a misty Ennerdale

Plate 11. Bill Teasdale, Tommy Sedgwick and Keith Summerskill
at Kilnsey, 1970

Plate 12. Tommy Sedgwick jumping a fence at Ambleside
in 1982

Plate 13. Tommy Sedgwick and Fred Reeves at Grasmere, 1973

Plate 14. Fred Reeves celebrates winning Grasmere in 1974

Plate 15. Fred Reeves leading Kenny Stuart at Grasmere in 1979

Plate 16. Kenny Stuart leading from Mick Hawkins at Grasmere 1980

Plate 17. Billy Bland and Pauline Stuart, 1980 Fell Runners of the Year

Plate 18. Pauline Stuart winning the Ben Nevis race in 1984

Plate 19. Sarah Rowell winning
the Three Peaks in 1991

Plate 20. Angela Mudge at the
Anniversary Waltz, 1999

Plate 21. Billy Bland and John Wild, prolific record breakers, at Wasdale

Plate 22. 1994 Ben Nevis winner Ian Holmes in between Jonathon Bland
on the left and Gavin Bland on the right

Plate 23. Joss Naylor on his 60 at 60 traverse in 1996

Plate 24. Joss Naylor on Fairfield – in the 1999 Lake District Mountain Trial

Plate 25. Billy Bland in the Ben Nevis race in 1984

Plate 26. Kenny Stuart on Whernside on the way to winning the Three Peaks in 1983

Plate 27. Kenny Stuart winning the Glasgow Marathon

Plate 28. Rossendale Fell Race – Jeff Norman leads Dave Cannon in 1970

Plate 29. Phil Davidson, Bob Graham and Martin
Rylands at Dunmail Raise, June 13 1932

Plate 30. Billy Bland at the end of his record-breaking BGR in 1982

Plate 31. Rob Jebb leading from the Addisons on Reston Scar, 2012

Plate 32. Alistair Brownlee leads brother Jonathon and Javier Gomez in the
2012 Olympic Triathlon in London

Yet another endurance effort by Naylor was undertaken on 14 April 1979. Joss ran from Carlisle to Barrow (88 miles, mostly on roads) for the Lions charity, raising over £10,000 in the process. He trained for five months for the effort. Commenting on running on the roads he said: 'I have no blisters or anything. In fact I never changed my shoes or socks on the road, which I thought I might have to. I would rather be on the fells.'

Another challenge instigated by someone else caught Naylor's eye in 1986. Chris Bland, Billy's cousin, had tried to 'do the Wainwrights' day by day, book by book. There are 214 summits recorded in Alfred Wainwright's classic series of seven *Pictorial Guides to the Lakeland Fells*. Chris Bland did 192 of them in a great effort, raising money for the repair of the Borrowdale church roof. Alan Heaton completed the whole set in 1985, but now not in book by book fashion. Getting away from the book by book approach improved the logistics and he completed them all in 9 days 16 hrs 42 secs – despite suffering from a septic foot from mid afternoon on the fourth day. Naylor reduced this to 7 days 1 hr 25 secs in 1986. The story of this epic is told by Naylor himself in the booklet *Joss Naylor MBE was here*, published by Ken Ledward's company KLETS, of Braithwaite. Just the numbers involved make you wonder – 214 Lakeland tops, ascents totalling 121,000 feet (more than four ascents of Everest) and a total of approximately 391 miles, the equivalent of 15 marathons.

Read the booklet and marvel – this was over a period of scorching hot weather, by the way. Joss sums up both this effort and his feelings for his support and his surroundings.

We had to drag from ourselves not only our accumulated fitness and basic strength, we had to reach even deeper into ourselves when natural physical abilities had been drained, deeper than I had ever had to reach even in the most serious winter mountaineering conditions. I just do not have words suitable to describe the discomfort, the physical pain, the frustration and the worry we all had to suffer ... We had our problems, sometimes disagreements, but not once was a cross word spoken – some colourful words, but never an angry one. I've found in the fells that there is a common purpose, whether I've been with a climber getting sheep off a crag, with a fell runner or even walking visitors, our bond is our love for these beautiful hills.

As a footnote, Naylor claimed at a later date that he would have done the Wainwrights in six days, but had trouble with his feet – the flesh on both ankles was cut through to the nerve. At 10-01pm on Friday 20 June 2014 Steve Birkinshaw set a new record of 6 days 13 hours.

Joss Naylor has a wicked sense of humour. Some of his natural humour comes out in his writing in the Wainwright's account. It is also evident from other incidents that he has an impish streak in him, and can even be a mite spiky. I have heard tell of a story from the days when no one could beat Naylor. Harry Walker and Jeff Norman decided to gang up on Joss and put their combined weight against him in one Ennerdale race. They were going to just stick to Joss and try to outsprint him. Joss got to know of this and used the misty day to his advantage. Coming off High Crag Joss rushed down Scarth Gap (deliberately going off course) and hid behind a rock. The other two duly followed, but were then Buttermere bound by mistake. Joss re-emerged from hiding and got back on course, taking half an hour out of both his rivals.

In conversation with me, Jeff Norman responded:

> I am not sure that story is factually correct. People say that is what he did. If I remember rightly we got to that area and I remember he took off in a burst on this very rough contouring path as that was his forte. I was useless at that, and he knew it. He just went away from me and I lost sight of him in the mist, and may have gone a little off course. I certainly don't remember finishing half an hour behind him. I have heard that story before though, about him hiding behind a rock.

On another occasion Joss ran in a race at Whitehaven and was beaten by John Kirkbride, who was an Olympian. In an interview for radio afterwards he was asked why he hadn't won. He replied that he had run there from Wasdale and was about to run back. Behind the interviewer's back he got in a car and drove off.

So, it may come as no surprise that on two occasions he has won the World's Biggest Liar contest. This event takes place at the Bridge Inn, Santon Bridge, and Naylor won in 1979 and again in 1982. Later, the 2004 winner was Mike Naylor, Joss's nephew, who brews beer at Wasdale's micro brewery, including his own Liar Ale. When Mike Naylor won it was reported[45] that he entered the room in his best dungarees and green wellies and told the noisy audience he was Micky Mandela. Mike told the audience and BBC camera crews that he was from South Africa, but thanks to a Teach Yourself Cumbrian course he was able to address the gathering in Cumbrian. He said a local firm called Bang! No Folk Left (BNFL) were flooding Wasdale and that Herdwick sheep would be replaced by fish farming, monitored by new organisation, the Ministry of Underwater Fisheries and Food (MUFF). The http://www.cockermouth.org.uk/Wasdale show was to be replaced with spectator events such as sea horse racing. He did say that residents whose homes were to be flooded would be allowed to keep their homes, with air locks at the door and cat or dog fish flaps.

Mike Naylor won the title again in 2005. On another occasion the Prime Minister (Tony Blair) was visiting nearby Sellafield on the same day as the World's Biggest Liar contest and some of the audience thought he might turn up to claim the prize. However, under the competition rules, politicians and members of the legal profession are banned from taking part as 'they are too practised in the art of lying'.

Joss Naylor's spikiness is evidenced by his contrary reaction to Mark McDermott taking his 24-hour peak record from 72 to 76, which he did in 1988. In a profile published in *The Independent* in 1996 Naylor noted that

> he's hardly won a race in his life, before or since – you'd think if
> he was capable of doing that, he'd be winning every big race in the
> country.

This comment, and his reported reaction to Mark Hartell adding one more peak in 1997, suggests he thought they were somehow not deserving of the recognition, as they were not traditional fell types, as neither were really from the traditional fell running areas or backgrounds. The fact that they ran computer programmes to determine route choices won't have helped. Joss had either just reconnoitred his long runs in the field in advance or even just done them blind.

However, the latest edition of the *42 Peaks* leaflet notes that Mark McDermott planned for his 76-peak effort meticulously in 1988, and that he 'had an intimate knowledge, and love, of the fells, and reconnoitred every section by day and night.' On Crinkle Crags someone asked him if he was doing the BGR to which he replied that he wished he was. Mark commented:

Soon we were on the ridge to Causey Pike with the moon beaming, the stars twinkling, and the lights of Keswick glowing invitingly down in the valley. The edges of the sky were still tinged with red. What a night!

The world moves on and records are only there to be beaten.

Age is no barrier to Joss though, and he has carried on setting himself targets and creating new legacies, when most normal people would be winding down in life. In 1990 he established 'Joss Naylor's fun run' or Lakeland Challenge as it is formally designated. It is from Pooley Bridge to Greendale Bridge, Wasdale. The route traverses 31 summits in 48 miles, with 16,000 feet of ascent. Aged 54, Joss did it in 11 hrs 30 mins. Veteran runners are now challenged to do it within set times that relate to their age.

Then in 1996 Joss did 60 peaks at 60 in 36 hours (over 100 miles and 40,000 feet of ascent), and in 2006 70 peaks at 70 in under 21 hours, covering more than 50 miles and climbing more than 25,000 feet – in both cases raising masses of money for charity. The *Westmorland Gazette* reported the former event in considerable detail in a piece entitled 'Mountain king becomes a conquering hero at 60'. Four days beforehand Naylor had lifted two gates off a trailer, badly pulling his back muscles, meaning he could barely walk, let alone run. Coming off Wetherlam, after 21 summits and over nine hours on the go, pacer Hugh Symonds is quoted as saying:

He is a man on fire. I am very tired. Joss has just an amazing level of fitness and an unbelievable competitive urge.

His GP David Clarkson treated him for severe muscle spasms in his back and legs en route and commented:

Fifty per cent of this is physical and fifty mental. If you believe you are going to do it you will do it.

Joss did do it. It took longer than planned, as he couldn't run at all towards the end. Over 36 hours on the go, and Joss summed it up:

Two great mornings, two great sunsets, it was something out of this world. I was mentally sick when I hurt my back, but knew I had to see this through. Too much was riding on it, so many had helped to organise it. That is all I have to say now, big thanks to everyone and that I don't think I will be doing it again.

Then added, 'well not that anyway, but maybe something else'.

Naylor is also not above criticising authority when he sees fit. For instance, the National Trust were taken to task thus in an interview in *The Independent*[46] in 1996.

The footpath on Black Sail there, it was kept right by the council until 1970 ... now it is eroded to nothing. The Trust leave things too late. And you can't tell 'em. Sixteen years ago I went specially to see the man in charge of the area and told him exactly what was wrong ... Nothing was ever done, and it's meant thousands and thousands of pounds' worth of damage to a good bridleway.

Considering the perceived dangers of nearby Sellafield, where he of course worked, he has had more real danger in his farming life, acknowledged as one of the most dangerous jobs you can do these days. In the same interview he said that a few years ago he inhaled sheep-dip, which is highly toxic, by mistake.

I had a dust mask there, but I got careless and didn't put it on, and I was breathing these particles in ... I got real low, like. It's taken about three year to get it all out of my system but I was lucky to get away with it, lucky I didn't get enough in my system to drag me right down, like ...

Joss Naylor keeps a few sheep still at his new home at Low Greendale. However, he also has a small place in the Costa Blanca, which he and Mary escape to in order to avoid the worst of the winter weather. He has circulatory problems in his lower limbs and feet which are helped by the more clement Spanish weather. These circulatory problems have been with him since his early running days. He has had cramp so bad in the past that he has passed out. The problems he has risen above to achieve the performances illustrated surely justify tagging Joss Naylor as what he is – a Legend.

To show that there is some justice in the world, the *Eskdale & Liddesdale Advertiser* carried a headline in January 2008 stating: 'Fellrunner Joss named as one of Britain's top 100 sporting heroes in new book'. The article noted that Joss Naylor had been named one of Britain's top 100 sporting heroes in a new book, alongside footballer George Best, cricketer Geoffrey Boycott, and Welsh rugby hero Gareth Edwards. The book *Best of British: Hendo's Sporting Heroes* had been written by Jon Henderson, a former *Observer* journalist.

Henderson says those included in the list of sporting greats are there 'in recognition of their making something less ordinary of themselves – and illuminating the lives of millions'. Other iconic figures in the book include ice skaters Torvill and Dean, and darts player Jocky Wilson. Naylor ousted stars including David Beckham, Paula Radcliffe and Barry McGuigan, all of whom failed to make it into the book. The *Best of British* book trailer concludes:

> Being immortalised in a book which also includes sporting all-rounder Henry VIII (whose sports included tennis, wrestling, bowls, sword fighting and horse racing), and even the deadly accurate archer Robin Hood, must surely secure his status as a legend.

In the 1970s Joss Naylor was awarded the MBE for his services to sport and charity, which have always run hand-in-hand for him, and he has been honoured by two universities, Manchester and Lancaster, and has had songs written about him.

Naylor was granted a place as a torch-bearer for the Olympic Torch Relay prior to the 2012 London Olympic Games. Also, when the Olympic Games were handed to Britain for 2012 there were celebrations to mark the end of the Beijing Games and the handing over to London, in August 2008. Cumbria's Everest mountaineer Chris Bonington joined Joss Naylor in climbing to the summit of Scafell Pike to symbolically fly the Olympic flag that day. One unknowing dignatory looked at Joss and said 'will you be alright to get up the mountain'.

In modern parlance then: Joss Naylor. Legend.

CHAPTER 12

Two more greats – Billy Bland and Kenny Stuart

There's no such thing as bad weather, just soft people.

Bill Bowerman

There are two other greats I wish to nominate. They are Billy Bland for his phenomenally consistent results in races, and in particular his records – including the outstanding Bob Graham Round time; and Kenny Stuart, for his relatively short career in which he absolutely tore up the record books.

So, the second of my 'greatest' is **Billy Bland,** who still holds the course records for two of the Lakeland classics – Borrowdale and Wasdale. These were both set at his peak in 1982, and have resisted all attempts since then. In the same year he also set the fastest time for the Bob Graham Round, of 13 hrs 53 mins. Memorably, this was the Bob Graham Round's golden jubilee year, and Billy Bland took nearly four hours off the record on his amazing run. Surprisingly, perhaps, he only won the British Fell Running Championships once, in 1980. He had been runner-up to Andy Styan in 1979. He also set records that have since been beaten at Ennerdale, Duddon[47], Northern Counties, Half Nevis and Sedbergh Hills, and holds the fastest time for the Lakes Four 3,000 Peaks. He was the first person to win Ennerdale, Wasdale, Borrowdale and Langdale in the same season, something which even Joss Naylor didn't achieve.

Billy Bland was born in Rosthwaite, with a father who was a guides racer, and has lived in Borrowdale all his life. Billy first raced in a professional race at Keswick Sports aged 17, coming virtually last. Interviewed in *Fellrunner* at the time of his British Championship win he commented:

> I used to go out training, but I never competed regularly. I used to get very nervous before races. I used to do the training and go to meetings, but sometimes got so nervous I didn't run, so I'd end up running about three races a year.

He obviously conquered the nerves to a great extent as he became a quite prolific, and very successful, racer over the years. He also said at one point that Colin Donnelly was a 'bag of nerves' who could have achieved more.

He reckons some of his physical attributes came from his father, Joe. In a profile published in *Cumbria* magazine in 2003 he commented on their respective pulse rates:

> He had a hellish slow pulse rate, which I inherited. I've had it down to 32, now it's maybe in the 40s. But my father's was always in the 30s. Good, that.

In the early days he was also a good standard footballer, representing his county (Westmorland). For ten years he worked as a quarryman at Honister Slate Mine. He ran originally as a professional guides racer, and wanted to run in his local Borrowdale race when it was started by his cousin Chris Bland in 1974, so ran 'unofficially'. He applied for, and was granted, reinstatement as an amateur and ran many, many other races as an amateur. By 1976 he had improved enough to come eighth in the British Championships. He followed this with sixth, third and second in the next three years, before sealing his 1980 championship victory at the Langdale race.

Always reckoned to be a hard trainer, Bland often trained on his own. This was partly because of the unavailability of suitable training partners nearby and also because he struggled to find people willing to train his way. He trained virtually always off road, and clocked up around 80 miles a week when in full training. He made a point of never doing more than 99 miles – yet he still rivalled many marathon runners of the time for mileage, and certainly for intensity. At his peak he was working as a self-employed builder and stone-waller. Consequently much of the summer training was on the fells in the evenings after work, and when nights came in it was on the roads or concentrated at weekends.

His training arena of Borrowdale has plenty of steep fells nearby and he developed into a fearless descender, particularly over rough terrain. He once cheekily noted about his relative abilities that he liked races with 'a good steep hill so that I can get a walk now and again'. He didn't like training on the roads, saying his legs wouldn't stand it. Significantly, he chose not to take his phenomenal fitness to serious road racing. Having said that, in his fell running championship year he did finish fifteenth in the Barnsley Marathon in 2 hrs 32 mins 21 secs. One can only surmise what level he might have reached in this sphere. That marathon was won by Jeff Norman, who also beat Bland in the Skiddaw race that year. By his own admission Billy Bland was never going to be especially good on the roads as he just didn't have the required pace.

Bland was ahead of his time in several ways, and also showed a strong individual streak. Firstly, he used a carbo-loading diet (similar to that of many marathon runners) before many of his longest distance events. This 'endurance diet' came about in the late 1960s, when the first carbo-loading protocol was developed by Swedish physiologist Gunvar Ahlborg. He had discovered a positive relationship between the amount of glycogen (carbs stored in the muscles and liver) in the body and endurance performance. Ahlborg devised a seven-day carbo-loading plan in which an exhaustive bout of exercise was followed by three or four days of extremely low carbohydrate intake (10 per cent of total calories) and then three or four days of extremely high carbohydrate intake (90 per cent of total calories).

Bland is 5ft 10ins tall, weighed 10st 10lb at his peak (claiming he'd got down to 10st 7lb and would have liked to have been 10st), and had a resting pulse of 32. He applied a moderated version of carbo-loading that concentrated on the loading part, and not the extreme bleed-out. He commented 'maybe it just works for me better than other people, but it certainly does work'. Many marathoners – and personal experience bears this out – find that the low-carbo intake period is very disorientating and find the effects of the bleed-out and supercompensation swing too much to cope with before a major race event. I remember only too well the effect of a 14-mile run, followed by a set of 400m reps, on the last Sunday before a marathon. More pertinently, there was the weird faint feeling for a couple of days, induced by not being able to replenish my glycogen levels, because of the self-imposed low carbohydrate phase. The theory is that this bleeding out allows a greater store of glycogen to be assimilated in the carbohydrate loading phase, just before the event.

Secondly, Bland advocated representative honours for fell running, including international competition, wanting something further after reaching Fell Runner of the Year status. He was selected for his country a few times, but eventually fell out with the selectors. Thirdly, he left Keswick AC in 1991, considering it wasn't developing its most able members to their full potential. With his nephews Gavin and Jonathan he formed Borrowdale Fellrunners, causing not a little acrimony in the area at the time. Although quite a small club it has subsequently won many team events, including the British Championships.

In several ways then, Bland was something of a trail-breaker, although he himself fully acknowledges that his actual training regime was very unscientific. No room for a coach, track sessions, repetitions, or even tapering down for races with him – just hard training. A typical training run was up Glaramara, Allen Crags, Esk Hause, down to Angle Tarn, on to High Raise, and finishing down Greenup, a two to three hour effort. For a change he might do the five tarns – Styhead Tarn, Sprinkling Tarn, Angle Tarn, Blea Tarn and Watendlath Tarn – 15 miles in around two and a half hours. He was especially good at reading rough ground and making steep descents, sometimes deliberately taking to rough ground to try to throw others off his tail. In a profile in *Cumbria* magazine in 2003 he stated:

> The rougher the going the more I aimed for it. That doesn't mean
> to say I really enjoyed it. But if you're travelling across ground
> faster than somebody else then you sort of like it. I got a reputation
> for being able to find my way around a course.

He had various other tricks to discourage runners from tagging him. He once started Ennerdale five minutes after everyone else to foil would-be followers and because he wasn't feeling on top form. He ended up finishing second, three and a half minutes behind Hugh Symonds, but in fact had run faster than him by a minute and a half. He told me that his general philosophy was 'I'll show you the way and if you can beat me to the finish then good on ya!'. He admitted that people used to say that he knew all the short cuts, but he responded to me that he would say to them that 'we all start on the line together'.

Billy Bland stayed at the top of the fell running pile for approximately a decade, winning many of the major races at least once, and favourites like Borrowdale and Wasdale ten and nine times respectively. He won every classic except Snowdon in his career. As a mark of how special his time for the BGR is, consider the fact that the unofficial best time for a relay round is only about 30 minutes faster. More details of his BGR are to be found later, when discussing that event (see Chapter 15). Billy Bland certainly has to be considered one of the greats of the sport.

When profiled in *Cumbria* magazine in 2003 he summed himself up, and his success, thus:

> My secret was simple. I had the will to train where other more talented runners who had the ability to knock spots off anything I ever did lacked that will. But one day someone will work hard at it who isn't as talented and get to break my records in the end and that's what happened to me.

That may be, but Billy Bland still towers over the sport, and his Bob Graham Round still remains as amazing testimony to his considerable talent and obvious dedication.

Bland's elder brother Stuart was a fine fell runner too, being particularly noted for his descending ability. His younger brother David also competed to a reasonably high standard for a while. David once memorably commented on his not having a whistle when being kit-checked for a race that he whistled sheep all day in his job and he certainly didn't need to carry one for a race. Note that the Borrowdale Blands are not directly related to the 'Blands of Kendal' – Pete and Dennis.

Thirdly then, **Kenny Stuart**, but not necessarily in that order. Stuart was born in Thelkeld in 1957, and is 5ft 5ins and weighed a mere eight stones at his adult racing peak. At school he was a good standard cross country runner, rising to represent the county. His first fell race was as a junior at Thirlmere, where he came fifth, but he didn't win much as a junior. His first senior fell success was over a cross country style course near Wigton in 1974. He originally competed on the professional circuit.

Stuart's early seriousness was shown by his reading coaching manuals from which he adopted interval work and fartlek sessions, adding these to his existing endurance sessions. By 1977 he was challenging Reeves, Sedgwick and Moffat, but not yet beating them. In 1979 he had improved enough to take second in the professional championships, with Reeves winning for the tenth successive year.

Kenny Stuart's two brothers, Gary and Colin, twice ran in the Ambleside junior guides race, but were really not that interested. His other brother, Duncan, was two years younger than Kenny and reached district standard at cross country at school. He had limited success on the Guides circuit, not winning any of the races he entered, although obtaining a good number of seconds. Joining the amateur ranks in 1981 Duncan had reasonable success, such as twelfth in the Half Nevis, and he also dabbled in road racing. Duncan achieving 1 hr 12 mins for the Great Cumbria Run (half marathon) was perhaps a precursor to his brother Kenny's later marathon exploits.

Kenny Stuart emerged as a serious player on the professional circuit in 1980, taking third at Alva. He also won Grasmere that year in 12 mins 37.5 secs in appalling conditions, and won 18 races to take the championship for the first of two occasions. In 1981 he had a remarkable season, champion again with a remarkable record of 30 victories in total in 32 races. However, as champion Guides racer in that year he is reckoned to have won a mere £687 from his racing.

In the process he lowered Tommy Sedgwick's Alva record to 18 mins 39 secs. At Kilnsey Crag, Sedgwick and Reeves have progressively brought the record down to 8 mins 1.7 secs. Stuart smashed this when local runner Mick Hawkins challenged him all the way, resulting in a sparkling 7 mins 46 secs record. The next year Hawkins took the record with 7 mins 35.8 secs. Stuart also set records for the races at Helvellyn and Braemar (24 mins 30 secs), where crowds of 25,000 were not uncommon. The Braemar race had been won by Queen Victoria's gillie (professional fishing and hunting guide) in the 1850s. When it was found that he had damaged his heart and lungs the Queen asked for the race to be dropped from the Braemar games.

In 1982 Stuart 'guested' in a pre-season low-key road race, the 22-mile Buttermere Round, which went over Honister Pass and Newlands. He dead-heated with Jon Broxap in a record time of 2 hrs 5 mins 30 secs. Stuart's reinstatement, the uncertainty of his status for a while, and first race as an amateur have already been commented on. His early amateur races produced variable results. In his first Ben Nevis Race, Stuart led from Billy Bland at the summit. Bland regained the lead on the descent, but Stuart surged past when Bland fell near the Red Burn, and eventually won in 1 hr 27 mins 12 secs. A week later he only managed to finish eleventh in the Lake District Mountain Trial. His navigation was not so good yet, and Bland won in very poor conditions. In that first season Stuart won at Langdale, Thieveley Pike, Tour of Pendle, Butter Crag, Blisco Dash and Wansfell. He also finished second in the by-no-means flat Derwentwater 10 mile road race, in 49 mins 51 secs.

Stuart was inspired by Bill Teasdale, and also by running against his heroes – Fred Reeves and Tommy Sedgwick. This was all in his professional days. His reasons for seeking amateur reinstatement were twofold. Firstly, to compete with his brother Duncan for Keswick AC, as they often trained together but were by then going to different race venues. He also was increasing his training and wanted to have increased competition, by competing in the larger amateur fields, over greater distances and to have the option of competing on the roads or at cross country if he felt like it.

Stuart's training is fairly well documented, and looking at it closely might perhaps cause surprise as the detail is revealed. He trained at a lower mileage than many fell runners, limited his running on the fells so as to maintain leg speed, and included interval sessions on road and grass. All of this was influenced by his having a manual job and limited daylight training hours.

He thus often used to train on woodland trails in his lunch breaks. His weekly mileage was approximately 60–70 miles in summer, and 80–90 miles in winter. Interviewed in *Compass Sport* in 1983, just prior to his peak, he commented:

> most of my training in winter is done in darkness, very little quality work on grass or fell can be done, and tarmac therefore becomes my main training surface. Mainly 'aerobic' running plus two speed sessions a week. I've added slightly more mileage and one extra long run a week.

His summer sessions were listed, however, and showed sessions such as six miles with 4–5 x 1 mile on grass; 6 miles with 8 x 0.5 miles on grass; 4–5 miles sustained effort on the fells. Typically he was running every day, with double sessions on five days within the week.

He has a light frame, weighing just eight stone at his racing peak, and had an incredible ability to ascend well. This was one of his greatest assets, and he was reckoned to be one of the very few that could run all the way up Thieveley Pike for instance, which he confirmed when I spoke to him. He certainly trained hard though, often feeling leg fatigue from his Tuesday session on a race Saturday. As to the intensity, he reckoned that his mile reps would have been run at a pace of around 4 mins 20 secs to 4 mins 30 secs per mile.

His approach to racing was that if you were on the start line then you ran hard, to win. There were no easy races and thus he limited his racing programme. It was noted in a previous chapter that Stuart holds course records across the race length range, but he felt he was best on medium courses with steep runnable ascents and descents. His navigation wasn't the best, nor did he perform well on extreme rocky terrain. The very best descenders have naturally quick reflexes, agility and confidence, although the skill can be improved somewhat with practice, especially one's confidence. In an in-depth piece about him, published in *Northern Exposure* magazine in 2003 he comments:

> during long races it is very important to maintain a positive attitude
> to help block out the inevitable pain. Try to stay in a good mood
> by focusing on pleasant thoughts such as the pint of cold beer that
> you'll drink in the pub after the race! Don't show discomfort when
> you are under pressure, always look like you are in control.

He was convinced he had won races against stronger opposition when feeling awful simply by looking like he was stronger than his rivals.

The 1983 season was a milestone for Kenny Stuart, as he won the British Fell Running Championship, in what is considered the best ever competition, with two men going into the final race needing to win. John Wild needed maximum points and Kenny Stuart, with enough points already, needed to just prevent Wild from winning. Wild had won the championship in 1982, trained well over the winter, and had come fifteenth in the National Cross Country Championships that spring. However, he broke a bone in his foot and missed six weeks training and also had to miss the Kentmere, Blisco and Three Peaks races early in the fell championship contest. Though Stuart had been well beaten by Wild at Burnsall the year before, he had upped his training, particularly the longer stuff. The season was 15 races, over a hundred miles of fells.

The following are the results from the races that counted, together with some comments from Kenny Stuart on them, which were originally published in an interview with him on the Championships that year in *Fellrunner* magazine.

The first race was Kentmere in April. Wild was injured and Stuart dropped out, having led at the first checkpoint.

> It was a blizzard. The thing is I'd set off without much clothing and basically I was too frightened to go on. I was losing more heat than I could keep.

A week later Wild also missed Blisco, and Stuart won, although being mindfull that Wild had beaten him in the race the year beforehand. Another week on and Wild was still out, leaving Stuart to win the Three Peaks.

> I'd looked over part of the course. Still, I didn't want to go it alone and went out with Hugh Symonds as far as Whernside where I made my effort ... I'd have liked a better time but they told me afterwards it was the heaviest going for years.

John Wild returned for Ben Lomond early in May and surprised himself by winning, in a new course record, despite only just being back into decent training.

> It was a gruelling race. I broke John going up but then on the way down we passed each other two or three times until he finally got 15 yards on me. When he gets yards on you that's it.

This is another example of two top performers pushing each other to a new best time. A week on and Wild's lack of preparation showed. In the Northern Counties race he could only manage fourth, while Stuart won on what he claimed to be his favourite long race.

> It's steep and I enjoyed the climbs. I was a bit surprised to win as I had flu the week before ... I made a break up Causey Pike. I thought if I kill myself there I'll kill a few others too and really put an effort in.

By now the races were coming thick and fast. Fairfield was the sixth championship race in seven weeks, and Wild showed great powers of recovery by taking this one with Stuart in second. Wild admitted that these medium cross country type course may have suited him more than Stuart, who had superior climbing skills.

Another two weeks on saw them both contesting the Welsh 1000m race. Stuart was competing in it for the first time, and his tactic was to follow whoever took the lead. Going up Snowdon, with 18 or so miles under their belts, there were Wild, Stuart and Billy Bland slogging it out up the PYG track, with Wild just out-sprinting Stuart.

> the three of us climbed Snowdon together. Billy dropped off three quarters of the way up and I thought it was mine. In the end it was nothing to do with fitness – John was just harder.

Billy Bland was running because he was apparently getting stick for NOT running any long races outside the Lakes, but he met his match on this occasion, although obviously giving an extra edge to the race by his presence.

Two more weeks and over to Buckden Pike, a course that was more cross country and described by Stuart as not really a worthy fell championship course. Needless to say Wild romped home after breaking away early on and produced a new course record into the bargain. They both took a break from racing and passed on Wasdale, which Stuart felt was Billy Bland's territory anyway. So, a month after Buckden Pike it was Kinniside, which once again Wild felt was his for the taking, with plenty of grass running. Stuart in fact won, having disillusioned Wild by managing to run every step, which Wild couldn't. Two more weeks and up to Scotland for Melantee. Wild didn't go well, and in fact had a very sore ankle afterwards, making him doubtful for Borrowdale a week later. Stuart won at a canter:

> It's a steep hill and I walked some although I don't think you'd gain much by running … No one was going to beat me coming down there that day.

A week later and Wild was fit to run the long Borrowdale course, which he was secretly hoping Billy Bland would win, to take points off Stuart. It is Bland's local course, which he had often won, but he had taken the trouble to show Stuart over the course in advance. Stuart won, but was looking over his shoulder all the way down the last descent as Wild was in second and could still spring a surprise.

Going up Scafell we tried to get away from Billy and dropped him although he came back down the Corridor. Out towards Styhead we got him again. He turned round and said it was no good and he doesn't say that unless he means it ... up Dale Head first Sean [Livesey] went then John, slightly. I felt bad. It was my hardest race ever and I pushed myself beyond the limit really.

It seems there were a few shared beers later that evening. John Wild was also not above a certain amount of practical joking, it should be noted.

Two weeks later the show had moved on, this time to Burnsall, where Wild was hoping for a hat-trick, which he achieved in a new amateur record (over a slightly longer course than Reeves' pro one, which was one second quicker). Stuart had realised he had to push it uphill if he was to win. Wild hung on, got in front after the cairn and literally and metaphorically never looked back, taking about 20 yards out of Stuart in the descent. Two more weeks and up to the Ben Nevis race, where Wild won, setting a new record in slightly bizarre circumstances. There was mist from Red Burn, and Jack Maitland and Stuart got away from Wild and Shaun Livesey on the ascent. They must have taken a wrong line on the descent as Wild came out of the mist in the lead, and strode to a new record for the course.

We went astray slightly coming down which is a pity because I feel I could have held my own with John back down the road. When we got back to the Red Burn we thought we were in front and in fact Jack Maitland went over the line still thinking I'd won and he'd come second.

So, to Thieveley Pike, three weeks later and the decider. Wild had won the last championship races and needed this one to win overall. Wild used the weeks beforehand to recover, then did a last speedwork session midweek before the race. In the race Stuart pulled clear going up the last climb, and just couldn't be caught, even though they both thought it was a Wild kind of course. Stuart only had to come second to seal the championship but decided to go all out to finish on a win.

Honestly I'd hoped to have it all sewn up ... on the day I set off and decided to take as much out of myself as possible. Every race had been hard so I thought I might as well kill myself on this one

too. At the finish I was 20 seconds clear and I must admit I felt
exceptional that day.

Stuart had beaten Wild at his course, had beaten the course record by 1 min
42 secs and had sealed his first championship. Stuart felt he would go for
the championship again 'in a roundabout sort of way'. He duly won it again
in both 1984 and 1985. He also had started thinking more about road
racing.

> When I am sick of hurting myself on the fells I might have a go
> [on the roads] I've only ever done two road races, both 10s and I
> found them different. Of the two I think I find road the hardest
> but then I've trained to hurt myself on the fells.

Leaving aside the fact that he seemed to have forgotten about the Buttermere
Round, it certainly gives an indication of where his career would eventually go.

The quotes, and the manner in which Wild and Stuart (and Maitland,
Bland and Livesey) approached each race and each other speaks volumes
about their character and the fantastic season's races that the sport witnessed
in that year. In passing, it is worth noting that the fifteen race format was
changed in 1986, to four from six, and it has never been as hard again to
win the champs as it was in that era.

Nineteen eight-four was even more successful for Stuart. He won a whole
tranche of races, and set records at Black Combe, Blisco Dash, Coniston,
and Butter Crag, which have subsequently been beaten. What is more
remarkable are the records he set that year at Latrigg, Wansfell, Eildon,
Skiddaw and Ben Nevis, none of which have been beaten in the years since.
It was reckoned that he was so in control in his local race at Skiddaw that
he could possibly have pushed himself if required to, and might have pushed
the 1 hr 2 mins 18 secs much nearer the hour mark.

That year's Ben Nevis race was held in wet weather and the going was
slippery to say the least. Stuart won in 1 hr 25 mins 24 secs, a time which
no one has come remotely near since, and it has a large organiser's bounty
on it for anyone who beats it. Talking with me about Ben Nevis, Kenny
added the following:

> What people forget is that John Wild had only lost the record by
> just one second. Colin Donnelly is the only one who has come

anywhere near it. I thought I was going to win the Ben quite easily. I was with Hugh Symonds and I drew away from him to get quite a lead by Red Burn. Until I heard this steamroller coming from behind. It was Jack Maitland, and I thought where the hell has he come from. He actually went past, just like that, left me for dead. I gathered myself and by just before the road I was reeling him in and once I hit the road I just dropped him. Jack was one of the best descenders I ever saw. They called him the rolling crab. A talented runner but a nutter downhill. He never seemed to have any work, a perpetual student.

In 1985 Stuart won the British Championship again, setting records at Snowdon and Ennerdale. His Snowdon and Ennerdale times have still not been beaten, leaving him still with seven major records, the most prolific of all the record setters. This doesn't take into account other records such as the Three Peaks and Buttermere Sailbeck which had their courses altered so his records there no longer stand.

In 1986 Stuart finally decided to have a crack at a road marathon. He entered Glasgow and with a time of 2 hrs 14 mins 3 secs he not only won but also set a new course record. At the time the world best was 2 hrs 7 mins 12 secs – a tantalising seven minutes faster. In 1987 he started having breathing problems, which affected his London Marathon debut. The next year he had issues again, but achieved 2 hrs 13 mins 36 secs in fourteenth place in London, and later came second in the Berlin Marathon (which is now acknowledged to be one of the fastest in the world, and has a course record of 2 hrs 3 mins 38 secs).

Stuart fitted in more training, now being advised by Dave Cannon, and went Stateside in 1989 and ran 2 hrs 11 mins 20 secs in Houston for second place. Stuart was starting to make money from his running. He was paid to run the London Marathon after his time in Houston, achieving 2 hrs 12 mins 53 secs in fifteenth place in 1989, and was receiving some sponsorship from running shoe companies. By then things had started going very wrong for him. In 1990 he dropped out of the London Marathon and his illness virtually stopped him running. Medical tests were inconclusive, and ME was the handle given to his situation. In talking to Richard Askwith for his book *Feet in the Clouds* Stuart revealed that

the doctor said I was lucky to get in as much training as I did …
It was all linked to the immune system. I was born atopic, which
means you're prone to allergies, so even as a kid I had lots of colds
and was bothered a lot by pollen. But all that marathon training
didn't help.

He also suggested that never seeming to get injured may have had some
influence, in that he trained mighty hard and never really gave himself rest
and recovery time, which is often forced on athletes who have minor injuries
and stop training temporarily for that reason.

Stuart's self-confidence shows from this quote about the Snowdon record
race day, from a recent video interview as part of the race publicity[48]:

Every fell runner knows when he starts the race the first half mile
he knows how he is going to feel, and I felt good right from the
start.

Although he took part in the international races, as they were becoming
prevalent during his peak, he reckons they had been detrimental to fell
running in Britain. Although he approves of runners having a go, he feels
that cash is pulling the better runners abroad. He also reckoned that his Ben
Nevis record might actually be a better one than his Snowdon one.

In his time Stuart was unbeatable. He won the professional guides title
for two years in 1980 and 1981, and then had a transition year in 1982, as
he was seeking reinstatement and adjusting to the different races. In 1983
he started his three consecutive British Championship wins, a feat of
consistency that was repeated by both Colin Donnelly and Rob Hope. He
was also the first British Fell Running Champion to go on and win a World
Mountain Running Trophy title. The longevity of his records for Snowdon
and Ben Nevis are a measure, and continual reminder, of his greatness.

He made a half-hearted comeback in 1991 but his post-viral fatigue meant
that he couldn't perform as he would wish and it was a short-lived effort.
His son and two daughters were very successful junior fell runners in their
teenage years, but sadly they dropped out soon after that. Emma was possibly
the most successful, coming eighteenth in the World Trophy in Otaly 2004
in the U18s age group. Having given up his previous job to concentrate full
time on his running career, Kenny returned to college to study horticulture

and now works as a gardener at the University of Cumbria. He lives in a house called Fellside, near where he was born, and says that he is now enjoying his running for the first time in his life.

A *conversation with:* **Kenny Stuart,** Keswick AC

Blencathra looms over the back of Kenny's house and I am thinking that Bob Graham Rounders come very close by here without necessarily knowing that it is where two of the greats of fell running live. Kenny makes me coffee and we sit down to flesh out some more detail of a fairly well documented story. At the end of the session, after the recorder has been turned off, we carry on talking for ages, covering some interesting ground that is not for this volume. At one point I comment on the difficulty I am having sourcing a photo of Bob Graham. Kenny says 'I think I have one'. He comes back with a fascinating photo from the 1930s of a group of men, including Bob Graham, about to follow the hounds from outside the village pub. Unfortunately it is not a sufficiently clear photo to be of use in my image search, but a very interesting record nonetheless.

'Whoever breaks the Ben Nevis record is going to have to be a damn good runner.'

Looking into Kenny Stuart's family background and athletic roots showed no real athletic prowess in the family. *'Me mum and dad never really did much. Me dad worked and me mum looked after the family as local families did in those days. Me dad played a little bit of local football for Threlkeld football club. He packed that in when he was in his mid-twenties. Me grandfather was a different breed, and did a bit of fellrunning. He also played full-back for Penrith football club when they were in one the Northern Counties leagues, which were a very high standard in those days. He was a fairly talented footballer. He was also well known for his strength and athletic prowess. He was known as Little Ji, because he was small feller. He didn't go to the sports as you couldn't travel in those days, there were no cars. He used to be renowned for his strength as he worked in the quarries, breaking rocks. He always had a good constitution for a small feller.'*

When Kenny was at school they decided to revive Threlkeld children's sports, which were held on the recreation field. There was a cross country race, which was up the hill. *'The first race I ran I won. It was under 12s, up to the white house you can see up there and back. I got to Laithwaite Secondary school and they started cross country racing and I was entered into the district champs and came second in that. I went on to the County champs and was about tenth, just scraping into the county team.'*

That was the height of his career at the time. He didn't go to the inter-counties, which was at Parliament Hill, in London. *'There must have been seven runners and two reserves. I had to wait until I was into my late twenties until I got to the inter-counties, when I was moving from fells to the roads.'*

At the time all there was on the fells were the short races. It was in the late 1970s when amateur races started up in the Lakes. *'They created the Skiddaw race and the Latrigg race. Apart from those there was nothing. The big thing was what was known as the professional scene, the guides races. That is basically what there was.'*

Kenny described the professional racing scene and his entry into and progress in it. When he left school he ran for the county and when he turned 16 he got a letter from the Northern Counties AAA to tell him he had to make a decision as to whether he was going to carry on running in guides races, which was deemed professional, or whether he relinquished a professional career to stay amateur. *'Because I was into fell running and there wasn't much road running and things up here I decided to go into the guides race scene. I had no idea of the implication. Obviously I wasn't running that well at the time. I was quite happy to say finish sixth in a field of 20. It was the local shows and it was part of my life, and that was it.'*

He says Sedgwick and Reeves were both runners to look up to, and both had relative strengths on different courses. *'Sedgwick and Reeves were already up there because Fred Reeves is around ten years older than I am, and Tommy Sedgwick seven years or so older. Fred started a little older, being about 24 when he first won Grasmere sports. Fred was the go-upper, and Tommy was the renowned descender. If there was any rough stuff and it was a short descent he would kill everybody. And kill himself as well.'*

Sedgwick rarely finished a season, as he was always injuring himself. But, Grasmere at that time was THE race though. *'It started to go off slightly. Just as we were juniors, there was Fred, Tommy and mebbe a couple of others. There was always talk of the sport having to go amateur to save it. We, as the young generation were coming through – a hellavu good group, and once we got with Tommy and Fred the times started to come down and there was a bit of excitement. It was like a circus that went around the local shows. It was a helluva competitive era.'*

Pauline Stuart chipped in with a comment about betting which took us briefly into that topic, and Kenny commented. *'There was a bit of betting. What you got at the big sports shows were hound trails as well, so the bookies were already there. I never once had a bet on myself or on anyone else. Once I had a bloke approach me at Ambleside Sports and said 'you don't want to win today'. I said "I have trained all year and have a good chance". He said "no, you don't really want to win, do you". And then I did, and I beat Fred Reeves for the first time. Then the same man came up to me later and said "I think you have had the wool pulled over your eyes, I think Fred must have been betting on you".'*

In the old days there was a lot of underhand stuff. It was reckoned to nearly destroy the sport in the 1950s. *'The old runners used to talk about going to a sports meeting and it being 'your turn'. It was like six or seven blokes backing this one runner. There are stories of the winner coming in and he wasn't supposed to win because they had all backed on the second feller. He had to stumble and hide behind the wall. There was quite a bit of that going on. Another thing that destroyed the whole betting syndrome in the old days was the fact that Fred and Tommy started to train twice or three times a day, like professionals. Dennis Beavins was supposedly coaching Fred. Because they were training like that they weren't interested in throwing races for a couple of quid, and that destroyed the betting.'*

Kenny's move to the amateur ranks was prompted by a search for a greater challenge of race distances, different types of races. *'It was becoming a big thing was the amateur side. My brother had already been reinstated. When the running boom was happening in the late 1970s I was being reinstated and Ron Hill Sports started importing books from America. Being fascinated with the sport and liking to read, I bought a few books, which proved groundbreaking for me. All the time I was on the fells I was self-coached.'*

Kenny Stuart set many fell race records (seven are still held by him), and he commented on records in general, and who he is impressed by. *'I am impressed by Ian Holmes, who has won Ben Nevis five or six times.'* For himself, he has lost a few records, as most people have, because courses change, and they then set a new record. *'I admire feats like Joss Naylor has come up with, Billy Bland running the BGR in that sort of time. I paced the first section of that run, around here, and I reckon he knew he was in shape for that result. I was always going to do BGR at a later date, when slightly older, but unfortunately things didn't materialise that way.'*

Kenny reckons that people from this background had a constitutional advantage, being fit and healthy to start with. *'Take the likes of Bill Teasdale, who was a guides racer and professional all his life. With the training he did and the times he was doing it is amazing. If he had been let rip to do the distances in longer amateur races like Naylor and Bland had done he would have been a world-beater. As a professional he somehow ran in the Mountain Trial and beat the field by an entire half an hour. He was changed and ready to go home by the time everyone was coming in. He was just a Lakeland shepherd but he had the constitution.'*

Kenny has strong views on training then and now. *'To be fair Joss and Billy were always prepared to give advice or even show you round some parts of a course. My training was different because I wanted it to be different. I wanted to do what I thought was best. The fell running times aren't coming down because the youngsters that are coming through aren't in the same numbers, they are not so keen, there are more things going on for kids, constitutionally they are brought up in a much softer way. Sounds daft, and this is the way older people talk, and I feel old when I say it. There is a mollycoddling effect now on kids, they are dragged around in cars.'*

He was also pretty forthright in describing how the likes of Coe and Ovett specialised in their particular events by adopting an approach of periodisation. *'Everything was linked to that specific target. It is not happening now. An example of focus is Charlie Spedding, who didn't run many races (and couldn't get under 49 mins for 10 miles) because of his commitment to the marathon.'*

We discussed today's marathon runners and the times they are achieving. For example, the fastest Brit in the London Marathon in 2012 was Lee Merien in 2 hrs 13 mins 41 secs, when the Olympic standard being sought was 2 hrs 12 mins. Sometime fell runner Andi Jones was fifth Brit in 2 hrs 18 mins 29 secs. *'I can't comment really on why Andi Jones is not coming up with the times in the marathon. I would think Andi can't run faster at Snowdon as he isn't a great descender, I might be wrong. He certainly has the talent to do it.'*

Kenny had medical tests to see what was going wrong, when he was ill. He went down to Northwick Park in Harrow to be tested, which included having a VO2 max test. *'I couldn't finish it actually, I had to just stop. Could have been higher if I had been fit still. It was 80-something (ml/kg/min). They had only had one higher score in the centre. There was a programme on TV a while ago about British milers, where Tom Lancashire was saying he went through the same thing, being completely shattered, every race he went into.'*

Dave Cannon had the same issue, and he persuaded Kenny to be tested. *'I was what they called atopic, which meant I had allergy problems, probably had them all my life. Yesterday I had a serious reaction to something at work which came up in hives, red weals. I do try to keep off wheat. It is a combination of food and pollen; there are all sorts of possibilities. Basically, I think my immune system started to rebel. I was working full-time and trying to train full-time at the same time.'*

The amazing 1983 British Championships race sequence against John Wild is recorded elsewhere in this volume. I wondered if Kenny thought he would win those champs. *'No, I was hopeful, knowing that Wild had won the year before, and he was running well. I would have been satisfied if I had come second that year. It got to the last race of the season and I thought I had nothing to lose. It was his type of race, at Thieveley Pike. I hit it from the front and just went and went, and he never came back. I was feeling my way a bit with longer races, but was quite confident that I could manage in the end.'*

Kenny thinks his optimum range was probably medium races. *'Being a guides racer I was also used to doing the short 12-minute sort of stuff. Bearing in mind I never ran Wasdale, as there was always something coming up near it, usually it was the week before Snowdon. Borrowdale was always difficult for me, as Billy knew it like the back of his hand. If the weather was fine I knew I had a good chance with him.'*

He acknowledges that he was a very average navigator. *'I didn't run many long ones outside of the Lakes where navigation skills were important. I did the Welsh 1000s and was beaten both times I ran. John Wild beat me on the sprint to the finish on one, and Billy Bland and Bob Whitfield beat me when it was a really horrendous day.'*

He reckons his Ben Nevis record is stronger than his Snowdon record. *'I think the Ben was more of a specialist race, say against Snowdon. Whoever breaks the Ben Nevis record is going to have to be a damn good runner, and a good specialist as well. It is very rarely that you find that sort of runner. Snowdon, you could get a top class Kenyan or someone like that come to beat it. One tried when we were down there in 2010, who was Commonwealth champion, and he only came about fifth in the race. He couldn't come down hill. It is a very difficult road race really.'*

Kenny has no especial regrets about not winning any particular races, or beating records. *'The Three Peaks maybe. I beat the Grasmere Guides record in a different race, over exactly the same course. Also the Butter Crags amateur race in October I did 12 mins 22 secs too, which is one second off Reeves's record, on the same course. I think that when those times were being set, Tommy Sedgwick and Fred Reeves had a competitive edge and specialised over that course, they used to train over that course. It was their lives really, it was the big thing they wanted to win.'*

I was interested to know how the Houston Marathon came about. *'I don't know how I got the invite. There was an offer of some sort. I think Dave Cannon had something to do with it – someone had been in contact with him. It seemed a good time to get one in, in January. I had done Glasgow in 2 hrs 14 mins and London in 2 hrs 13 mins, and I think Birmingham in 2 hrs 15 mins or something on a heavy course too. I came second in Houston to Richard Kaitany from Kenya.'* What thoughts did he have after achieving 2 hrs 11 mins there? *'At that time, being in work, and the environment I was in, I thought I could at the very least get to 2 hrs 10 mins, I was more than capable of that.'*

He had done a 62 mins 55 secs half marathon. Houston coincided with a quiet period at work, and he made sure he didn't exert himself too much. *'I also recall having about six weeks of very competitive training, with four weeks at 100 miles per week, then started to drop it down slightly. I went into that race and at five miles I was running so easy I was almost excited. I knew that something special was on. Sometimes you get to 10-13 miles, you just know.'*

Kenny Stuart was tempted to do Bob Graham Round later, but later never arrived. *'At the end of the day it is quite an organisational carry-on. I wouldn't have needed to do much reconnoitre work. It was something that needed to be done in mid-season, so it would probably ruin the rest of your competitive season.'*

I'd heard it said that Kenny was possibly the only one who could run up Thieveley Pike all the way. *'Yes I could. I won it twice. I used to prefer running if I could. The only place it would have been faster to walk was on the first steep bank by the railway bridge there. Harry Walker could run all the way up the Big End on Pendle, but it was slow running.'*

What was his greatest running achievement? *'Race wise, I suppose Ben Nevis. That was helluva time to run. Some of my races in Italy maybe. I ran a race they called the Grand International of Europe, basically an Italian version of the European Championships, and I won quite easily. I won the first World Mountain Running Trophy.'*

In conclusion Kenny gave his thoughts on fell running today. *'No one is outstanding for the men at the moment. You almost feel that someone needs to step onto a higher plain. I think it is diluted by the number of races. Mid-week races, bunny runs. However, it is a good thing in some ways. The leisure runners have a chance to have a go. I also like the fact that there is no other sport where grass roots competitors can compete against the best, at least in most races.'*

CHAPTER 13

Death on the fells

To die will be an awfully big adventure.

J.M. Barrie

There has long been controversy about the dangers that people voluntarily face when indulging in their chosen sports and recreations. It is there in many sports, and tends to be the subject of discussion whenever hill walking, climbing or fell running in particular come up. On the one hand there is the right of individuals to take risks upon themselves, and on the other there is the devastating effect that a major incident can have on the families and friends of individuals involved. Equally there is the cost of, and possible risk to the members of, the Mountain Rescue service when they are involved in any situation that arises. It is a thread that runs through the history of the sport of fell running.

Accidents on the fells are of course nothing new, as the following two examples from the Lakes demonstrate. John Ruskin, in *England's Lakeland – a tour therein* describes meeting in the summer of 1859 a young gentlemen 'attired as though for a lounge in Bond Street' attempting to climb to the summit of Scafell Pike. When the young man did not appear in the evening, some of the locals, in thick mist, went to try and find him. They found him on the summit:

> dead beat ... lying breathless upon his back and watching the awful curtain of night and death descending upon him.

Even the rescuers lost their way in coming back down in the dark, but they carried the man back to safety.

Hunter Davies in *A Walk Around the Lakes*, describes the following accident in Piers Gill, on the side of Scafell Pike:

> ... no place to wander into. Apparently someone did in 1921, falling and breaking both ankles, and lay at the bottom for 18 days, he was brought out alive, thanks to having landed beside a pool of water.

One of the earliest fell race fatalities was in 1957 when Ben Nevis suffered its first, and only, fatality when competitor John Rix died of hypothermia. He had lost a shoe at the Red Burn, and strayed off the main footpath. The rescue parties had to search for nine hours through the night, before finding him at two o'clock in the morning. He was still alive when he was discovered, but he died while being carried down the mountain by stretcher.

After the tragedy, the Ben Nevis race committee decided to discourage recreational runners who might be unprepared for the rugged conditions by implementing qualifying standards and by imposing time limits:

1. runners who do not reach the halfway point on the ascent in one hour are turned back
2. runners who do not reach the mountain summit in two hours are turned back
3. runners must complete the course within 3 hours and 15 minutes.

The race committee also decided to limit the size of the race to five hundred pre-registered runners, the maximum number of participants that they felt the race-support personnel could safely handle. Each competitor must carry full body waterproof cover, hat, gloves, and a whistle; otherwise he or she is immediately disqualified. The equipment is necessary because the weather on Britain's highest mountain can change rapidly and drastically. Like other races, the Ben Nevis event takes safety very seriously, now requiring entrants to have run at least three 'A' category fell races.

There was also a fatality at the Three Peaks race in 1978. The race report in *Fellrunner* magazine included these sentiments:

The thick mist over parts of the course resulted in many competitors going astray, including Edward Pepper of Blackheath Harriers, who died from exposure. Let those road and cross country runners who competed on this occasion be warned that this course is far from being the toughest, as claimed by some uninitiated writers, and that the strong wind and mist produced only mildly unpleasant conditions by comparison to the really bad weather which can prevail on Britain's hills.

Race organisers have always taken these matters very seriously. The Three Peaks fiftieth anniversary race leaflet included the following comments on safety:

Our systems and procedures have meant that the race has been relatively safe. We have had injuries but, fortunately, these have been relatively minor. We have had cases of hypothermia but these we know how to treat. In 1978 we had the particular misfortune to suffer a fatality in the race, fortunately a very limited experience in fell running. This came as a wake-up call not only to us but to fell running in general. We looked carefully at what we did and made sure that we responded constructively wherever possible. The Three Peaks has been at the forefront of developments ever since. We were the first to operate a substitution system; the first to introduce a tag system; the first to combine this with radio contact between Race Control and checkpoint; the first to use the labels system to display results and one of the first to employ the Sport Ident electronic timing system with laptop computers installed on the summits of Whernside and Ingleborough, which this year will be the first to be networked by radio to our control centre.

There is not a significant number of fell running fatalities. While being mindful that you can use statistics to make almost any point you wish, and that you and I are at risk just crossing the road, the following are figures that the Lake District Search and Mountain Rescue Association (LDSMRA) have compiled over a number of years. The table lists over a 14-year period the number of incidents they have had to respond to that are categorised as fell running, mountain biking and rock scrambling.

1993	1994	1995	1996	1997	1998	1999
Fell Running Casualties – fatalities in brackets						
7	11 (1)	2	3	2	4	3
Mountain Biking Casualties						
15	9	9	9	9	5	2
Rock Scrambling Incidents – fatalities in brackets						
6 (1)	5	9 (1)	13	8 (1)	8	8 (2)

2000	2001	2002	2003	2004	2005	2006
Fell Running Casualties – fatalities in brackets						
4	1	6	2 (1)	2	4	2 (1)
Mountain Biking Casualties						
8	6	8	10	10	7	6
Rock Scrambling Incidents – fatalities in brackets						
2	2	4	1 (1)	6	4	5 (1)

From Lake District Search and Mountain Rescue Association website:
http://homepages.enterprise.net/ldsamra/ldsamra/statistics/accident_
summary.htm

In that period there were more fatalities from rock scrambling than from fell running (seven against three), and far more non-fatal incidents mountain biking than in either of the other two sports (conveniently ignoring the different numbers of participants in each sport). Furthermore, if you read the full reports, where they are available, they give details of the specific incidents. The 2006 fell running fatality was listed as 'Man (64) – Subject collapsed while running. FATAL Heart attack. On Kidsty Pike'; and the 2003 one as:

> Location: Ullscarf. Equipment: Good. Cause of Accident: Fell runner (years of experience) collapsed without warning. Companions

immediately commenced CPR and team used AED, both without success. Outcome/Injury Details: FATAL – cause not known at this point.

Behind the figures then is the fact that of the three fatalities recorded that were categorised as 'fell running' two were not actually in races, but were just individuals out running on the fells. A full LDSMRA report is not available for the year of 1994, but the incident reported is likely to have been at the Kentmere race, where in that April an uncharacteristic and violent blizzard resulted in the unfortunate death of Judith Taylor.

Judith Taylor was an experienced fell runner, and had completed the Kentmere race on a number of occasions. Although she was found some way from the race route it would appear that she had attempted to escape from the dire weather conditions prevailing by finding her way off the fells to safety. Doug Brown was competing in that Kentmere race, and recalled later on his club's website[49]:

> About a third of the way round I passed Judith Taylor, the wife of a friend at Clayton Harriers. We chatted briefly. She was going well. However, as the field reached the open plateau of High Street we were engulfed in a terrible blizzard. It was freak weather. Such was the strength of the wind it was almost impossible to stand and visibility was virtually nil. I found the summit wall and, following it, staggered and fell across snowdrifts to reach the checkpoint, a tent at the cairn. I turned and fought my way to the comparative safety of Nan Bield Pass. I managed to finish the race. More than half the field dropped out, many arriving back late after being lost. Judith did not return. She had been swept right over High Street by the blizzard and had attempted to descend into Patterdale. Eventually she collapsed and died on the open hillside only a few hundred yards from safety. She was found a couple of hours later by a search dog from the mountain rescue team. As the last person to speak to her during the race I had to go to the inquest in Carlisle to make a statement. Such an experience puts our own selfish pleasure into a true and sharp perspective.

The latest annual report of the LDSMRA was published in March 2012, showing that the number of incidents and fatalities fell sharply in 2011. Cumbria's 12 rescue teams were called out 424 times in 2011, compared to 600 in 2010 – a decrease of 29 per cent. The number of deaths from all activities dropped 43 per cent – down from 30 to 17. 499 people needed help in 2011, down from 676 the previous year, with falls, and people getting lost the most common calls. The lower numbers were put down to a drop in visitor numbers and a less severe winter.

However, mountain bike accidents, including one which led to a death, have jumped 160 per cent. Ged Feeney, incident report officer at LDSMRA, said such accidents were rising because of an increase in the number of mountain bike trails in the area and more people taking part. The report also revealed that water sports incidents had risen since 2010 with three of the seven call-outs last year being fatalities.

The table below gives similar breakdown to that above for the last five years, again from the LDSMRA[50].

2007	2008	2009	2010	211
Fell Running/Orienteering casualties				
6	9	10	7	4
Mountain Biking Casualties – fatalities in brackets				
15	18	9	8	20 (1)
Climbing/Scrambling casualities – fatalities in brackets				
12 (1)	19 (5)	21 (1)	31 (3)	14

There were no fell running (now combined with orienteering) fatalities in the Lake District area in the period reported. Again, there are consistently more injuries in biking and climbing than running, with one biking fatality and ten in climbing/scrambling. Rescuers said it highlighted the need for better training and supervision. This should be a warning to be heeded by fell runners as well, in particular those new to this tough and potentially dangerous branch of athletics.

What is perhaps more of a problem for the sport is the situation that race organisers find themselves in, and the subsequent reactions from runners, when inclement weather hits an event. Different scenarios are possible, as the following three cases from the 1980s illustrate. The actions of some of the entrants to the first two races could have resulted in incidents that would have involved the rescue services, which is pretty ironic when you consider that it would have been on their advice, and that of the police, that the decisions the organisers made were taken.

In 1980 the Carnethy International Hill Race (category 'B', 10 miles, 1,300m climb) was held in February. On the day there was dense fog. Because the race crossed the A702 road and fog was causing problems the police decided it warranted calling off the race, which the organisers reluctantly agreed to do. The organisers quickly substituted an eight-mile cross country race, with hardly any climbing. Around 120 runners left the start line, with 17 running the official (new) cross country, while the rest crossed the main road and ran the original hill course unofficially. Some top runners went the unofficial way and there was some acrimonious discourse after the event. It did result in the organisers choosing an alternative course that started the other side of the main road. However, it does highlight the fragility of organised fell racing, and the 'right to choose' attitude to danger often shown by individuals drawn to the sport. This is just one example of runners still taking to the fells at an event when it has officially been cancelled.

Later the same year there was a similar situation at the Ben Nevis race, with cold, wet and extremely windy conditions. The race has support from radio equipped mountain rescue members at the summit, but on this occasion they failed to reach there and radio back by the start time. The race was delayed and finally 30 mins later the 400 runners were told:

> The police and medical authorities, taking note of conditions on the hill as reported by the mountain rescue, advise us that anyone getting into difficulties would be dead within 25 minutes. Gentlemen, we cannot take that chance with your lives. The 1980 Ben Nevis race is cancelled.

An alternate route, or postponement till the Sunday, were not considered appropriate by the organisers. Observers counted 138 entrants running to the half way point as training, and nine went to the summit. Again recriminations and differing views were expressed in the various media, including comments about fees refunding, which weren't forthcoming from the organisers. The numbers of inexperienced and under-equipped runners entering was also a catalyst for the FRA thinking again about its rules on entries and clothing requirements. As it happens, that is the only time the Ben has been cancelled since 1951.

On a slightly lighter note, the 1981 Kentmere race (Category 'A', 12 miles, 3,300ft ascent) was run in thick mist. Several of the biggest names in fell running got lost in the mist and added an extra summit to the course in their confusion. The *Fellrunner* magazine report jokingly records a separate Harter Fell race result for them, and also the fact that on the actual course John Wild took 30 seconds off Andy Styan's three-year-old course record, which had been set in mist and snow.

A more recent event shows how good the support at races is these days, although unfortunately there was still an unavoidable fatality on this occasion. A 45-year-old fell runner died while taking part in the 2009 Snowdon race. The man, from the north-west Wales area, collapsed 300m below the summit while on the way to it. He was airlifted to hospital in Bangor, but medical teams were unable to revive him. The event safety was noted as being 'second to none' on the day, and the organisers were commended for that. There were two mountain rescue teams, Aberglaslyn and North East Wales Mountain Rescue, on the course, as well as five doctors and two paramedics. The runner had received medical assistance 'within seconds' of collapsing, and was rapidly airlifted off the mountain. It was a tragic incident, and the reason for the death appeared to have been heart related. During the race, mountain rescue teams dealt with another five incidents involving competitors, mostly cuts and bruises.

One of most annoying problems for race organisers is that of runners retiring from an event, not thinking to inform the organisers of this fact, and causing all sorts of unnecessary complications. This can include rescue searches being set in motion, as the runners may be feared lost or injured. All competitors should be familiar with the rules as laid down by the FRA and the particular race event they are entering. These are the current FRA instructions about retirement:

> Retirement may occur due to either competitor or organiser decision. Race control should be informed as quickly as possible. This must be done by either:

a. Reporting to a checkpoint and then returning directly to the finish to report to race control.

b. Reporting directly to race control when retiring between checkpoints.

c. Telephoning the race emergency number or the police. (This may be necessary when getting completely lost and arriving in the wrong valley.)

In light of all the above it is worth repeating here the relevant section of the FRA 'Safety Requirements for Fell Races' on equipment[51]:

Competitors should arrive at races prepared to carry any or all of the following equipment:-

a. Windproof whole body cover.

b. Other body cover appropriate for the weather conditions.

c. Map and compass suitable for navigating the course.

d. Whistle.

e. Emergency food (long races).

These requirements constitute "best practice" and are mandatory at all Category A Long and Medium races. However any race organiser is free to impose additional safety requirements (e.g. waterproof as distinct from windproof whole body cover) and competitors must be prepared to accept such requirements as a condition of race entry. In the event of settled fine weather, confirmed by a local weather report, the organiser *may* decide to waive some of the above requirements for races of other categories. Organisers must ensure that whatever requirements they specify on the day are met by holding complete or random checks before and after the start of the race. Race organisers should be aware of the dangers of hypothermia if injury to runners causes them to stop or slow to a walking pace. Body heat is lost quickly and in cold, wet or windy weather the onset of hypothermia can be very rapid unless sufficient warm clothing is carried. This factor should influence decisions on the extra equipment runners are required to carry in poor or unsettled weather conditions. If necessary the fact that the weather creates a high risk of hypothermia should be stressed to competitors.

I'll finish this chapter with the poignant story of the death of Bill Smith, the author of *Stud marks on the summits*. He died in September 2011 aged 75, having apparently fallen in a peat bog as he ran across Saddle Fell. His body was found by a walker, but in this remote area there was no mobile phone signal, so it was some time before he could raise the alarm. A Mountain Rescue team returned the following day to recover his body by helicopter. Smith had been due to marshall at the Thieveley Pike race and friends became concerned when he didn't turn up. It is uncertain exactly when he died but Lancashire Police said they believed he may have fallen into the bog and his body lain undiscovered for up to three weeks.

Bill Smith began running after meeting Stan Bradshaw in 1969. He ran up to 100 miles a week and competed frequently in long-distance fell races, such as Wasdale. In 1973, Bill Smith became the twelfth person to complete the Bob Graham Round, and set a new record (with Boyd Millen) by finishing in 20 hrs 38 mins. He built on the effort by traversing 55 Lakes peaks in 24 hours, and the following year he scaled 63 peaks in 23 hrs and 55 mins, a new mark that was later taken higher by Joss Naylor.

As well as being FRA Press Officer for a while Smith also put much back into the sport, being an avid photographer and supporter of races. He began what turned into the classic book *Stud marks on the summits* in 1978, and seven years later it was published by SKG Publications (the initials standing for Smith himself, plus Peter Knott and Peter Gildersleeve) after being rejected by the traditional publishers approached. The influence of the book is evident if you talk to almost any fell runner. Now the long-out-of-print book is being sold for well over £200 on eBay. Such was Bill Smith's stature that the major national newspapers all carried stories of his tragic death.

Among the runners who took inspiration from Bill Smith was Boff Whalley, of the band Chumbawamba. The Burnley-born guitarist is possibly known by the general public for being part of the band that carried out the stunt of tipping the icy dregs of a champagne cooler over the Deputy Prime Minister John Prescott at the Brit Pop awards in 1997. Whalley has been prominent in the fell running scene at a relatively high standard. He was instrumental in the production of the *Fellternative* fell running 'fanzine' in the early 1990s (part of *Up and Down* magazine). Chumbawamba recorded a song called 'Stud Marks on the Summits' and another called 'Joss' (the lyrics are in Appendix 1). Whalley is further profiled later in this book.

Footnote

Unfortunately there have been two fatalities in fell races in the period that I have been writing this book, the first since 1994.

The first happened at the Buttermere Sailbeck race on 29 April 2012. The body of Brian Belfield, who was 63, was discovered by mountain rescue teams the day after the 9.5 mile race. One hundred and fifty runners had set off in freezing rain and high winds to compete in the event. Belfield had taken part in the race four times previously, but sadly never returned this time. Fifty volunteers from the Cockermouth and Keswick mountain rescue teams, along with search dogs and police, took part in an initial search which was postponed at 3am on Monday when conditions became too difficult. At 7am the search resumed with support from Penrith, Kirkby Stephen and Wasdale mountain rescue teams and an RAF helicopter. Belfield's body was found at 9.45am. It was off the race route on steep, rough ground and in a spot sheltered from the wind below Scar Crag. Rescuers were unclear how Brian Belfield met his death, but believed he could have fallen or may have been sheltering there from the wind and rain.

Mike Park, the leader of Cockermouth Mountain Rescue Team, ran in the race and also joined the search for Belfield. In the *Westmorland Gazette* he was quoted as saying:

> Wind was gusting on the tops, with sleet and freezing rain. The weather changed during the day, it was getting worse and became windier from 1pm onwards. Everyone signed a declaration and race organisers gave a briefing at the start which mentioned the weather conditions. There was a kit list for the race which said you must have waterproof cover, a hat, gloves, map and compass, and there were kit checks.

Secondly, on 7 October 2012 Darren Holloway collapsed while competing in the Ian Hodgson Mountain Relay, which was being run over the Fairfield Horseshoe fells. Fellow competitors battled in vain to save his life by administering CPR. A helicopter was flown in to provide assistance, with the crew collecting a defibrillator and member of the Ambleside mountain rescue team from its base. Holloway was taken to Furness General Hospital but, despite efforts by doctors to resuscitate him, he unfortunately died. He was just 42 and a fit and experienced fell runner. A post mortem suggested his death may have been caused by an underlying heart condition.

In a report in the *Westmorland Gazette*, the Langdale Ambleside mountain rescue team leader commented:

> I believe some of the runners who stopped to help were quite experienced medics, including a couple of doctors. There was also a member of another mountain rescue team. The CPR administered was to a high standard, it is just unfortunate that it is one of those cases when nothing anybody could have done would have made a difference.

The Darren Holloway Memorial Race has been established in Darren's memory, with the first running taking place on 29 Saturday June 2013. It is a resurrection of a former epic Lakeland race, the Buttermere Horseshoe, to reflect his love of racing in the Lakeland Fells.

We must move on from these unfortunate incidents, and now consider the relative successes of fell runners coming off the fells to take on the marathon, and of road runners taking to the fells.

CHAPTER 14

Coming off the fells

Running would be better if it was only ever downhill
Moira Chilton

When considering writing this book, one thought that struck me was why more fell runners hadn't followed Kenny Stuart's example and come off the fells and put their undoubted endurance capabilities into running fast marathons. Maybe there is some subtle difference between the running styles, race rhythm or the training required to make that change. The following section details some of those who did just that, or even in some cases took their proven marathon form on to the fells, with varying degrees of success in both directions.

My first example is a runner who didn't come down off the fells, or take to the fells after the roads, he just included the fells as part of his usual training and racing. **Ron Hill** achieved considerable success as a marathon runner in the late 1960s and early 1970s, and included fell running in his seemingly insatiable desire to compete at track, road, cross country and off-road disciplines throughout his career. His two volumes of autobiography are perhaps the most detailed accounts of training and racing by a world-class athlete to be published. Like *Stud marks on the summits,* getting published seems to have been an issue with Hill, when he produced his manuscripts. In the end they were published by Ron Hill Sports Limited, rather than by a mainstream publisher. The two volumes[52] are out of print now, but Amazon partners had secondhand copies available for between £30 and £50 at the time of writing.

Ron Hill was raised in Lancashire, and his first athletic club was Clayton-le-Moors, who have always had a fine fell running tradition. Luminaries of the club at the time Hill was coming through included Stan Bradshaw (described in Hill's book as a tripe manufacturer), Alf Case (membership No 1 of the FRA when it formed, and its first Chairman), George Brass, and Alan and Ken Heaton, who all had backgrounds in fell running.

In 1958, at the age of 20, Hill entered his first fell race and came fifth at Rivington Pike. A week later he was fifth in the Pendle Hill race and shortly afterwards won the local Pendleton race. Even at this young age he was running 70 meticulously recorded miles a week, including training runs over the moors of two hours plus. He also often ran straight over the fells to work as this took 30 minutes, against the one-hour bus trip round the valleys.

Over Easter in 1959 he came sixth at Rivington Pike and concluded that he lacked strength going uphill, but was good on downhill. In the first part of his autobiography he commented:

> in fell races there are always a frightening ten seconds or so, after the turn round at the top, when my legs feel lifeless and virtually out of control. After that my success depended on style, a long stride, a degree of recklessness and an ability for my eyes to look, automatically, a few feet ahead, knowing exactly where each foot would land. I can't say I enjoyed fell races, but I was always drawn to them. They were competitions and I was attracted to competitions.

He continued in local races, including winning Pendleton again, after coming second earlier in the day in a 100-yards race. In September that year he also went on a club trip to the Ben Nevis race, his eighth place showing his strength and affinity with longer races. At halfway on the ascent Hill was third, but his relatively weak climbing left him twelfth at the summit. His descending skills re-gained him four places but he had nothing in his legs once back at the road for the run-in. He concluded:

> I was glad to see the finish line and felt sick once I stopped ... when I recovered, I was quite pleased with my position.

In 1960 he returned to the Ben but dropped out due to taking a flyer on the descent, having to then hop off the mountain. He changed clubs to Bolton, and upped the mileage to eighty miles a week. In 1961 he had his first victory in what he termed a 'proper fell race' – Rivington Pike. He also entered the Three Peaks Race and typically raced, and won, a three-mile track race the day beforehand. In the Peaks he took the lead for a while, but ended in fifth in 3 hrs 11 mins 55 secs, seven minutes behind the winner. He also entered the Liverpool Marathon, as he couldn't find a race that weekend. He duly won the race in 2 hrs 24 mins 22 secs. Two weeks after this debut marathon he won Pendleton again, with his warm-up being 'running to the top and back'. The following years he gradually increased the mileage even further, eventually experimenting with a 160-mile week in 1967. Hill not only survived this huge training mileage, but also once being treated by the infamous Hyde GP Harold Shipman.

> I had some stomach problems and brought some samples in and he did tests and gave me antibiotics. Everybody said he was a good doctor, even the people that he killed thought he was. But he was on a mission of some sort.

There was a definite change in emphasis towards marathons, yet three more times he ran the Three Peaks, achieving ninth in 1963 (having got lost following Alan Heaton), a best of fourth in 1964 and another ninth in 1966. The marathon times gradually came down, and bigger successes followed. These included winning the European Marathon in Athens in 1969, the Boston in 1970 (in a course record of 2 hrs 10 mins 30.1 secs), and culminating in winning the 1970 Commonwealth Marathon in Edinburgh in 2 hrs 9 mins 28 secs, a time which was the second fastest in the world at the time.

In the next phase of his career Hill reverted to running all distances and surfaces again, with many lesser marathon wins. He returned to the Three Peaks a couple of times, including a 2 hrs 59 mins finish for thirteenth in 1972 – achieving his fastest time for the event in a self-proclaimed 'training run'. As his international career wound down he returned to his roots and used fell races to satisfy his need to race frequently. An indication of the appetite for fell races is the second volume of his autobiography, recording results from 14 fell races for 1980, along with many road and cross country races. Not exactly a marathon runner who came down off the fells, more a distance runner who used fell racing (and training) as both a motivation and a challenge.

Also, as I write this, his streak of having trained at least once every day has lasted 47 years. Even more remarkable is Hill's little known streak of running **twice a day** (once on Sundays). On 6 March 1991 this particular streak came to an end after 26.2 years. *Up and Down* magazine noted at the time that the decision came suddenly, after Hill became more and more tired in training. In a piece in the magazine he said:

> I could have carried on but it was becoming counter-productive, and looking for a significant number I came up with 26.2 years, 26.2 miles being the distance of the marathon.

Not long after Ron Hill, an athlete from Appleby came on the scene. **Dave Cannon** had considerable success as a youngster, competed superbly on the fells for a few years, and then took to marathon running. Cannon was arguably the best fell runner in the UK for a couple of years in the early 1970s. He is one of four athletes who were interviewed in the very first typescript FRA newsletter in 1971.

He was Cumbrian schools Champion at cross country and took up fell running as a teenager, initially running in local races, and joining Kendal AC. He was a contemporary of Tommy Sedgwick, who was the only one who could beat him on a steep descent in those days. In an *Up and Down* magazine article he describes competing in the Whernside Junior race:

> You have a wall to get over when descending. Well I was coming down so fast, I was not going to stop to climb it, so I took off a few yards from the wall, got one foot on top and over! There was a fell race follower watching the race at this point and he said to me afterwards that he had never seen anything like it before. I hadn't the heart to tell him it hadn't been intentional.

Cannon precociously won several senior amateur races while still a junior, including Ben Nevis in 1971. He had a considerable number of victories in shorter fell races, and despite his later marathon prowess never really encompassed the very long fell events. As noted, he was a daring, breakneck descender and specialised in shorter up-and-down races, claiming Burnsall and Thieveley Pike as two of his favourites. In the same interview he claimed:

> The race my descending skills most helped me to win was the 1970 Burnsall. Harry Walker pushed me all the way to the summit, but even with two falls on the way down, I won by over a minute ... A few people remarked to me after the race that I must be crackers to come down that fast. As you know, they can see the whole course from the village green.

He used to develop his descent speed and technique by doing downhill repetitions on Dufton Pike and Murton Pike. He used to train about 70–75 miles a week when fell racing, but did have some injury issues due to turning his ankle a couple of times. Despite having a slightly limited race range he was the first British Fell Running Champion in 1972. He is 6ft tall and weighed 10st 7lbs when racing.

Cannon won Ben Nevis five times between 1971 and 1976, setting the then record of 1 hr 26 mins 55 secs in 1976. He also set a record at the time for the Skiddaw race, which he was very proud of. In the FRA interview he replied when questioned about any particular targets, that they were 'to break all the fell race records and to run for England'. However, looking back at his career he never really realised his potential as a long-distance fell runner. Actually, he only competed in three of the really long events. In 1972, the year he was British Champion, he retired in the Three Peaks, came third in the Chevy Chase, and also third at Ennerdale, having blown up in the latter stages.

Recently Cannon was interviewed by Alistair Aitkin (published on the Highgate Harriers website[53]) and he rationalised his change of focus thus:

> because there were no international honours to be gained from fell running, I decided to take a new challenge and see if I could run for Great Britain and took up the marathon. In 1977 I became British Champion at the Marathon. It progressed from there.

The first challenge was at the AAA Marathon in Rugby, which Cannon won in 2 hrs 15 mins 2 secs. He improved to 2 hrs 13 mins 29 seconds at the trial race. This enabled him to go to the European Championships (in Prague in 1978) in which he finished ninth in 2 hrs 14 mins 31 secs. Then he concentrated on training for the 1980 Olympics. To try to gain selection he raced in New Zealand, finishing second to Dick Quax in 2 hrs 13 mins 44 secs on a blistering hot day. The selectors still made him run the Olympic trial race, but he was ill and finished fifth Brit, missing out on selection. In the Aitkin interview he takes up the story.

> Then because I did not go to the Olympics they invited me to the Montréal International Marathon in 1980 and because a lot of countries had boycotted the Moscow Olympics the field in Montreal was exceptionally good. My best time of 2 hrs 13 mins 29 secs was only the thirteenth fastest in that field for that day but I managed to win it. A lot of determination for being left out of the Olympics and a natural progression and I ran 2 hrs 11 mins 21 secs. After that I ran another couple of 2-11s, one in Paris and one in Japan.

Paris was a victory, and Fukuoka a dead-heat with Ron Tabb, because they were together up to about 41km, but were impeded by traffic and agreed to the tie as a true sprint-out had been thwarted. He also ran in the European Championship Marathon in Athens in 1982 but finished a disappointed twelfth in 2 hrs 21 mins 33 secs, after feeling good earlier and being with the leaders at half-way[54].

Cannon stopped training on the fells completely when he moved to marathon running. His rationale was that it was using different types of muscles. He also gave this as a reason that he took so long to really make his mark as a marathon runner. Strangely, for someone who was reckoned to be one of the sport's greatest ever descenders, he eventually took to road racing remarkably well. He also found that the flat road stretch at the end of the Ben Nevis race, for instance, played into his hands when racing there. In fact he won Ben Nevis three times after he had virtually forsaken fell running for the roads. He set his fastest time of 1 hr 26 mins 55 secs in 1976, which was the record for seven years, with Billy Bland only being able to get within one second of it, before John Wild took it to 1 hr 25 mins 35 secs in 1983.

Sadly, Cannon had to cease racing in 1986 because of a bad viral illness that was later diagnosed as ME. What had started as just a heavy cold developed into something much more serious. It destroyed his athletics career and devastated his life. Doctors were baffled why a super-fit athlete couldn't shake off a simple cold. After months of feeling completely drained of energy, a fellow runner suggested he might be suffering from ME. It was a little-known condition back then, and was often referred to as yuppie flu. He strongly believes it was his punishing training regime that triggered the ME. With doctors unsure about how to treat him, Cannon turned in desperation to less conventional ways to tackle the condition. He consulted a homeopathic practitioner, who eventually helped him rebuild his immune system.

Cannon took up coaching with some considerable success, claiming to have five athletes faster than 1 hr 3 mins 30 secs for the half marathon at one stage. Most significantly he guided Kenny Stuart in his transition from the fells to marathon running. He may have first realised Stuart's road potential when he lost to him in the Derwentwater 10, a tough course that Stuart completed in just under 50 mins. Ironically Stuart achieved a very similar marathon PB, travelled to North America to achieve it, and had to end his career in similar circumstances, as has already been seen. When interviewed in 2009 in the *Cumberland News*, Cannon tells an interesting tale from the day he won the Montreal Marathon.

> As my weary legs pounded the Canadian city street lined with spectators, from the crowd came a distinctive Cumbrian voice: 'Go on, Dave Cannon, you can do it – use your experience of running up them fells'. That was nearly 30 years ago and to this day I don't know who that man was – but I reckon he won me that race. I still wonder who he was and what a Cumbrian was doing there.

Olympian **Jeff Norman** is from Leigh in Lancashire and started running cross country and track for Altrincham AC when he was 17 (in 1962). Within two years he was running on the fells too, coming fourteenth in his first race at Rivington Pike. He was inspired by stories of the Three Peaks Race, which he first entered in 1966, finishing fifty-fourth in this his first really long event. He swiftly progressed, through twenty-seventh next year, third in 1968, to a close second in 1969. Then, in 1969 he won his first fell race at Three Towers.

He finally won the Three Peaks in 1970, in 2 hrs 48 mins 11 secs, in a year when snow was on the ground on all three peaks. The following year there were ideal conditions and he broke the record of 2 hrs 40 mins 34 secs, finishing in 2 hrs 36 mins 26 secs. He won again in 1972, and in the next year reduced the record to 2 hrs 31 mins 58 secs. Despite poor weather in 1974 he brought it down to 2 hrs 29 mins 53 secs. He won on the revised route in 1975, giving him a fantastic sequence of six consecutive wins.

As well as his Three Peaks success Jeff Norman also had victories in a range of other fell races over different distances. He won Skiddaw and Ben Nevis in 1970, as well as the shorter Gale Fell race in 1972. Not only that but he won Skiddaw five times, Three Towers five times, and Gale four times, and Fairfield three times in a total of over 60 wins overall. The year of 1974, when he set his fastest Three Peaks time, was also the year that he won the Fell Runner of the Year award.

The following year he came only ninth in the fell championship, but there was a change in emphasis. He had moved to the roads, winning the AAA Marathon in 2 hrs 15 mins 50 secs. Consequently he was picked for the Olympics, achieving 2 hrs 20 mins 4.8 secs for twenty-sixth in the 1976 Montreal Olympics. He also competed in the Commonwealth Games Marathon two years later. He has a marathon personal best of 2 hrs 12 mins and 50 secs from 1978, and set the world record for 50km on the track – 2 hrs 48 mins 8 secs in 1980, which still stands, and for 30 miles (2 hrs 42 mins exactly), within the same race. His 2 hrs 16 mins 13 secs from Maasluis (Netherlands) from 1986 is the second fastest British Vets Marathon time, after Ron Hill's 2 hrs 15 mins 46 secs. At shorter distances his PBs were – 5000m: 14 mins 30 secs; 10000m: 29 mins 57 secs and 10 miles road: 48 mins 20 secs.

Although he changed to marathons Norman kept up the fell running as well. In 1978 only a week after coming second in the AAA Marathon he came second in 1 hr 15 mins 55 secs in the Darwen Moors fell race, in a time inside the previous course record. He had no fell wins in the Olympic year, but won Kentmere the year before, and also came second to Joss Naylor at Ennerdale that year. In the Commonwealth games year he won at Stoodley Pike, and took Snowdon for the second time the year after, but his training was more road focused. He went altitude training before the 1976 Olympic Marathon and claimed in a recent interview[55] that it

felt really good at first when I came down. Unfortunately the timing was wrong – I caught a cold in the Olympic village. Was there too long and it all went out of the window. I used warm weather training a couple of times – I think it was useful for preparing for races in warm weather.

He liked to train in a group, often with runners from Bingley Harriers. He always tried to hang on and usually tailed off at first, until eventually he was comfortable in the group. He often used races as training – sometimes flat out, sometimes trying different tactics – either starting fast or deliberately taking it easy early and trying to finish hard. He claims weights caused him injuries. In the same interview he commented:

> Cross country is important to build that tenacity to keep pushing when the going gets tough. I did enjoy cross country and felt that this and the fell running were vital early season conditioners. For me it was essential to work on my strength and run 100+ miles per week. While not ignoring speed work, running shorter mileage at a fast pace never worked for me. Mileage varied from 20–40 miles per week in early winter to 100–140 in March–June. I once reached 188 miles. In winter most running was on road. In summer I tried to get on hills/grass as much as possible. Speed sessions tended to be on the track or road in the winter, and on track or off road circuit in the summer.

In an earlier interview in the very first *Fellrunner* magazine Jeff Norman responded to the question on special training for particular events with a comment that he

> always starts the season with a couple of outings over the 'Peaks' course in about 4 hours and Sunday runs over hills every week I can manage for 6 weeks prior. Also like a fast fell run (eg Rivington) shortly before. When my legs stop being stiff running on hills I know I am ready to race.

Jeff Norman is still competing to a high standard as a V65 athlete, and his sons Andy and Dave are literally following in his footsteps, both having 65 min half marathons to their credit.

In the 1980s several other fell runners had a go at marathon running, with varying degrees of success. Were they possibly, like me, inspired in some way

by the first London Marathon in 1981. These early Londons certainly raised
the profile of marathon running greatly. The results for that first London
Marathon show Veronique Marot in ninth place with 2 hrs 46 mins 51 secs,
Anne Bland fourteenth in 2 hrs 51 mins 56 secs, and Bridget Hogge
twenty-third in 2 hrs 59 mins 21 secs. These three all had fell running
backgrounds, or moved on to the fells.

Veronique Marot ran Ennerdale two years before this, and won Sierre-Zinal
a little later (in 1985), although she was never a mainstream fell runner.
Marot went on to a long and brilliant marathon career, winning several
marathons, including London and Houston, and competing in the Olympic
Marathon in 1992. Her best time was 2 hrs 25 mins 56 secs when winning
London in 1989, a British Record. Anne Bland started running in her mid
thirties. As a fell runner her most notable performance was probably winning
the Elite Mixed Team Class, with her husband Pete, in the 1978 Karrimor
Mountain Marathon held that year in Peebles. She became the first woman
to complete the Elite class in the Karrimor. Anne then moved into running
road marathons and became very successful, running 13 sub-three-hour
marathons. All these marathons were completed when she was in her forties.
She also competed in the World Masters Marathon in San Diego, California
in 1984.

Bridget Hogge had a long and successful fell career. She won the first
ever Snowdon race in 1 hr 40 mins 11 secs, and went back in 1983 to win
again in 1 hr 39 mins 32 secs. Hogge was one of the pioneers for ladies in
races, coming second in the inaugural Three Peaks ladies race in 1979, and
then winning in 1984.

After these pioneers, along came Sarah Rowell. She won her first marathon
at the early age of 20. It was the North Kent Marathon in 1982. She then
was selected for the World Student Games in 1983, where she won the
marathon in 2 hrs 47 mins 37 secs. She had a relatively short marathon
career, which culminated in her second place in London in 1985, in a new
British Record of 2 hrs 28 mins 6 secs, and included Olympic Marathon
selection for 1984. She also took on off-road marathons, first entering the
Seven Sisters (now Beachy Head) in 1982, an event she won outright in
1986.

Her fell running credentials are impeccable too. From 1989 she started
running long fell races. She achieved a second place in the World Mountain

Running Trophy in 1992. Rowell also had a remarkable return from her Three Peaks racing – winning in 1991, 1992, 1994 and 1996, the last time in a new course record. She was British Fell Running Champion in both 1995 and 1996. She won at such diverse courses as Burnsall and Ben Nevis. She still holds two course records, Skiddaw from 1989, and Dale Head from 1995.

On the men's side Fraser Clyne did a 2 hrs 14 mins marathon in London in spring 1984, and then at the beginning of June won the Scolty Hill race in a new course record. In September of that year he ran 2 hrs 11 mins 44 secs in the California International Marathon. He wasn't a major force in fell running, but did end up winning the Scolty Hill race 16 times.

More recently Andi Jones is a runner who has flattered to deceive in his marathon attempts. Despite PBs of 29 mins 28 secs for 10k and 1 hr 4 mins 22 secs for the half marathon he has so far only managed 2 hrs 15 mins 20 secs in the marathon, in the 2009 London. Andi Jones first started running at the age of 18 by entering the London Marathon. With an aim of breaking four hours he ran 3 hrs 58 mins. His fell running pedigree is good though. In 2003 he was fourth in the WMRA (World Mountain Running Trophy) World Mountain Running Trophy in Alaska. In July 2009 Jones became the first male to win the Snowdon Race four times in a row, and he returned in 2011 to win again. You could argue that he needs to decide on EITHER fell running OR marathons to achieve his true potential, but he begs to differ. On his own blog[56] he says:

> I kept getting told that marathon running and mountain running didn't mix even though there were some very good examples around of runners who have ran awesome marathons and ran well on the mountains.

Kenny Stuart was arguably the best fell runner ever to have a serious tilt at the marathon. Stuart peaked on the fells in 1985. In 1986 he turned his attention to road running and won his debut marathon that year at Glasgow in 2 hrs 14 mins 3 mins. He went on to set his best marathon time of 2 hrs 11 mins 36 secs at Houston (Texas) in 1989, but as has been noted his career was curtailed by increasing allergy and virus problems. That PB is still thirtieth on the all-time UK list, with only fourteen athletes having beaten that time since 1989, and only two in the last six years. Kenny Stuart's road credentials were certainly good too: 10km in 28 mins 51 secs, 10 miles in 48 mins 13 secs, and a half marathon in 1 hr 2 mins 55 secs.

We must now take a short diversion, for a bit of physiology. VO2 max is a measure of the maximum amount of oxygen in millilitres one can use in one minute per kilogram of body weight, and can be used as a predictor of performance. However, having a high VO2 max does not necessarily mean that you will be a successful endurance athlete. Although the athletes listed below have been successful in their chosen sports, there have also been others equally successful who have not recorded such high VO2 max scores. There are obviously other factors to consider for success in aerobic based sports. But, in tests Kenny Stuart was reported to have a VO2 max of 80 ml/kg/min, when tested in June 1990. Comparable VO2 max figures reported for other top athletes across sports are: Fred Reeves at 79, former 10,000m world record holder and London Marathon organiser Dave Bedford at 85, and cyclist Lance Armstrong at 84[57]. It is worth noting that Matt Carpenter, the Pikes Peak Marathon course record holder, has a VO2 max recording of 92 ml/kg/min[58].

Another option for fell runners who have achieved all they can in standard races is to tackle some of the extended fell challenges, such as the Bob Graham Round. For some this is an end in itself, and ordinary fell races take second place or aren't even considered challenging enough. I shall firstly look at the Bob Graham Round though, as it is probably the best known challenge and is a serious target for many fell runners.

A *conversation with:* Jeff Norman, Altrincham AC

Another interview, another café. Perhaps I should write a good café guide. I am waiting for Jeff Norman in the Costa Coffee inside Tescos in East Didsbury. As my wife and I were travelling to the Yorkshire Dales for a short holiday the former Olympian has agreed to meet me – the day before going on his own holiday. Major delays for accidents on the motorway have made us late, but a chain of phone calls got us Jeff's number and he kindly agreed to meet us slightly later. It was another case of recognising someone from decades-old photos I have seen. We began reliving Jeff's athletic story.

'I did run 188 miles in a week once.'

Jeff Norman was born in Leigh. All he did at primary school was 60m at school sports. The longest distance race was 80m. He was last every time, and says he was useless at all sports. He just couldn't sprint. When he went to secondary school you were allowed to do rugby. *'When I was about 15 I got a chance to do cross country. They said you are no good. It is the ones that are good that get a chance to do cross country, so I had to wait another year.'*

Then he showed he was reasonably good at cross country, and did well in the house sports. He joined Altrincham 50 years ago, a year after it was formed. He is still going strong. *'They are having a little do for us (me and two others from that era) next month.'* At school he wasn't even county standard. He was in the school cross country team and ran a couple of times for school on the track. He wasn't at a particularly good standard just then.

He also wasn't really aware of anything to do with fell running. He used to like climbing. The first he knew of mountain/fell races was reading an article about the Three Peaks Race in a magazine. *'It said stuff like "enter at your own risk", blowing it up as something dangerous. At 17-18 years old I was taken by that sort of idea.'*

There was no evidence of his parents being very sporty. His two sisters liked walking, but never did any running. *'We were getting the club going and another of the 50-year club members is Alan Blinston, who went to the 1968 Olympics. We decided that we wanted to do the Rivington Pike race, which was tough enough for a starter. It was the sort if race I did best at in the early days.'* Now he says it was probably a bit too short for him actually.

As he got older he trained more. He was 21 when he first did the Three Peaks, and first won it on his fifth attempt. He actually wanted to do a marathon as soon as he was old enough. *'The first one entered was a couple of months after I turned 21, but I got injured. I was never fast enough for track. It seemed the further I ran the better I got.'* When it first started Altrincham was mainly a harrier club. Even now it has difficulties getting a track team out. Jeff doesn't remember looking up to anyone in particular in fell running. The early fell races he did were mostly composed of road and cross country runners that just did fell too. *'When I started I was inspired by skinny Bruce Tulloch, but I saw him run but never raced against him. I remember going to run in the juniors at the East Lancs Championships, and watched the Senior race which was won by Ron Hill.'*

The first fell race he won was the Three Towers, in the snow. *'I think it was in February that year. It was quite something to win my first race.'* Looking back, he says all the fell greats impress him, in different ways. *'Well Kenny Stuart really, his times for Snowdon and Skiddaw are just brilliant. Ricky Wilde too, I saw him on Thursday. He was so laid back, if he had trained better he could have been a world beater. John Wild was brilliant too.'* In his early days there weren't that many races. *'Often a new race came along and I would have a go at it. Kentmere is one I did and liked.'*

Jeff set the Three Peaks record several times. *'On the old course I set the record and lowered it four times, to get the 2 hrs 29 mins in the end.'* The following year it changed to a different place and a longer course, moving from the Hill Inn to Horton, and he set the original record on that. He set the Skiddaw record a couple of times. *'I think Dave Cannon took that and then came Kenny.'* A lot of new races were being set up in his peak years and he set a few records because of that. *'I ran against Billy Bland, and on his type of course I had no chance, nor did I against Joss Naylor.'*

He was working as a pharmacist when he was running his best, indoors all day long. Billy and Joss were doing manual work. They got some training advantage from their jobs, Jeff suggests. *'I used to like to do some fells when in marathon training. I tended to avoid the really rough ones. I was also a bit careful when I put a fell race in. For instance it would take quite a while to get over something like Snowdon.'* He was doing a mix of road and track sessions, his long runs were pretty long compared to most – some on the fells and some on roads. He did speed sessions with Alan Blinston on different surfaces.

His first marathon was Preston to Morecambe, aged 21, and he ended up walking. He had been injured, and had only just got round the Three Peaks. *'I wasn't really fit enough to do it really. I knew I had to do more training to last out better.'* At the time he did get some advice from a guy called Wilf Richards, who coached at Manchester Athletic Club, and who lived about 100 yards from him. He gave Jeff a bit of advice, not coaching as such. There were also a few at the club that were doing long distances. By the time he was 24-25 years old he started to improve his marathon times. *'Two-forty was the first one, then 2 hrs 32 mins, and I stayed there a short while, then did 2 hrs 28 mins, and 2 hrs 22 mins. Then I thought I should get some recognition when I knocked six minutes off for a 2 hrs 16 mins time. A minor invite out somewhere, but nothing happened, which was disappointing.'*

He claims his navigation is OK. He always does the navigation leg on the FRA relay. *'Having said that I got lost on Thursday night. I used to do the Mountain Trial. When I first started I wasn't that good at that aspect.'* He used to go back to races that he liked. The Three Peaks was always one he had to get fit for. That was at the end of April. *'Then I might do a marathon in June. My favourites were fell races like Three Peaks, Snowdon and Skiddaw.'*

Jeff's view was that if you don't like roads you are not going to do well at it, but that some of the better fell runners have phenomenal endurance and could come down to the marathon. *'The real endurance rough stuff specialists would find it difficult to translate as you need the speed. As well as myself, Alan McGee, Dave Cannon and Kenny Stuart all did good marathons after the fells.'*

He says he was a better descender than climber in the early days, but that he did improve his climbing over time. *"I used to reckon that if I was within reach of them at the top I would win the race. The one I worried about though was Ricky Wilde, every time. Jack Maitland and Andy Styan were also great descenders on rough terrain."*

He had his VO2 max tested when he was in the marathon squad, and he was also told he was a bit fat. Of course your performance is a combination of things, such as your VO2 max and the way you are able to use it. *'The result wasn't anything exceptional, but I was very efficient. For instance, Derek Clayton had a very low score and look what he did[59].'*

Norman's two sons run and have particular strengths. They have both done good half marathons, and both did fell running for a bit. *'David was third Junior in the British Championships one year. Andrew was lying second till he got injured. He still has issues with injuries."* David has already done several marathons, and has won the Manchester Marathon.

Jeff certainly packed the mileage in at times when training for the marathon. *'I did run 188 miles in a week once. I wanted to see how much I could get in. I ran a good relay leg shortly afterwards. I remember being tired. I would have been on 100-mile a week for eight weeks, and build-up a little.'* He was crowned Fell Runner of the Year just once, and claims he did try to win it then. *'The Championships then had many races though. From next year you can win it without even doing a long race.'*

When asked about his greatest achievement on the fells Jeff cited two particular ones, the Three Peaks and Sierre-Zinal. *'I got more pleasure from fell races than roads, but the sense of achievement from doing the Olympics is something else.'* He competed in the marathon at the Olympics in 1976. He did the AAA race in 1975 and won, but loads of people were missing (Ian Thompson, Ron Hill for instance), and they said 'you won that but you won't get in the Olympics'. He thought 'I'll show them'.

The Olympic trial for 1976 was at Rotherham on a tough course. Ian Thompson and Ron Hill went off quite quick with Barry Watson, who always was a fast starter. *'I laid back a bit, but started coming through. Thompson and Hill were going backwards. I took the lead at about 23 miles. Coming to a big downhill at 25 miles and I got cramp. I thought "oh no, out the window". So, I am sure I could have won the race, but I wanted to be sure to keep in first three to be selected. Time was not important. I had done 2 hrs 15 mins 50 secs the previous year and that day did 2 hrs 15 mins 17 secs.'*

In the Olympics in Montreal he did 2 hrs 20 mins. He looks back on a not particularly good experience. *'Everything went perfectly till about two weeks before. I came down from altitude, had done some great sessions, lovely long runs, and felt really fit. Came down and got a cold, which wasn't helped by being 14 to a room in the village. We had to wait till end of the week to run.'*

His first Three Peaks was done just to do it, off hardly any training. He actually went to sleep during the race. In those days you started at the Hill Inn and did Ingleborough first. *'I got to Whernside and struggled up it. Going down my legs were in such bad shape and I was so tired I kept falling. I got part way down and had fallen so many times I just felt like having a little sleep – just ten minutes. I lost about half a stone but got such a sense of achievement by finishing it, and ate so much after.'* In the early days it took a more direct route straight through fields from Horton. The last bit was very steep. It is gentler now and quite a lot longer. *'The year I did the 2 hrs 29 mins I just remember I was running out in front, having left Harry Walker on Pen-y-Ghent. It felt like I was on a training run, I felt so great.'*

The Bob Graham Round was in his mind at one time, although he knew it would mess up the whole season. *'I did think of it. I started getting a team together and we did a reconnoitre over the first part. There was no way that lot were going to do it. We were only on the first part and we fell apart basically. I wanted to do it but by the time I was able to do it I wasn't bothered any more.'*

As well as having one of the fastest Rivington Pike times Jeff is still ninth fastest for the Lantern Pike race. He is in pretty good shape but does have a few issues these days. *'A race like those is not good on the knees now. So, I have not raced since a cross country in January.'*

CHAPTER 15

The Bob Graham Round

Anybody should be able to do it – provided they're fit enough
Bob Graham

Not content with participating in organised fell races some athletes have taken to the hills to set endurance records over known routes, or to complete ever increasing numbers of peaks in a given time. One of the most famous of these challenges is the **Bob Graham Round,** which some define as a long walk/run over 42 Lakeland summits, the Round originally being made in 1932. However, other remarkable feats of hill endurance were noted well before this.

Possibly the first round of the fells was by Rev. Elliott of Cambridge, who in 1864 (or thereabouts, sources vary) departed from Wasdale Head and returned there eight and a half hours later after going over nine of the highest mountains in the Lakes. These were Scafell, Scafell Pike, Great End, Great Gable, Kirk Fell, Pillar, Steeple, Red Pike and Stirrup Crag, making a distance of about 15 miles.

Six years later Thomas Watson from Darlington, together with a man called Wilson (a Borrowdale guide), went for 20 hours and covered 48 miles, with 10,000-plus feet of ascent. Starting from Keswick they walked to Scafell Pike and then cut across to traverse the Helvellyn range, followed by Blencathra and Skiddaw, finishing in Keswick. They did all this in nailed boots, experiencing thick mist at one point, snow showers on Scafell Pike and gales that forced them to crawl to the summit of Blencathra. Bob

Wightman's website lists several others that he calls 'proto-rounds and attempts'[60] from the 1880s and 90s.

The one-day record was pushed in 1902 to 70 miles and 18,000 feet of ascent by one S.B. Johnson of Carlisle. Then in 1905 Dr A.W. Wakefield from Keswick, wearing rubber shoes, shorts and his Sedbergh School football jersey, increased this to 70 miles, 23,500 feet, and 22 peaks in 22 hrs 7 mins. Wakefield swam in Derwentwater every day, and his climbing exploits got him invited on the 1922 Mount Everest expedition. At the age of 45 he reached Camp 3, 1,000 feet or so below the North Col, but suffered badly from altitude sickness. Wakefield later coached Eustace Thomas to repeat his Lake District route in 21 hrs 25 mins in 1920. The following year Thomas added the ridge north from Helvellyn over the Dodds to Clough Head, giving over 25,000 feet inside 24 hrs. He was 54 at the time and always wore hobnailed boots on these efforts. Thomas was the first Englishman to ascend all of the Alpine 4,000m peaks. He also gave his name to the Thomas mountain stretcher, which was adopted in 1934 and was very widely used by mountain rescue teams until the 1970s.

Several attempts to beat the record took place in the next decade or so, including one by Bob Graham in 1931. In 1932 Graham eventually set what is now the standard for his eponymous round. According to Roger Smith's *The Story of the Bob Graham Round*, it was '42 peaks representing one for each year of Bob's life'. The peaks included are illustrated p235.

The round was completed in 23 hrs 39 mins. In the BGR booklet Roger Smith records:

> The stocky figure in shirt, shorts and plimsolls, padding through the dark Keswick streets with his four trusty friends, had set a record that was to stand for 28 years. There was no great celebration; no reporters met them. They shook hands and retired to Bob's guest house, and at 6am he was up as usual to cook them breakfast.

According to Ronald Turnbull's account of the event in *Cumbria* magazine:

> he ran in shorts, pyjama jacket and gym shoes; he dined on bread and butter, lightly boiled eggs and sweets. At Dunmail Raise he was photographed by the Abraham Brothers [the photo is on the cover of the BGR booklet]. The weather closed in: heavy rain on Red Pike, mist on the Derwent Fells, also thunder and lightning.

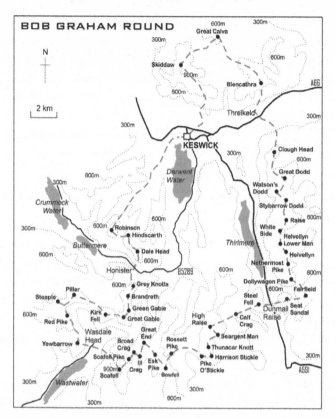

Bob Graham's pacers were Martin Rylands, Phil Davidson, and Messrs Deans and Hewitson. The pacers carried a pair of boots for him, but he never bothered to use them. It is reckoned that Bob Graham reconnoitred each summit in bare feet, to toughen up his feet and to avoid unnecessary wear on his plimsolls. Graham was no great athlete, but had an excellent knowledge of the fells, and was teetotal, and a non-smoker. He walked all the uphills, and ran the downhills. According to Ronald Turnbull, who quotes Graham in a *Cumbria* magazine article 'Following in the Footsteps of the Record Breakers', as saying:

> The uphill bits gave me a rest, and if I felt tired going up I thought to myself: I can always get a rest running down the next bit ... I'd no time to do much thinking. We were laughing and telling tales all the way. We thought it great fun. Yes, it was a good day.

He went clockwise, on George Abraham's advice. On subsequent attempts the trend for a while was to go anti-clockwise, but has more recently reverted to clockwise being more popular. This is mostly due to the long 'run-in' from Newlands to Keswick being the last section when going clockwise.

Others attempted to repeat, and even beat, this feat. Meanwhile in the 1950s, long distance walks (such as Lands End to John O'Groats) were very popular, and there was even an organised race between those two points, sponsored by Billy Butlin, of holiday camp fame. Noted author Harry Griffin wrote in the *Lancashire Evening Post* that

> anyone could do Land's End to John O'Groats provided they were modestly fit, indeed they could get fit on the way.

Griffin added that the **Lakeland 24-hour fell record** was more like a real challenge.

Alan and Ken Heaton from Clayton-le-Moors Harriers took up the challenge and in June 1960 organised a backup team from the running club as support. Despite various setbacks en route (including Ken breaking his glasses), Alan turned out to be strongest and reduced the time for the traverse to 22 hrs 18 mins. Roger Smith noted in *42 Peaks* that arriving 18 minutes ahead of schedule at Honister

> they were met by Harry Griffin and Bob Graham, a fit looking 71. Graham expressed the view that the hot weather was ideal (a view not shared by the others!) and wished them the best of luck.

In June 1961 Ken Heaton raised the stakes by planning a route that raised the summit total to 51 peaks, and in bad weather managed it in 22 hrs 13 mins, starting this time from the Old Dungeon Ghyll (ODG) pub in Langdale, in order to add more peaks in that valley. Alan Heaton was injured that year, but in 1961 he raised the record to 54 peaks, covered in 23 hrs 48 mins, with Joss Naylor helping pacing, and perhaps having his own thoughts about tackling the challenge later.

Eric Beard set about this target in 1963, and was blessed with pacers of the calibre of the Heaton brothers, Stan Bradshaw and Joss Naylor. He chose to do the traverse in light climbing boots and not running shoes. He went so well that he was able to add Greatrigg Man and Grisedale Pike to the previous summits list. He ended up doing 56 summits, about 88 miles, and around 34,000 feet of ascent, coming home in 23 hrs 35 mins.

Beard was a multi-faceted character. He is remembered by some as a raconteur and singer of ballads, but there was more to him than that. He was born in Leeds and left school at fifteen. Initially he was small, weak and puny in physique, being just five feet tall. He had jobs as an office boy, trainee salesman, conductor on Leeds trams, and greenkeeper at a golf club. Dennis Gray's *in memoriam* piece in the *Alpine Journal* noted that when working on the trams,

> he was voted number one in a poll for courtesy and cheerfulness by the travelling public. By one of those coincidences which are the turning-point in any life, he started to run at the age of 24 when involved in a bet with his tram driver, a former athlete of note.

The long distance bug bit him, and gradually he built up his physique and stamina by rigorous training, becoming as dedicated as any marathon runner. In 1958 he competed in the Doncaster to Sheffield Marathon and suffered a stress fracture of the fibula. The race was for the Northern Counties title, and Beard was in the leading group for 15 miles. He began to fall off the pace, complaining of leg pain. At 18 miles he collapsed, and was driven to hospital where x-rays revealed he had been running for ages with a fractured fibula. To strengthen his legs he went on to the hills – to Snowdonia, and then Chamonix. Beardie (as he was known) was a member of Leeds City AC and the Rock and Ice Climbing Club, though he never wished to be, or was, an extreme rock climber. At Leeds he had the idea of building up a team of road runners for the many events then being added to the athletic calendar. Primarily, his life revolved around ensuring he had enough training time.

Beard worked at various times at Glenmore Lodge and Plas y Brenin national mountain centres, stoking the boilers, as general factotum, and as a temporary instructor. Without a teaching qualification he could not become a permanent instructor at the time. Gray also noted that he was

> dedicated, besides running, to helping backward or deprived youngsters: a genius with children, he had that same kind of essential simplicity which is usually only the child's.

He loved racing over the fells and brought the time for the Welsh Fourteen 3,000-foot peaks down to 5 hrs 13 mins in 1965. He also set many more long distance records, such as the Snowdon Horseshoe and the Cairngorm 4000s. He recorded a fourth place in the Three Peaks race in 1965. In 1967 he set a record for the Skye Cuillin Traverse of 4 hrs 9 mins. This ridge is possibly the finest mountain challenge in the British Isles, being a chain of peaks seven miles long, many of them over 3,000 feet, with a total of over 10,000 feet of ascent, and a couple of stiff climbs and one abseil involved. Some later commentators have suggested that Beard may have by-passed the Inaccessible Pinnacle, although that view has been challenged. The possibility certainly shouldn't be discounted. However, he was a good standard climber, having been tutored by Joe Brown and Don Whillans, amongst others. We do know he climbed the Basteir Tooth on his traverse, and he actually failed to meet up with his sole supporter.

Sadly he died in a motoring accident in 1969, aged just 38. At the time he was in training for an attempt on the world record for a 24-hour run, which was also intended to raise money for the Save the Children Fund. He was having a drink in the ODG when his lift arrived. On getting up to leave he left half a pint, which he was told was bad luck, but he didn't want to keep the driver waiting. In the last year he had run from Leeds to Downing Street in aid of the Save the Children Fund – well before the likes of Ian Botham and Eddie Izzard were doing this sort of thing. Being stupendously fit at this time he also ran from summit to summit, Ben Nevis, via Scafell, to Snowdon; and a roof of Wales traverse from north to south. He completed the John O'Groat's to Land's End (JOGLE) run in 18 days, bivouacking each night. In his excellent book *Rope Boy* Dennis Gray tells many stories of Beard's climbing and running exploits. One is of meeting him at Land's End at the end of his JOGLE. Gray comments:

> He was fresh, and could have run to America if the sea hadn't been in the way. As he came down the last half-mile his long arms and legs, on a disproportionately small body with its barrel chest, moving effortlessly in unison, and he was singing at the top of his voice, just with the joy of being fit and alive. Dave Gilmour, the driver who had accompanied him in an open jeep, looked in far worse fettle.

Beard was also planning to have a go at running the Pennine Way. He laughed at the carbo diet that was becoming popular at the time. His version was honey butties and mugs of tea half filled with sugar.

He was a significant enough person to have his obituary in *The Observer*. In it Chris Brasher had this to say about Eric Beard:

> He was the simplest, kindest, most unselfish man I have ever met; a hard man, yet hard only on himself; a man whose death diminishes everyone who knew him. He had little education, no formal qualifications whatsover, except for the greatest qualification of all – the ability to make people, especially children, happy when in his company.

After Beard's efforts others took up the challenge. In July 1965 Alan Heaton set off from the Old Dungeon Ghyll to try to raise the 24-hour total to 60 peaks. He had with him his brother Ken and the support of ten other pacers at various stages during the attempt. He achieved his 60 in 23 hrs 34 mins and claimed at the time that would be his last effort. However, five years later he agreed to pace Joss Naylor to a 62-peak attempt, by adding Fairfield and Great Rigg. However, conditions were poor and it was unsuccessful, but it does show the continued trend of record setters helping others to attack those records. A year later, in June 1971, Joss himself set out from Wasdale Head, just up from his own farm. Despite cloud, wind and rain, he came home in 23 hrs 37 mins with a new record of 61 peaks in the bag.

As well as extending the absolute peaks record there were attempts to lower the best time for the original Bob Graham Round (BGR) too. A month after Joss completed 61 peaks, in July 1971 Pete Walkington completed the 42-peak BGR circuit in a new fastest time of 20 hrs 43 mins. Earlier that year Fred Rogerson, who assisted in many attempts, proposed a club be formed for successful 'rounders'. The Bob Graham 24-Hour Club was formed to: specify and define the 42 summits; provide details; encourage and advise intending members; and record in detail all registered attempts. In an article in *The Observer* Chris Brasher called it

> the most exclusive club in the world because you cannot buy your way into it, you cannot join because something has happened to you; you can become a member only by accepting the challenge of those 42 peaks to be traversed inside 24 hours.

The details are all now recorded on a comprehensive website. The early dissemination of information in printed form acted as a massive impetus to

people attempting the BGR, as is shown by the numbers being successful in
the next few years:

1971	4
1972	2
1973	5
1974	13
1975	14
1976	13
1977	33

It should be noted also that in 1973 many more long fell races were appearing
in the calendar, mirroring the increase in the numbers of fell runners.

A new fastest BGR time was set in July 1973 when Bill Smith and Boyd
Millen came home in 20 hrs 38 mins, beating Walkington's time by five
minutes. Joss Naylor raised the record to 63 peaks (23 hrs 35 mins in 1972)
and then set an absolute peaks record of 72 in 1975 – 100 miles of mountain
travel and 37,000 feet of ascent, all within 24 hours. In August 1976 Billy
Bland shot round the standard BGR in a superb new fastest time of 18 hrs
50 mins, with Anthony and Dennis Bland also completing in just over 20
hrs. The next year Mike Nicholson reduced the fastest time to 17 hrs 45
mins, Alan Walker completed a completely solo (unsupported) round, and
Jean Dawes became the first female to join the BGR club, completing her
round in 23 hrs 27 mins. To top it all, Boyd Millen completed a double
BGR. A clockwise run in 21 hrs 30 mins was followed 30 mins later by an
anti-clockwise traverse in 30 hrs 30 mins[61]. One year later Anne-Marie
Grindley achieved a BGR time of 21 hrs 5 mins, and Helene Diamantides
brought it down to 19 hrs 10 mins in 1989. Then in 1991 Anne Stentiford
took the ladies BGR record to 18 hrs 49 mins, which at the time placed her
a magnificent eleventh fastest on the all-time list. That was just four weeks
after setting a new Paddy Buckley Round record of 19 hrs 19 mins, also
taking 49 minutes off the time Diamantides took for that round.

There is some classic reporting in *The Observer* in an article entitled 'On
the peaks of satisfaction' by Chris Brasher, describing Ken Ledward's
successful round in 1977, supported by Joss Naylor and in part by Brasher
himself on the Scafell leg.

So there I was last Sunday night, ensconced in a warm sleeping bag with an alarm set at 05.20, waiting for Ken Ledward, an unlikely applicant for this exclusive club. He is the very antithesis of the lean, lanky, strong-sinewed image of the great fell runner. Indeed, his legs are so short that they disappear in deep heather, and as he came down off Seat Sandal in the early morning light I thought he looked like Cleator Moor's third team hooker after a heavy Saturday night in the clubhouse.

Brasher then gets quite lyrical as he records their leaving of Dunmail Raise:

After a breakfast of bacon butties, hot sweet tea and some tinned pears which created an awful stink later, we were off up Steel Fell into the early morning sunlight. Now I knew why I had driven 250 miles through the night and slept under the stars. Here we are, three friends on the fells, the sun warming our backs as it burnt away the mist of the night, chattering about the distant views and the solitude, thinking of the tourists down in the valleys below sleepily stirring towards breakfast and we, up high, moving freely over the most beautiful land on earth.

Full details of the Bob Graham Round are available in the *42 Peaks* booklet and on the website. The following are just some of the amazing stats from this challenge:

Fastest time	Billy Bland	13 hrs 53 mins	1982
Fastest female	Nicky Spinks	18 hrs 12 mins	2012
Youngest person	Ben Squibb	23 hrs 51 mins	age 12 (1992)
Youngest female	Alison Wright	23 hrs 19 mins	age 19 (1985)

Nicky Spinks set the current ladies record on 28 July 2012, beating the 18 hrs 49 mins by Anne Stentiford from 1991. Spinks was on schedule for sub-18 hours at one point but the weather turned against her, meaning she lost a fair bit of time on the Wasdale-Honister leg. Her top-rope on Broad Stand had also been put in the wrong place, but she was brought up on it anyway. In her blog report[62] she concluded:

I was very pleased to have finished in style and to have broken the record. My only disappointment is being over 18 hours but in these conditions I couldn't expect more. It was a very hard day out in fantastic company.

Over time details of the distance covered have varied. The detail for the Round is normally stated as being: a 72-mile circuit, with 27,000 feet of ascent, over 42 of the highest peaks in the English Lake District within 24 hours. In *Long Days in Lakeland* Ronald Turnbull reckons that if:

measured with string or a little wheel it is 60-62 miles[63]. However, factors can be added 'for wiggles', or 'distance up the slope' or 'to make it more exciting'. The generally quoted figure for the Bob Graham is 72 miles. I've used the distance as measured, of 62 miles. The climb of 27,000ft is found by counting contour lines.

At the time of Bob Graham's original completion of the round the achievement was reported in some sources as being 140 miles and 30,000 feet.

The Bob Graham 24 Hour Club website[64] currently states:

The use of mapping software and GPS devices has led to a re-evaluation of the distance of the Round. Mapping software gives figures as low as 61-63 miles. GPS systems (which have been carried and operated throughout several successful attempts) give a figure of between 65-66 miles. The traditional ascent figure seems to be more accurate, though some calculations have produced a figure of 26,000 feet. The distance continues to stimulate debate depending on how it is measured, but a figure of something between 60 and 66 miles is more accurate than the traditional 72.

The report[65] of Billy Bland's 1982 sub-14 hour round has some interesting comments that sum up both the camaraderie involved, and also the phenomenal fitness that Bland had at the time. He was going so well that one of his pacers (Tony Cresswell) only just managed to get to the appointed place in time. When Cresswell met Bland at Ill Crags he was going brilliantly and he commented that Bland:

graciously declined my offers of tea, coffee, squash, milk, butties, cakes, having humped them all the way. I could have made a fortune flogging it on Scafell Pike.

Reaching Broad Stand, which Billy chose to scramble up with his brother Stuart and Jon Broxap, Cresswell noted it as:

> the riot it commonly is. Stuart was shoved up to pull up Billy then Jon who went on for the Scafell summit. I was last and nearly had me and Stuart down Mickledore Chimney! 'By lad, yer 'eavier than our Jon' he said.

They shot down ridiculously fast to Wasdale Head where:

> Billy only stopped a very short while, but I recall him with a butty and bottle of Mackeson as I stood croaking behind Joss's car. Only Joss continued with Billy on up Yewbarrow leaving me trying to flog those drinks and things to Joss's kids.

On Yewbarrow apparently Bland had a weak moment that was resolved by Joss applying a 'Naylor shake'. On the run-in from Newlands even freshish legs struggled to stay with Bland as he raced in to knock 3 hrs 51 mins off the record. It has been reported that Bland had apparently told his pacers that 16 hours was the target. However, he was even fitter than anyone suspected, as evidenced by his winning the long Ennerdale fell race the previous weekend, and then the Wasdale race a few weeks later, with a new record time. When I asked him, he informed me that he 'didn't actually put a predicted time on his BGR attempt, but just ran as fast as I could with the minimum of stops'.

What is not very well known is that Billy Bland decided to have another attempt, vowing that he would walk every step of the way, and not run – not even on the downhills. This he did in 1989, accompanied all the way by witnesses to verify the feat, and he walked round in an astonishing 20 hrs 48 mins, nearly missing his supporters at Wasdale. For this walk he was accompanied by 17-year-old Gavin Bland. Billy wore road shoes and got blistered feet. In the report in *42 Peaks* Billy Bland says:

> I started getting fed up as I couldn't get it over as fast as I wanted
> … after running fell races for 15 years with virtually no injuries,

two days after the walk I had a problem with my knee – torn ligaments, most likely caused by holding back downhill, which was the hardest part of the round.

The two Blands separated by ten minutes during the walk-in to Keswick (they went anti-clockwise), both getting under 21 hours without running a step.

The second fastest Round ever was set by Mark Hartell in July 1999, with 14 hrs 54 mins. On the Macclesfield Harriers website[66] he describes it thus:

> I set off with a schedule based around Billy's 1982 time of 13 hrs 53 although I don't think I really believed I could better this. So it proved, I was on my schedule up to Dunmail but lost a little time over the Langdales and more on the Wasdale to Honister section. Final time was 14 hrs 54 mins which is 2 minutes inside the 2nd fastest time (as was) set by Stuart Bland – 14 hrs 56 mins. Anyone interested can have minutes of fun looking at the attachment which shows my splits compared to those of Billy and Stuart. [See website] One nice thing about the day which saw perfect weather and excellent support from a cast of many (15-20) was that both Billy and Gavin Bland turned out to see me suffer.

The web link shows full splits for Mark, Billy and Stuart's efforts. Comparing Mark to Billy shows that Mark wasn't on schedule early on at all. On all the standard sections Mark was slower, with differences of nine minutes to Threlkeld, three minutes to Dunmail (where Stuart was actually the fastest), 20 minutes to Wasdale, 18 minutes to Honister, and 12 minutes to the Moot Hall. An even more interesting comparison can be made from Mark to Stuart, where the end result was a two minutes faster round by Mark. Mark was five minutes up on Stuart by Threlkeld, but this was reversed when he lost seven minutes to Dunmail (overall two minutes down). To Wasdale, Mark lost another minute, and to Honister another three minutes. However, Mark regained eight minutes from Honister to the finish, five of them in the long run in from Robinson, thus in fact only getting back ahead in that last stretch.

The other interesting comparison is in their acknowledged rest times at the various support places. Mark shows zero minutes at Threlkeld, then three minutes at Dunmail, zero at Wasdale, zero at Honiston – so three minutes in total. Billy's record shows respectively three mins each at Thelkeld and Dunmail, two at Wasdale, and a massive 13 minutes at Honister. He explained this to me as having been necessitated by his 'having run out of gas on Grey Knotts'. Acknowledging that there could be differences in the ways the timings were recorded on the attempts, this does seem a remarkably different approach by these two athletes. Incidentally, Stuart's rests were respectively two, two, ten and three minutes. For anyone thinking of a super-fast round, this data provides a fantastic starting point for considering the planning of their pace.

Billy Bland's 13 hrs 54 mins had been preceded by a 18 hrs 50 mins round by him in 1976. Stuart Bland's 14 hrs 56 mins (noted above as second fastest before Hartell took two minutes off it) was Stuart's first round. Coming as it did in the August of the summer that Billy did his record, and using many of the same pacers, it has not really had the credit it deserves, as a mighty impressive achievement. On his round Stuart was reluctant to eat, and faded coming off Scafell. Tony Cresswell's report in *Fellrunner* takes up the story:

> Part way down Stuart lay down and Billy saw his chance to try the 'Naylor shake' – a delightful little remedy performed by the said bod on Billy when he wavered on Yewbarrow [on his record round]. It was as much as I could do to obey instructions, but with Billy holding his arms and me his legs we picked him up and shook the living daylights out of him. Gripping a Mars bar between his teeth for anaesthetic poor Stu was shaken like a rag doll between two guard dogs. It worked though; his eyes were all over his head but on we all trouped to Wasdale!

In correspondence recently Tony Cresswell recalled the occasion and commented 'It was sickening, it really was. Every joint, muscle and sinew in his wretched body cracked and tweaked and I nearly passed out, never mind Stuart'. Having lost a bit of time Stuart and Billy set off up Yewbarrow, meeting Joss on the way. Stuart picked up the pace and came into Keswick just under the 15 hours.

Finally, the 24-Hour Lakes Peaks record was raised in 1988 by Mark McDermott from 72 to 76. McDermott reckoned that his planned schedule, which several people had already failed at, was the equivalent of a BGR in 17 hours. Since his BGR had taken him 18.5 hours he got down to serious training, and further planning. Helped by pacers such as Colin Valentine, Dave Hall, Mark Rigby and John Blair-Fish, he arrived back at his Braithwaite start point in 23 hrs 26 mins, to a hot bath and a champagne breakfast.

Then in 1997 Mark Hartell raised the total to 77 peaks in 23 hrs 47 mins, again starting and finishing in Braithwaite. Mark Hartell did not show early promise as an athlete. His early interest was gardening rather than sport, and he even smoked for several years. He progressed from climbing, through orienteering to fell running. He found he had an ability to compete well at endurance events and a passion for long days in the hills. Then the records came for him, with the second fastest standard round following shortly after the maximum peaks record. For the women, the 24-Hour Peaks Record was set by Nicky Spinks, with 64 peaks in 23 hrs 15 mins in 2011.

On another level, there had been a moment of comedy in 1976 when Dave Meek claimed to have scaled 81 peaks within 24 hours. Joss Naylor said he frankly disbelieved this, as he didn't think Meek could have done it off the training he was known to be doing. Meek responded in the press[67] by saying

> It appears to me that Joss thinks I did the same thing that he did, but that is not so. I altered the route and made it more compact and easier. I agree I don't think I could have done the route he did.

The Bob Graham Club 'rules' state that for any new 24-hour record you must traverse all the peaks conquered by the previous record holder and finish in a faster time or add more summits. The implication is that Meek added several easier (and lower?) peaks, and even possibly missed out some of the major ones in his effort. Being something of a maverick he concluded that it was against his principles to have all these rules and he was just going to go out when he felt like it and do what he fancied. This didn't stop him from making a public 'record' claim, mind you.

Some people like to extend the challenge by doing the Bob Graham Round in winter conditions. What constitutes 'winter' is open to debate[68]. The official Bob Graham 24 Hour Club website states:

The Club perceives that there are two distinct types of winter Bob Graham Round which are:

> the 'Mid-winter' round which, taking its inspiration from the earliest attempts on a winter round by Pete Simpson and Martin Stone in the early 1980s, is attempted at any time from the weekend before the shortest day through to the first period of decent weather after the shortest day but to be completed no later than 10 January; and

> the 'Winter' round, which is a round not falling within the definition set out above, attempted during the period starting on 1 December and finishing on 1 March.

Even this distinction is artificial, because conditions on the shortest day could be quite benign, whilst full winter conditions could well be experienced at any time before or after within the wider definition of 'winter'. Ultimately, though, if records are to be kept, someone has to set parameters to keep them by. The Club is persuaded by the view of the early winter pioneers that the challenge represented by maximum hours of darkness puts the 'Mid-winter' round into a category of its own.

Is that clear then? The website then proceeds to list the records. Pete Simpson did a round of 26 hrs 22 mins, with Martin Stone supporting most of the way before having to drop out back in 1979. Selwyn Wright did a solo mid-winter round in 1985 in 27 hrs 38 mins (which he wryly noted was about ten minutes short of double Billy Bland's record), despite Joss Naylor suggesting at the Bob Graham Club Dinner that he was ill-advised to do it.

The first 'mid-winter' 24-hour round recorded was by John Brockbank and Selwyn Wright in December 1986, taking 23 hrs 6 mins. That time was eventually beaten by Scott Umpleby and Brian Meakin, with 22 hrs 48 mins in 1999. The first 'mid-winter' ladies round was Nicky Lavery with 22 hrs 45 mins in 2000, which is technically the fastest mid-winter of all.

The first 'winter' sub-24 round was by Martin Scrowson and Barry Laycock, with their 22 hrs 8 mins in 1989. The first ladies 'winter' round was a supported one by Alison Crabb in November 1993, with a time of 23 hrs 51 mins. Scrowson and Laycock's time was beaten by Jim Mann in February 2011 with his 20 hrs 39 mins. Mann tells of the setting up of his round in a report on Durham Fell Runners website[69]:

> after an uncompleted attempt on the 18th of December last year I was ever more mindful of how quickly those Lakeland fells can turn nasty! With this in mind I had decided to wait till December 2011 for a further attempt where I would be fitter and more experienced but the BG has a strange way of eating away at you, teasing you when it has beaten you. I hadn't seriously considered another attempt until I had the good fortune of supporting Ian Taylor on his successful attempt on the 22nd of Jan. Conditions were near perfect, crisp cold but very runnable – I was extremely jealous and decided that I would go again as soon as I got a break in the weather. It finally looked like that break had come at the end of February BUT it was right on the deadline and I had a race on the Sunday before! I checked the rules over a winter round and asked for clarification and sure enough I had to be finished before the end of the 1st of March. Now just to get a crew and choose a time. I started pulling a crew together on Sunday morning (Sunday 27th February, about 36 hours before I set off!). It's a big ask ... 'hey do you fancy running with me up lots of big hills tomorrow in the cold?' and of course people were working etc. It was clear pacers would be very thin on the ground but I managed to get three nutters to join me on the fells.

This paucity of pacers meant that Mann had to do the Dodds and Helvellyn leg solo, where he was not overly confident of his navigation. Mann discussed Broad Stand with his pacer on the way round and he reports:

> Joe's a good climber and wanted to go up Broad Stand (not a chance! I have been up it but only in summer and on the end of a rope!) I wanted to go West Wall traverse so as not to lose the height but the rake was full of snow and after Bowfell we thought this might be tricky so went Foxes – what a big height loss that is!

Mann made good speed and duly set the fastest time for a winter round, by some margin. His cautious approach to Broad Stand is further justified by the experience of Simon Waller on his winter Bob Graham Round. In a piece in Peter Hooper's book *Best of the Fells* he writes:

> I was beginning to feel apprehensive about Broad Stand; I am not a climber and my fears were not helped by seeing the body of a walker at the bottom just as we arrived. I completed the climb with the aid of a rope. The walker had slipped coming down and we could hear the helicopter evacuating what was unfortunately a fatality.

In private correspondence with me, Jim Mann suggested that

> a round is only accepted by the BG club if it is witnessed on every peak or if the athlete is already a member of the club – so you must be accompanied for the entire round first time round in effect.

The Guidance Notes for the Bob Graham Club (which apply to both summer and winter rounds) state only that 'the contender **must** be accompanied at all times by at least one witness. During darkness it is advisable to have two or more for safety.' Either way, such 'rules' produce anomolies. Martin Stone's solo and unsupported 23 hrs 41 mins round in 1987 is accepted and listed, whereas Steve Ashworth's 18 hrs 45 mins round in January 2012[70], and his 21 hrs 4 mins in February 2012[71] are not. Ashworth's 18 hrs 45 mins is listed on the records website with the comment: 'The fastest time to date. Mostly solo on the fells so not ratified.' On 1 December 2013 Jim Mann set a new winter round record time of 18 hrs 18 mins.

Bob Graham's grave is in Stonethwaite, in Borrowdale. He is commemorated by the efforts of all these athletes who have followed him, but also by a small memorial cairn near Ashness Bridge, a traditional stone-built bridge on the single-track road from the Borrowdale road (B5289) to Watendlath, in the central Lakes. The cairn has an inlaid tablet, which is inscribed with the message:

In memory of Robert Graham 1889 – 1966 of Keswick who on the 13 -14 June 1932 traversed 42 Lakeland Peaks within 24 hours, a record which stood for 28 years.

It was placed there in 1982, 50 years after the original round, and is in what may seem a somewhat incongruous location, explained by it being on a piece of land formerly owned by Bob Graham.

A large number of other Lakeland challenges have been devised by different individuals, but none seem to have the same resonance as the BGR. One such is the Lake District 3000s, which is a 45-mile route taking in the four highest peaks in the Lakes: Skiddaw, Helvellyn and the Scafells, starting and finishing at the Moot Hall in Keswick. It was first completed in a competitive way in a Ramblers Association event in 1965. Predominantly a walkers event, there were 83 entrants, only half of whom finished. The fastest time was set then by Stan Bradshaw, with 11 hrs 11 secs. Subsequently Joss Naylor completed it in eight and a half hours, and then Billy Bland managed 7 hrs 35 mins in the event in 1979.

There are many other fell challenges around the United Kingdom, and the next chapter details some of these.

A *conversation with:* Jim Mann, Durham Fell Runners

It is the day before Easter and Jim Mann has agreed to an interview, before travelling to the Lakes for some more fell training time in preparation for the Calderdale Way. We are in the Moonlight Café in Cockfosters, North London, where you cannot believe the amount of noise a group of older people are making (are they ALL deaf?). My digital recorder faithfully records the interview, so all is well in the end. Jim cycles off back home to pack and to plot his next assault on the ultra fell records, having just lost his record time for a winter Bob Graham Round. I return home to the transcription task, with a better understanding of the mind and training of a top ultra fell runner.

'I don't think anyone has broken down fell running into a science yet, not properly.'

I had met Jim once before as he has trained with my athletic club intermittently. I first asked about his introduction to fell running, which he reckons he just 'fell' into. *'I used to run when I was at school, used to run cross country. I hated track athletics with a passion, to the extent of being caught on one occasion having used a sick note to get out of athletics and being caught coming back from a seven-mile training run. I used to enjoy cross country and was looking for a race one Easter and someone said go and do Pendle Fell Race. I would have been 14 or 15, so my mum took me over, as I lived in Burnley at the time. I turned up and there was an 18 years age limit, so I did the standard thing I did at the time at road races and lied about my age.'*

Jim did the race and has always wanted to run on the fells since. Literally, it was that one moment. Furthermore, he has never considered himself a runner since, always a fell runner. *'I did some of the shorter races as a teenager. I remember doing Tebay, Clougha Pike, which I won. I used to cycle and then eventually run out to Clougha Pike.'* At 17 and 18 he didn't think anything of doing a 20-mile training run, sometimes twice a weekend. *'Jogging out there, work over the fells, where I wanted to be, and then jog back. I did loads of races in the Trough of Bowland area.'*

We then discussed what happened since school, and what has brought Jim to where he is now. *'I had 15 years when I didn't run. I stopped running when I left school. I went to uni and discovered beer and girls, and drifted away, but didn't lose the desire.'* He also had a brief spell about five years ago when he trained a bit, and started properly two years ago. The catalyst was that he always wanted to do it, and he got some time again. Business commitments were sorted and allowed time for it. *'I went to Durham University, but actually joined Durham Fell Runners later because I am normally based in the North East. They are a friendly bunch of guys.'*

He gets some good coaching there, in a way that allows him to fit it around his life. They go out every Thursday throughout winter and train off-road with head-torches. *'In the winter when I was up in the north-east I was training for the winter Bob Graham Round. I didn't train in daylight for nearly six months, because I work seven days a week generally. Once you get used to the moors at night it is great place to be.'*

Mentioning issues that were faced by the likes of Gavin Bland, who worked on the fells as a shepherd, we discussed types of training. *"Some of your base fitness comes from being just out on the fells. I raced last Saturday and went straight from a 25-mile race to the Lakes to support a Bob Graham Round. I did a night leg on the Wasdale to Honister leg – all the big ones, slow but a lot of climbing. All very slow, time on your feet, time when you are tired."*

Jim reckoned that if Gavin Bland was on the hills all day – even if not running he was climbing hills day in and day out – the strength that gives you is phenomenal. Jim's training has changed since coming down to London. *'I have got a lot quicker. The guys I train with are always watching their times, want to know what minutes/mile they are doing, and are always pushing the pace because they are on the roads.'*

He has started doing weights three times a week to make sure he keeps up the strength. Last year he couldn't keep pace with the fastest guys, not on the flat. He'd pull them back on the hills and on the downhills, but on the flat they were away from him. He thinks that runners like Billy Bland had their best performances generally on the longer stuff. *'To a degree you can get away with the longer stuff. If you want to get quicker you need to work on getting quicker. It depends on where your strengths are. For me, I can run for ever but I am not quick. I don't need to work that hard necessarily on stamina, but I do need to work on the speed.'*

Jim has a race plan that involves racing short distance events, treating them as a high intensity session. *'This season I am concentrating purely on the off-road ultras. I will also do the longer Lakes races. I did Ennerdale a couple of years ago, and have done Wasdale the last two years, and got lost both years.'*

One day he would like to do the Lakeland Classics Challenge. *'Right now I am focused on the ultras, as I think if I get those right I'll be able to move back on to the fells with more strength. With the Lakeland Classics you have got to be on the fells every couple of days, you really have to be. The conditioning you get from the climbing, from the big hills and the time you need to spend working on the big hills, and knowing the routes is vital. Route finding needs to be second nature, you need to not have to think about it.'*

When he started he was inspired by Mark Croasdale who was at Lancaster and Morecambe. He won the British Championship around then. He was also a winter Olympics cross country skier, and used to train on his road skis for conditioning. *'The Three Peaks was the race that cursed Mark, but he got there in the end. I have never done the Three Peaks mind. I always felt it was a bit dull. I don't think it is great race, which for someone doing the ultras rather than classics is a bit of a contradiction. A lot of it is on tracks and trails and I really like free route choice. I like the Lakes ones where it is point to point and you can find your own best route.'*

Jim likes to find time to reconnoitre routes, as that can be fun as well. When he started again he was very much mid-pack, but started to work his way through. *'It is only two years so I have accelerated quite quickly, so I don't know half the guys, which is a bit bizarre.'* He certainly knows his endurance stuff, mind. *'I am impressed by Billy Bland's Bob Graham time which is amazing, and Mark Hartell's 24 hour-Lakes peaks record, something I'd love to have a go at. Mark was a very good ultra runner, and also did the second fastest standard Bob Graham Round. For the 24 hour he trained hard, got to know the fells and was very specific in his aims. It was a huge achievement, which no-one has got near.'*

We talked further about the Bob Graham Round, and Jim's winter round efforts. I suggested the record breakers for winter rounds tend not to be your 'standard' fell runners. *'Yes, some are orienteers crossed with fell runners, Steve Birkinshaw for instance. They have similar attributes, because they are very strong at running on all terrain, and often hilly and tough terrain. Mountain marathons now are dominated by orienteers, and for good reason. They are super fit, they are fast athletes, and to switch up distance is no problem.'* Jim did admit that navigation is his problem really, and has done some events like the Mountain Trial to sharpen up his navigation.

I asked him what he thinks with regard to Billy and Gavin Bland's training compared to current athletes. *'What I have heard about Billy Bland was that he had a love of the fells and was always up there, and that he got his fitness through what we would consider as over-training.'* Having said that, Jim is a big believer in heavy base mileage. He was up to 125 miles a week before Christmas because he was trying to come back quickly from an injury and to get fit for a winter Bob Graham. *'If you are trying to do the really long stuff I think you need the base mileage. I thought Billy did more mileage than you are saying. I don't think what he was doing was scientific, but then I don't think anyone has broken down fell running into a science yet, not properly. So, what I have been trying to do is adapt some of the road training schedules, breaking them down into what they are aiming to do, then try and build them into something that works for the fells.'*

That is where the weights come in, which are free weights as they work your core strength, which he thinks is absolutely crucial. *'If you do a long race your whole body suffers. I think that with Joss Naylor it was fell running that helped him deal with things like his back problems, with its emphasis on core strength. Guys that come from the roads to do the BGR, they come unstuck. Training like 13 flights of steps, ten times, is just not going to do it. You suffer most on the descents and your legs will go if you have not done the sustained descents, the big hills, you are not going to make it.'*

Jim had a few interesting thoughts about crossing sports, like Rob Jebb and the Brownlees are doing. *'I don't think it is particularly crossing sports with those guys. When you look at cyclo-cross the muscle sets you are using are the same. I cross train on a bike, as I can do that as base mileage without impact, but using the same muscle sets. When you look at triathletes they do running for speed, cycling for strength and swimming for core strength. You often see triathletes high up in ultra events. They do the mileage in training, they know they can sustain it, they are good on the eating, good on drinking and can transfer to ultras quite easily. Cross training is useful for fells but you don't particularly want to build quad strength from cycle training. Relatively, road runners use the same muscles to do the same thing and everything is out of balance.'*

He observed that fell guys rarely get serious injuries compared to road guys. When you look at the terrain they run over, everything builds up to make you stronger. Fell injuries can be more severe of course. Jim pointed out, for example, that Ron Hill did a lot of running on fells even from a young age, and this may be one reason why he didn't get injured. *'Ron Hill also did a lot of reps on grass, and much in bare feet to build up his muscles. I also did a lot of that to deal with shin splints.'*

With Jim having been to university, and with me having a mild fascination with lab testing as a base line for your training, I was interested to find that Jim had never been tested for VO2 max – or any of the other tests. *'It is not that important, because you are not working the VO2 max. It is the efficiency, the body degrading and the psychology that count. On the shorter fell races I accept it may be important. They are lung busters, and muscle busters. You need recovery to turn at the top to start sprinting again, because you have just gone as fast as you can up a steep slope. I used to do some of those type races when younger. I used to train for those. I would cycle three miles flat out in the highest gear on level ground till my legs were on fire, then get off and run a mile fast. First time you do it you can't even stand up, your legs are all over the place. It was a good way of simulating lactic build-up and trying to run with it, and clear it out. A couple of times a week I would do that.'* Now Stu Ferguson at Durham Fell Runners advises him a bit on the coaching side. Ferguson has written extensively about off-road running.

When asked about his greatest achievement, and future ambitions, Jim reckoned that he had just started really. *'I am 35 so may only have a few years to get to my best. I want my "winter" BG record back, definitely going for that, no two ways about it. I want to get a "mid-winter" BG in – tried that twice but not got round, in some horrific conditions but still terrific experience. My 20 hrs 39 mins time went this winter. It was a solo effort by the guy too. It may not count if the person had not done a BGR before, because you have got to have done one before you can self-authenticate.'*

On his winter round he did one leg solo – the Dodds and Helvellyn. He goes out on the fells solo all the time so has no real problems with it. *'I hate the cornicing and it scares me a bit. On the Dodds I could see the track and it was OK. Scafell was covered with snow which made it difficult, ankle-breaking conditions. We decided not to do Broad Stand, even though I was with a climber as pacer. We thought of Lord's Rake but didn't have crampons. We went down to Foxes Tarn and back up. All the way I was taking sensible safe routes.'*

He had sort of done a summer round, but had been tagged on to someone else. They didn't make it, he did. This was in late September, so it wasn't really summer, and less than a year since he started training. Then a December winter failure and then back in February, after a good experience supporting someone else. *'Everything was wrong for it, but I just wanted to do it. I did a shortish fell race 36 hours before starting the round, so no tapering, but I was in the right mindset, which is so vitally important.'*

Jim explained the real differences between summer and winter Bob Graham Rounds. *'Winter is so different. Firstly the darkness is psychologically really tough when you go into the second period of it. If you get a clear night the navigation isn't too bad, but it is going to be bitterly cold even if it is still. It is never still on those hills. Icy cold blasts coming across the fells are so debilitating, it just sucks the energy out of you. It is amazing how much harm it does, how much extra energy you are using, and the way you feel. The dark and the cold are the two things, even if you have perfect underfoot conditions it is so much harder than a summer round, especially psychologically. The pace you have to go for a summer round is really slow.*

As long as you keep going you will get there. That is not trivialising it, because it is difficult to do and you have got to be fit to do it.'

So, to get round in winter is a whole different game. He says that when you see darkness again after just eight hours of daylight that is hard to take. You are going to be doing some difficult bits in darkness. *'On my first winter attempt I came off Blencathra via Sharp Edge, in completely the wrong direction, in a blizzard, and had to go back up again. You have footwear issues. Crampons, micro spikes, which ones are actually viable? You need a nice break in the weather, and be in condition and ready to go. You get a load of supporters for your own efforts from pacing others. But, I do think the fastest time is doable though.'*[72]

CHAPTER 16

Some other fell challenges

Long distance running is particularly good training in perseverance
Chairman Mao

There have also been similar fell challenges to the Bob Graham Round established in other parts of the UK. The following are short histories of some of the most significant and well-established ones, in order of their inauguration.

The Welsh 3000s is a route of 26 miles from the top of Snowdon to Foel Fras, including some 13,000ft of ascent and 14 summits (15 if Carnedd Uchaf is counted). The challenge is to complete the route within 24 hours. It is uncertain who first completed the route, but it was probably one of the early Victorian mountaineers who were all prodigious walkers. The earliest known traverse of all 15 peaks dates back to 1919 when Eustace Thomas led a Rucksack Club group over the route. During the thirties, traverse times began to come down, with W. Stallybrass walking from Snowdon to Foel Fras in 13 hrs 20 mins. Showell Styles, the noted author, achieved a time of 12 hrs 44 mins and Frank Shuttleworth managed 10 hrs 29 mins. The existence and precision of these times suggests that these were not casual outings but record-breaking attempts.

In spring 1938 Thomas Firbank (who farmed on the slopes of the Glyders) along with his companions, including his then wife Esme, completed the route in 8 hrs 25 mins. It is worth remembering that there were far fewer clear footpaths at that time, adding to the navigational difficulties that the persistent fog caused. A fascinating account of this record is given in Firbank's book *I Bought a Mountain*. Firbank's attempt was frowned upon by the establishment and resulted in an apology by Firbank's companions being published in The Climbers' Club *Journal* for 1939. It was not the done thing for members of the club to take part in escapades such as this, as that produced some rather unwelcome publicity in the press.

After the Second World War the Welch Fusiliers, clad in full battle dress, used the Welsh 3000s as a training exercise. As numbers grew they were accused of contributing to the severe erosion on the mountainside and pressure was put on them to find an alternative. They chose the 'One Thousands', a route which visits the four peaks in Snowdonia that top 1,000m in elevation – Yr Wyddfa and Carnedd Ugain from the Snowdonia Group and Carnedds Llewelyn and Dafydd from the Carneddau. Shorter than the Welsh 3000s, this route begins on the seashore at Aber and finishes on the summit of Snowdon, being 19 miles with 8,900 feet of ascent. It later became established as a fell race.

The 1950s seemed to bring athletes to the hills. John Disley set a Welsh 3000s time of 7 hrs 24 mins and Chris Brasher's group reduced it further to 6 hrs. In 1965 Eric Beard traversed the route in the exceptional time of 5 hrs 13 mins. Just before his untimely death in a car crash in 1969 Beard was out on a training run with his friend Joss Naylor, whom he predicted would take his record. On a damp, misty June morning in 1973 Naylor had a crack and set off from the summit of Snowdon. It was only the fourth time he had been to Wales, and he became cragfast on the damp rocks of Crib Goch. 'Thirty-five minutes to the road,' he noted with a hint of dissatisfaction. Unfamiliarity led him to a poor route choice going up Glyder Fach's boulder strewn shoulder. On Carnedd Llewelyn he lost more time and only finding three locals coming out of the mist saved him from going seriously astray. Some 4 hrs 46 mins later, still in mist, he touched the summit of Foel Fras. Naylor's verdict was that there was about ten minutes to come off that time.

The record stood until 1988 when Colin Donnelly, who lived nearby and was a member of the Eyri Harriers, took on the challenge. He recorded a mightily impressive 4 hrs 19 mins, including Carnedd Uchaf, a new summit added to the earlier list of 14 by the latest Ordnance Survey maps. Colin was accompanied and paced by his team-mates from Eyri Harriers. Donnelly, like Naylor, wasn't entirely happy with his run. In Clayton and Turnbull's book *The Welsh Three*

Thousand Foot Challenges Donnelly comments that he 'shouldn't have been so tired on the Carneddau, really should have knocked a further ten minutes off.' He put it down to not eating enough earlier on, when he hadn't really felt like it. We've all been there. The record still stands though. His then wife Angela Carson has set the women's best time of 5 hrs 28 mins.

The Bob Baxter Round was first mooted in 1977. It was established by Baxter, and is a 52-mile challenge, which involves 11,000 feet of ascent, and climbs all 37 of the Isle of Man's peaks over 1,000 feet high. It starts from Laxey promenade and zig-zags to successive hills, which are not neatly arranged like some other rounds. Baxter's original round was more of a reconnaissance, taking nearly 15 hours. He repeated it in 1978 in 12 hrs 58 mins. In 1982 Colin Donnelly was over to do the Manx Mountain Marathon and four days beforehand recorded a new best time of 11 hrs 34 mins.

The Ramsay Round is considered to be the Scottish equivalent of the Bob Graham Round, taking in 24 Munros (mountains over 3,000 feet) on the ridges of The Grey Corries and the Mamores. The round is essentially an extension of Tranter's Round, which was a trip of 36 miles with 20,600 feet of ascent, which was completed by Philip Tranter in June 1964. Charlie Ramsay decided to make it more of a challenge and added 15 more Munros to make it 24 Munros to complete inside 24 hours. This version was established in 1978 by Ramsay, a member of Lochaber Athletic Club in Fort William. The route is 56 miles and has 28,500 feet of climbing, which he completed in 23 hrs and 58 mins. The next four rounds set successively faster times. They were:

June 1987	Martin Stone	23 hrs 24 mins (solo)
July 1987	Jon Broxap	21 hrs 24 mins
July 1989	Helene Diamantides	20 hrs 24 mins
	Mark Rigby	20 hrs 24 mins
August 1989	Adrian Belton	18 hrs 23 mins

Since then many people have successfully completed the round, but no one has got near Belton's time. In fact Helene and Mark's time has not been beaten either, according to the website[73], and there were no completions in 2012, and just 5 in 2013. On 31 May 2014 Nicky Spinks set a sparkling new record time of 19 hrs 19 mins. She now holds the ladies record for all the 'Big Three' rounds, and is the only person to have done all three rounds under 20 hours.

The Paddy Buckley Round is a circuit of just over 61 miles with 28,000 feet of ascent, taking in 47 summits in North Wales. Paddy Buckley devised the round with the help of Chris Brasher. Wendy Dodds was the first to complete it in 1982 in a time of 25 hrs 38 mins. Dodds had set out with Bob Roberts and Paddy Buckley himself. However, Roberts had to retire with stomach trouble and Buckley with cramp. The first sub-24 hour round was on 30 July 1985 by Martin Stone in 23 hrs 26 mins. Pete Simpson recorded 22 hrs 51 mins in 1988, and this was reduced later that year to 22 hrs 2 mins by Adrian Belton. Helene Diamantides beat that with 20 hrs 8 mins in 1989, as part of a triple she did that year along with a Bob Graham Round (19 hrs 11 mins for a new women's record) and a Ramsay Round (20 hrs 24 mins).

Helene Diamantides/Whitaker claims that doing the big Three Rounds[74] in a year came about by accident. She wanted to have a go at the Charlie Ramsey Round as she was living in Scotland.

> I didn't know Mark Rigby at the time, but Martin Stone said this chap is prepared to pace you on the understanding that if he can keep up he will keep going. I said that is fine, and if necessary I will sort myself out. We set off up Ben Nevis and along the ridges, and took turns to carry one rucksack between us. We had one person doing road support for us. Martin Stone joined us for the last leg, so two of us got round and we had two supporters. In the car going back I thought I hadn't done the Welsh Round. It wasn't deliberate to be in the next month or so. I thought it would be nice to use the fitness and do that. By the time I had done the Welsh Round I thought it really would be nice to finish it off and do the three, so finished it with Adrian Belton on the BGR. I think he had set off to do the three from the start. Mostly what I did every weekend was to go for 12 hours plus Munro-bagging running sessions. That was normal background for ages. So when training for something specific I would do four days of that in a row.

In 1992 Mark Hartell recorded 18 hrs 10 mins for the Paddy Buckley Round, and this time was matched by Chris Near of Eryri Harriers in 2008. The current records are Tim Higginbottom 17 hrs 42 mins (set in 2009) and Anne Stentiford 19 hrs 19 mins (1991). On 19 May 2013 Nicky Spinks brought the record time down to 19 hrs 2 mins.

The seeds for the round were sown in 1977, when Chris Brasher and Paddy Buckley tried and failed on the Bob Graham Round. Buckley had the idea of using a similar round in Snowdonia, which was an area he knew very well, as training for the Bob Graham. In an article in *Compass Sport* in 1983, Paddy Buckley described the gestation of the route in Chris Brasher's cottage above Llyn Gwynant:

> Chris, mellowed by drams of Glenmorangie, examined my round on paper. 'Can't have Crib Goch,' he decreed, 'too dangerous for fell runners; might get cramp.' 'This,' said he, stabbing his pipe at Moel Cynghorion, '– this is the fell runners' ridge, – a classic, – absolutely essential. We could then drop down to Llanberis Youth Hostel and get Joan and Denis (Glass) to provide some tea. Then straight up through the Quarry to Elidir.' I pointed out that the CEGB had closed all rights of way in the Quarry, including the route from Deiniolen to the church at Nant Peris, which had been used for generations by coffin bearers, and that furthermore the quarry was patrolled. 'Go through it at night,' he said, easily dismissing the vast powers assembled against us.

As the idea developed Buckley envisaged being on Snowdon at sunset and Tryfan at dawn.

In 1980, having reconnoitred it all, an attempt was scheduled by Buckley and Ken Turner, a month after they had done the BGR. They didn't even start due to the weather. They tried again, this time adding Wendy Dodds, ran into problems and abandoned at halfway. Buckley, with Bob Roberts and Wendy Dodds, tried again in 1982. Wendy Dodds eventually made it to complete the first round, after one postponement due to terrible weather – which was so bad that two young Scouts camping on Snowdon died of exposure.

Chris Brasher's name has cropped up several times already in this story (first mentioned in the introduction). To many he was a heroic figure – a record-breaker, charity worker, a pioneer of fell-running and orienteering. He was also the inventor of the Brasher Boot, President of the Sports Journalists' Association for a spell before his death in 2003 and, above all, the founding-father of the London Marathon. He did have his wild side, and is proof (if needed) that top sportsmen misbehaving is nothing new. In

1956, after winning his gold medal at the Olympics he went for a liquid lunch with the media and according to *The Complete Book of the Summer Olympics* he arrived, in his own words

> blind drunk, totally blotto, on the Olympic podium. I had an asinine grin on my face and nearly fell flat on my face as I leant forward, breathing gin fumes all over an IOC Frenchman as he attempted to hang a medal around my neck.

Brasher was an advocate of, and participant in, both the sports of fell running and orienteering. He was also a very eloquent journalist, and wrote in his column in *The Independent* newspaper:

> The best fell-runners are athletes of real world class – if their sport lent itself to being held in a stadium surrounded by television cameras then they would be known the world over.

It isn't, and they aren't. Even for the hardy people who turn out at fell races to spectate the sport is really inconvenient to watch. Most of the action takes place out of sight, high on the fells. There have been attempts to film races, but none of them has really succeeded in capturing the scale of the locations, the difficulty of the terrain and the beauty of the runners' progress on film. Really, the only way to appreciate it is to do it.

Chris Brasher was also instrumental in the creation of the short course at the Lake District Mountain Trial – and ran it for several years. He tried the Bob Graham Round a couple of times, but without success. In his regular column in *The Observer* in 1997 Brasher described his first attempt, at the age of 49. He set off from Keswick with Paddy Buckley and George Rhodes. He started at night, being paced by Joss Naylor, and was mysteriously joined by a 'Charlie', who was holidaying in the Lakes with his family at the time. At Dunmail Raise Paddy Buckley retired, and Joss had to leave to catch a train to London as he was having lunch with Muhammad Ali. Ken Ledward, Frank Milner and Boyd Millen took over as pacers, all being BGR completers. Charlie was still there too. The BGR spirit is shown when it came to climbing Broad Stand:

> Terry Thorpe and his wife, who gave up city life to manage the campsite in Wasdale, had climbed 3,000 feet in the dawn to fix us a rope – a long hard trudge to give us a few seconds of safety.

After a break for a massage at Wasdale, Brasher continued up Yewbarrow, but was so ill when he met Stan Bradshaw at the summit he abandoned his attempt and dropped down to Joss's farm. George Rhodes carried on, paced by Bradshaw and Millen to finish in 23 hrs 9 mins. The story concludes:

> And Charlie? He gave up pacing at Wasdale and became a contender, taking off at great speed with our fittest pacer, Chris Brad … finishing strongly through the lanes to Keswick. 'Just an hour's jog up Skiddaw,' he had said to his wife and now he was back in Keswick 21 hours 57 minutes later … Charlie Ramsay is his name and he works at the Commonwealth Pool in Edinburgh and in his lunch hour he sometimes runs up Arthur's Seat.[75]

The South Wales Traverse is sometimes considered the South Wales equivalent of the Bob Graham Round. This 24-hour challenge involves 72 miles and some 17,000 feet of ascent. It is not a round but a linear traverse. It takes in 31 summits in the Carmarthen Fan, Fforest Fawr, Brecon Beacons and Black Mountains areas and may be completed in either direction.

It was launched in 1984, having been completed by Derek Fisher and Andy Lewsley the year before in 21 hrs 24 mins. Phil Dixon went round in 18 hrs 10 mins in 1986, and then Adrian Belton, Mark McDermott and Andrew Addis managed 17 hrs 15 mins in 1988. The fastest time is by Mark Hartell with 14 hrs 42 mins (set in 1993), with fastest lady being Debbie Cooper with 22 hrs 33 mins from 1990.

The Joss Naylor Challenge has become a sort of benchmark challenge for the older runner. It was inaugurated by Joss Naylor in 1990 as a fund-raising challenge to the over-50s. In addition to completing the route, contenders must raise at least £100 for a charity of their choice. Joss's challenge involves climbing 30 tops, traversing over 48 miles of mountain terrain and ascending some 17,000 feet. The route starts in Pooley Bridge, Ullswater and finishes at Greendale Bridge, Wasdale. Each age group has a specific time limit varying between 12 and 24 hours, with different times for men and women. There is no emphasis on record times and pacers are mandatory for safety reasons.

Over the Irish Sea, **The Wicklow Round** is the Irish equivalent, taking in the peaks in the Wicklow mountains region. It traverses 26 peaks, totalling over 60 miles and over 6,000m of climbing, with a 24-hour time limit. It is administered by a sub-committee of the Irish Mountain Runners Association, and has received some criticism for its rules (e.g. for any attempt to be recognised it must first be publicised in advance on the forum section of the IMRA website and afterwards you must supply a list of splits).

Moire O'Sullivan completed the round in 2009 in 22 hrs 58 mins 30 secs, and Eoin Keith in 2009 completed the fastest round of 17 hrs 53 mins 45 secs. http://www.imra.ie/ad-hoc/Eoin splits.doc On her first attempt, in 2008, Moire had to abandon with just two summits to go. In her book *Mud, Sweat and Tears* she describes this moment:

> Guided by my thin head torch beam, I painfully plod my way up the mountain side. As my body slows with every step my mind begins to run riot. Thoughts of success and failure, thoughts of people and far-off places. Having already physically destroyed myself, I am now emotionally ripping myself apart ... There are only two more mountains to climb. I have three and a half hours left. I have in theory plenty of time. But I don't move. I stay where I am. My mind and body have made their decision. I cannot go on. And with the relief that knowing it is all over, I crouch down on the mountain top. And one by one, tears of disappointment, relief, obsession, and exhaustion begin to trickle slowly down my face.

Eric Beard's records have already been mentioned, including that for the **Cuillin Ridge**. The traverse of the Cuillins is not really a fell challenge, as it includes climbing and abseiling. However it has attracted the attentions of fell runners over the years, and records have been set. By early in the twentieth century George Abraham, the climber from Keswick, thought that the traverse of the Cuillin Ridge in one day might be possible some day by a climber with the necessary endurance and technique. In *Long Days in the Fells* Harry Griffin writes that:

> in June 1911, two such men appeared on the scene, and although considerable sections of the ridge were unknown to them they succeeded in making the complete traverse for the first time, reaching Sligachan nearly 17 hours after they left Glen Brittle and taking 12 hours 18 mins along the ridge. The two climbers were L.G. Shadbolt and A.G. MacLean, members of the Scottish Mountaineering Club.

Apparently the two did not bother to lay caches of food and water along the ridge, carried their own ropes and supplies, and eschewed the aid of pacers or parties with provisions, and this was to be the pattern of most of the successful attempts that were to follow, in marked contrast to most approaches to the BGR. In 1920 T.H. Somervell, the Lakes surgeon who reached 28,000 on Everest, took less than 11 hours to traverse the ridge. In 1932 Peter Bicknell reduced this to eight hours.

Griffin also noted that Eric Beard on his 4 hrs 9 mins record traverse was:

accompanied to the first summit, Gars-bheinn, by a companion who then descended to Glen Brittle, planning to wait for Eric on the last summit, Sgurr nan Gillean, but the man from Leeds had got there first. In his international three-peaks effort (taking in the highest peaks in Scotland, England and Wales) he scorned the use of transport and did it all on foot. Eric Beard apparently subsisted in the hills on honey and jam butties. He lived a simple life, having no house and no car – just his tent, his mountain gear and his skis. He often had no proper job, but would turn up ready to turn his hands at anything to earn a crust.

A new record for the fastest time for the Cuillin Ridge was set in 1984 by Andy Hyslop. He brought Eric Beard's phenomenal record down by five mins to 4 hrs 4 mins 19 secs – peak to peak, Gars Bheinh to Sgurr Nan Gillean. Hyslop defined any record attempt as encompassing every Munro on the Ridge, and negotiating the main climbing sections un-roped, which actually means reverse climbing the Inaccessible Pinnacle. Eyri Harriers members Paul Stott and Del Davies attempted the record in a warm day in 1986. Del Davies finished in 3 hrs 49 mins 30 secs, with Stott a minute behind, having both taken different routes climbing over the Basteir Tooth.

Martin Moran brought it down to 3 hrs 33 mins in 1990. He went solo and unsupported in cool windless conditions, and survived what he described as a 'nasty tumble' on Sgurr Mhic Coinnich. Then in May 1994 Andy Hyslop came back after doing some serious reconnoitres on the ridge and brought it down to 3 hrs 32 mins 50 secs (those seconds being oh so important now). Hyslop tells a nice story about how early on, he had met a group whose

leader asked if he was attempting the record. 'Too early to say' was his terse
reply as he rushed past. He never realised his questioner was in fact Martin
Moran, who watched his progress for the next few hours.

The same August he came back and recorded a new fastest time of 3 hrs
32 mins 15 secs. Some suggested that a kind of physiological barrier might
have been reached, but in the spring of 2007 Es Tresidder comprehensively
proved the pundits wrong with an astonishing time of 3 hrs 17mins 28 secs.
In a report in The *Herald*[76] Es Tresidder reflected:

> It's a unique run, there's nothing else quite like it. I've run a circuit
> of the hills around Glencoe taking in the Aonach Eagach for example,
> but that seems like an athletics track compared to the Cuillin. You
> really need to be a climber as well as a runner, since you're quite
> often using all four limbs at the same time but moving very quickly.

Tresidder wore a pair of fell-running shoes re-soled with 'sticky' rubber for
his run, which helped his security on the climbing sections such as the slippery
basalt of the ridge's Thearlich-Dubh gap, the King's Chimney, the exposed
Naismith's Route on the Bhasteir Tooth and the Inaccessible Pinnacle.
Tresidder admitted to feeling nervous the night before, and confessed he feels
uncomfortable with solo climbing.

> ... the enormity of what you're about to embark on hits you and
> you can't help falling prey to self-doubt. But the funny thing is that
> once you get started the concentration blows a lot of the fear away.
> In the event, I felt fine on the technical climbing sections because
> I deliberately forced myself to take them steadily and not rush the
> moves – in reality the running sections are the dangerous bits – they
> are mentally exhausting.

Then, on 16 June 2013, Finlay Wild recorded a new record time of 3 hrs
14 mins and 58 secs for the Cuillin Ridge Traverse, under the Hyslop 'rules'.
As recorded on the UK Climbing website[77]:

> Amazingly, Finlay ran a time of 3:10:30 the week previously – but
> in an impressive show of discipline decided it didn't count because
> he'd failed to touch the summit cairn of Sgurr Mhic Choinnich,
> despite passing 10 metres from it. For his successful attempt Finlay

had no support on the ridge, which meant soloing all the graded pitches. He downclimbed the spots that are usually abseiled.

On 12 October 2013 Finlay Wild took his own record down to an amazing time of 2 hrs 52 mins 22 secs.

Having done the Cuillin Ridge myself, and been pretty much 'on the edge' for the whole of the traverse, I have a huge respect for these frankly amazing achievements. These achievements don't come easy either. In our team of four we had already experienced a range of failures on the ridge before succeeding. For myself, I had already been beaten back twice before succeeding. Once was through being under-prepared, and once when we were struck by a mid-summer blizzard on the summit of Sgurr Alasdair, and were forced to escape rapidly to the valley via the stone shute to avoid hypothermia. That occasion was itself a once-in-a-lifetime experience. Lifelong friend Mike Cambray has shared many mountain adventures with me, and was the inspiration for our successful effort in 1995. It was his second successful traverse, and he comments:

> there is nothing quite like it when the weather is fair – travelling light across Britain's greatest mountain range is pure heaven. However, on a cold and wet day navigation is extremely tricky and on more than one occasion I have descended to Glen Brittle in exasperation at the challenge of route-finding in zero visibility.

Finally, the **Man versus Horse Marathon** event is an annual race over 22 miles, whereby runners compete against riders on horseback. The race takes place from the Welsh town of Llanwrtyd Wells every June. It started in 1980 after some pub banter. The sponsor's website[78] says of its history:

> One night in the Neuadd Arms, Landlord Gordon Green overheard two men discussing the relative merits of man and horse. After several pints one was brave (or foolish!) enough to suggest that over a significant distance across country, man was equal to any horse. After several more pints, the inevitable challenge was made, at which point Gordon decided that rather than this be a private argument, it should be put to the test in full public view.

In 2004, the twentieth-fifth race was won by Huw Lobb in 2 hrs 5 mins and 19 secs. It was the first time that a man racing on foot has won the race, thereby winning the prize fund of £25,000 (money again).

What is the chance of some of these records being broken in the future? As we have seen no one has got within an hour of Billy Bland's phenomenal time for the Bob Graham Round, and that has lasted for 30 years now. Maybe someone in the next chapter could be the one to come over from Europe or the States to do so. We will see.

CHAPTER 17

Going global

Inevitably an international dimension has been added to the sport, with the relative ease of travel, and availability of more leisure time. When the Fell Runners Association was formed several high profile fell racers were pressing for international recognition to be available in the sport. There were already some 'fell-type' races held in other parts of the world by this time, as will be seen.

I must put my cards on the table at this point and say that I wouldn't count most of what is in this chapter as fell racing. The best fell races involve navigation and choices of routes, are rarely flagged and to a great extent are over courses that are designed not to always follow paths or trails. If you wish to descend a boulder field, or leap off a small crag you may do so, at your own peril. Mountain races, according to the governing body (WMRA) have courses that are 'designed to eliminate danger'. They are predominantly on trails and often have fully defined and rigid courses. Furthermore, IAAF (International Association of Athletics Federations) rule 250.10 defines the distances and heights for men, women, and juniors for both uphill only and uphill/downhill courses.

In the USA the Pikes Peak race (located just west of Colorado Springs) dates from 1956. The race started when three smokers challenged ten non-smokers to compete over the 26-mile (42 km) course. None of the three smokers completed the course. In 1966 a marathon was initiated there, with over 7,800 feet of ascent before the turnaround, the race being the third-oldest 'marathon' in the United States. Joss Naylor was invited to compete in 1975. Despite training over the course a couple of times in advance of the race he found it really tough as the summit is over 12,000 feet, and also dehydration was a problem. Joss was 39 years old at the time and finished sixth after being eighteenth at the summit, and had the satisfaction of having the fastest descent time, in fact being three minutes faster at descending than winner Rick Trujillo. The race has only ever had one UK winner, that being Angela Mudge in 2003.

In the early days the main international race in Europe was at Sierre-Zinal (in Switzerland), usually having 70 or so entrants at the time. The Sierre-Zinal race started in 1973, also being called the Race of Five 4000m Peaks, and is considered by some to be the finest mountain race in the world. It was once suggested that it is 'to mountain races what the New York Marathon is to marathons'. It is the oldest mountain race of its type in Europe. The race takes place in the heart of western (Valais) Alps, and is over a distance of 31km, and has 2,200m ascent and 800m descent.

With the formation of the FRA in 1970 there had been moves to send runners to races such as this, and Joss Naylor had already been part of this trend, looking as he was to do Pikes Peak. In the 1974 Sierre-Zinal Harry Walker was third, Jeff Norman fifth, Joss Naylor eighth and Pete Walkington twenty-third. The first three entered as a FRA team and they won the team prize. Jeff Norman didn't especially rate it, as it is basically all run on paths. Norman remarked to me: 'Sierre-Zinal was being touted as the International mountain race. Joss had already done Pikes Peak [it was actually a year later]. The organisers of the race wrote to the FRA to nominate a team I think.' John Blair-Fish must have liked the event as he ran the race 25 times, which is more than any other UK runner.

The globalisation of sport also caused fell running to look at itself, and some even questioned the participation in tough fell races by runners from other branches of athletics. It has already been reported that the 1978 Three Peaks Race was run in thick mist and resulted the death of Edward Pepper of Blackheath Harriers, who died from exposure. Let's remember the already quoted remark from the organisers at the time:

Let those road and cross country runners who competed on this
occasion be warned that this course is far from being the toughest,
as claimed by some uninitiated writers, and that the strong wind
and mist produced only mildly unpleasant conditions by comparison
to the really bad weather which can prevail on Britain's hills.

Despite these warnings runners from all branches of athletics were moving
in to fell running. The 1978 Sierre-Zinal result shows many British runners
in the results, including less likely ones such as Nigel Gates in seventeenth
place and Mick Woods[79] in eighteenth. So, while the setting up of the formal
Championships was being worked on, British runners were gaining more
experience by going to events abroad.

Notwithstanding this, the 1980 Snowdon race had what was reported as
'a significant continental challenge in the form of a crack Italian team [which]
added spice to the 5th annual Snowdon race'. The Italian Pezzoli won from
Andy Darby, with another Italian in third place, although the weather meant
it was a time 2.5 minutes slower than the 1 hr 4 mins 28 secs of the then
record holder Ricky Wilde (set in 1978) – who was ninth on this occasion.

In 1982 a party of 58 runners, mostly fell runners from England, went
out early to acclimatise and take part in the Sierre-Zinal race. Nigel Gates
had been second in the race in 1981 and the Brits were hoping to do well
again. In the end the first Briton home was Mike Short in eighth place,
followed not long after by Dick Evans and Jeff Norman. An issue of *Fellrunner*
at the time listed 68 races that comprised the Coupe Internationale de la
Montagne (CIME), as well as a report on the 1982 Pikes Peak (Hugh Symonds
coming second), and an article entitled 'Fell Running in the USA'.

The next year Scotland, England and Wales sent teams of four runners
to compete in the Italian International Mountain Championships near Verona.
The course was nine miles long over cart tracks and roads. Even with one
steep hill at the beginning it was not really mountain running, despite
ascending 1,700 feet. In comparison, the Snowdon race has over 3,000 feet
of ascent in the five miles to the summit turnaround. Italians took the first
five places, winning the team competition. John Wild was sixth, with Kenny
Stuart and Dick Evans (Wales) in the teens, Jon Broxap in the twenties and
Shaun Livesey in the thirties, England took second team. A report by John
Blair-Fish in *Fellrunner* noted:

discussions at the event initiated by the FRA were very favourable to a possible World Championship but this cannot be pursued further because the IAAF are not interested in an official mountain championship. The CIME mountain races in Europe are classed by the IAAF as fun runs mainly because everyone starts at the same time regardless of age and sex. Thus mountain or hill running is a long way from being a major official amateur sport.

The Italians tried to broker an inaugural world event for mountain running in September 1984 in Val d'Aosta. It was planned to be for teams of four and include men's long, men's short, ladies and junior races. This too did not come to fruition, so Italy arranged an International Fell Race in Zogno. They invited England, Scotland, Wales, San Marino, Switzerland and Austria. The English team received financial support from the AAA, with the team selected by the FRA. The Welsh team was selected by the Welsh FRA regional committee, and the Scottish by SAAA with reference to SHRA (Scottish Hill Runners Association). It was a 9.5km course with rough and rocky track all the way, finishing back down in the town square.

Kenny Stuart swept to victory ahead of six Italians, who were led by Fausto Bonzi – a local who lived at altitude and held the course record for Snowdon at the time. Malcolm Patterson was the early leader, with Stuart soon taking over. Stuart reached the summit with a lead of ten seconds, which had increased to 34 seconds by the finish. Not surprisingly the Italians took the first two team places, with England's team of Stuart, Malcolm Patterson (thirteenth), Hugh Symonds (fifteenth), Dave Cartridge (sixteenth) and Jon Broxap (seventeenth) taking bronze. The day before an International Mountain Racing Committee was formed with FRA's Danny Hughes as secretary. The plan was to work towards worldwide membership of the committee and to convince the International Association of Athletics Federations (IAAF) to authorise world championship events.

Following this, Danny Hughes organised the Reebok International Mountain Challenge in May 1985. It consisted of the Buttermere Sailbeck Horseshoe on the 12th, the Grasmere Dash (over the guides course) on the 19th and the Fairfield Horseshoe on the 19th. The invited international challenge only materialised in the last event, where the Italians Pezzoli, Bonzi and Rossi came 3rd, 13th and 18th respectively. Kenny Stuart won all three races from Jack Maitland, and Pauline Haworth all three from Wendy Dodds. The Grasmere Dash had a quality field and Kenny Stuart won in 12 mins 1 sec, beating Fred Reeves's professional record of 12 mins 21.6 secs, though it was not officially recognised as a new record by the FRA, who still list Reeves's time.

The well-established Sierre-Zinal event in Switzerland was again noted in August 1985 for featuring British wins from Jack Maitland and Veronique Marot, and a considerable number of British runners in the entry list. Maitland had apparently executed 'a mad descent with several falls and shortcuts'.

The first World Cup in Mountain Running took place at San Vigilio Di Marebbe in Italy in September 1985. England, Scotland and Wales all sent teams, with varying degrees of financial support. The two Senior races, plus the Ladies and Juniors were all won by Italy. England was the most successful home nation with second in the Senior short and Junior races, fifth in the Senior long races. Kenny Stuart won the Men's short course, which consisted of two laps of varying lengths in the hills around the village where it was based.

Following the first World Cup in 1985, FRA were invited to organise a second one in England in 1986, which they declined, mostly on the grounds of cost – the Italians admitting to having spent £42,000 hosting the first. There was also a feeling around that this international perspective was only relevant to the real elite of the sport. In 1986 FRA discussed a policy on international fell running, and set up a working party to consider the possibility of holding the World Cup a couple of years hence.

There was considerable enthusiasm expressed by Keswick Town Council for the event to be held there in 1988. The plan was for a longer race to take place on the Coledale Horseshoe, with a short course on Latrigg. There were objections from Switzerland, Germany and Austria on the grounds that they did not finish uphill, which were rebuffed. The planned style of race was finally accepted by those countries. It was decided also to include non-championship races to involve all fell runners in the event. The Saturday was to have Junior, Ladies and Senior Mens races all over the short course on Latrigg. On Sunday the longer course would have the open race, the Veteran's world cup and the Senior men's race for national teams. Responsibility for the short course would be with Keswick AC and the longer course with CFRA (Cumberland Fell Runners Association).

The race was eventually held on a sunny day for the short courses on Latrigg, described as cross country in style. The Junior race was won by Schoch of Switzerland who led his team to victory. Mark Rice and John Taylor were second and third respectively, helping England to second team. In the Ladies race, Fabiola Rueda of Colombia retained her title, with Switzerland again winning the team award (on countback from Italy). First Brits were Angela Carson (Wales) in sixth and Patricia Calder (Scotland) in seventh. The Senior Men's short race was over three circuits of the tough Latrigg course. Alfonso Vallicella led Italy to first team ahead of Switzerland, while the England team took a close third place, led home by Robin Bergstrand in fifth and Ray Owen in ninth.

The Sunday was misty for the Men's long course on the Coledale round. Dino Tadello led Italy to an overwhelming win, with their other runners in second and fourth places and an almost perfect score of seven points. Rod Pilbeam finished third, the best position by a Brit in the event thus far, leading Malcolm Patterson (sixth) and Shaun Livesey (fourteenth) to silver medals. The Veterans race was won by John Nixon, with Hugh Symonds a convincing winner of the open race which suffered from the removal of some marker flags on Grizedale Pike. A meeting of ICMR (International Committee Mountain Running) held in tandem with the event was dominated by superior numbers of votes from the 'Alpine' nations, who ensured that uphill finishes would be the norm in future World Cups. Finally, the accounts show that almost 50 per cent of the income was from sponsorship from Reebok, and a grant from the Sports Council, which did in fact mean that the event came out with a surplus of over £3,000 to be shared equally between the Sports Council and the FRA.

From 1989 selection races for the World Cup were instigated. In 1990 a special 7.5 mile 'Uphill Only' Snowdon race was used as the trial. It was won by Nigel Gates of Brighton and Hove AC, who as it has already been noted, had already had some success in international events. Runners considered by many to be 'proper' fell runners – Mark Croasdale and Paul Dugdale – came second and third respectively.

The World Cup almost floundered in 1993 over a huge row about 'Up and Down' and 'Uphill Only' courses. A compromise was reached to alternate them year on year, and the re-badged World Mountain Running Trophy seemed to have a future again, and has been run ever since. Indeed there is now a proliferation of such championships. Browsing the World Mountain Running Association website[80] shows that there now are World Championships; European Championships; World Long Distance Mountain Running Challenge; and Commonwealth Mountain Running Championships. The latter was held in Keswick in 2009, with the Men's (uphill) race won by a Kenyan athlete. Since then there have been an increasing number of athletes from African nations, and from less 'usual' other nations figuring highly (and sometimes winning) in this and other WMRA races. The World Long Distance Mountain Running Challenge started in 2004 and is a one-off event that moves around the major races. The first was in Sierre-Zinal, and has been held at the Three Peaks in 2008 (and won by Scotland's Jethro Lennox) and Pikes Peak in 2010.

Someone making waves in this arena is the Catalan, Kilian Jornet. His CV is most impressive, with entries such as World Skyrunning Champion in 2007/2008/2009; winner of Climbathon Malaysia three times; Skyrace Andorra three times; and Ultra Trail Mont Blanc three times. He also holds the record for up and down Mount Kilimanjaro, the GR 20 (see Glossary) in Corsica, and the Tahoe Rim Trail (280km with 14,000km of ascent in 38 hrs 32 mins). Looking ahead to the next chapter he is also an extremely accomplished ski-mountaineer. So impressed with this portfolio of achievements were *Athletics Weekly*, that in January 2012 they proposed him as the 'world's greatest runner' in an extended feature article. When questioned about what he might achieve if he ran a road marathon Jornet replied:

> I don't think about running a marathon. I've never run on ashphalt and I'm never going to run on it. I've always said that running is only a medium. The mountain is my goal.

Jornet is very much the modern athlete, regularly updating his 'fans' via social media sites. He conducts interviews in several languages, is invariably seen with sunglasses atop his head, is lead athlete for a major sponsor, and has videos aplenty on the internet. For instance Salomon, the outdoor shoe and clothing company, helped him produce his own series of online videos called 'Kilian's Quest', and they have built a team of trail running racers around him, including UK fell runners Ricky Lightfoot and Andy Symonds (Hugh Symonds' son).

The *Athletics Weekly* article on Jornet produced some letters of response in the magazine, some questioning the relative difficulty level that these 'trail' races have. You only have to see some of the terrain on the GR 20 to realise that that is not an especially sound argument. *Athletics Weekly* also published a letter I wrote pointing out how poor their coverage was of fell running, questioning how you might compare Jornet's feats with some of the supreme endurance efforts of Joss Naylor, Mark Hartell, Billy Bland and Es Tresidder, which have been detailed in this volume. Slightly tongue in cheek, I posed the question of what Jornet might achieve if he was to tackle Tresidder's Cuillin Ridge record of 3 hrs 17 mins. Subsequently I came across a Jornet video interview[81] where he is questioned by fell runner Ben Abdelnoor on the Run247tv YouTube channel. In the clip Abdelnoor asks him if the Bob Graham Round was something he might attempt in the future. He replied that he knew the course

> and it is one of the best in the world. I like it also because it is
> technical, it's climbing. Why not, in some years time.

On the video he is then symbolically presented with a copy of the *42 Peaks* BGR booklet for his further research.

So, could Jornet approach or even beat Billy Bland's BGR time, or take Es Tresidder's Cuillin Ridge record? I suspect not; as he is an ultra endurance runner his major efforts have not even been in the recognised mountain races, and traditional long fell races would be a whole new experience for him. Having said that, I would love to see him try. I stick with the conclusion to my *AW* letter, which is that Naylor, not Jornet, is the 'world's greatest runner'. I would now like to consider some athletes who have excelled at fell running and made a significant mark in other sports.

CHAPTER 18

Crossing sports

Rapid motion through space elates one
James Joyce

It is difficult to know where to draw the line when considering which sports have a close affinity with fell running. There are the obvious comparisons with walking and climbing from the early days. More recently, there has been the development of trail running, and the trend for runners to try triathlons, and for triathletes to try adventure racing, and so on. In fact, there is now a slightly artificial series of events that can be undertaken that add an extra level of extremeness, but usually in a 'controlled environment'. Some examples are: Tough Guy – twenty-five obstacles over an undulating course in mud and cold; Brutal 10 – a 10km cross country race over hills, streams and undergrowth; and Tough Mudder – a 10 to 12 mile obstacle course featuring mud, ice baths, barbed wire and electric shocks.

It is worth looking at what might be behind this 'extreme' trend. In a piece in the *BBC News Magazine*[82] in January 2012 sports psychologist Dr Victor Thompson suggested:

> I think we are becoming extreme in both directions. Humans are essentially animals and animals are, by nature, lazy. But some people choose to do something about it. For years people will have been pushing themselves in their careers, but after a while you need a new challenge, another goal. They've been to the gym, they've done that, time for something new.

I question whether the addition of artificial difficulties is really necessary. Perhaps for some the challenge of a tough run over the fells is not enough. In his book *Running: a Global History*, Thor Gotaas has an 'extreme' view of these events and those who take part:

> The participants in these extreme runs are a travel-insured and pampered version of the explorers of the past. Runners have invaded the farthest outposts of the world and raced in them, they have colonised every geographical zone and declared them conquered. There is almost no natural environment on the globe that remains untouched by the feet of joggers. Is a marathon on the moon the next step?

In 1991 *Fellrunner* magazine carried a piece on a proposal for a Trail Racing Association, and this organisation now runs that side of the sport, through their affiliation to UK Athletics. None of this need necessarily bother students of fell running history, but for the fact that one of the top fell runners of today also excels at the sport of cyclo-cross, and that Britain's two top current triathletes (who are now global superstars after the 2012 London Olympics, as both of them won triathlon medals) also happen to be top quality fell runners.

Firstly then, a particularly good example of an athlete crossing sports is **Rob Jebb.** He is from Bingley originally, and was born in 1975. He was encouraged to take up running by his father Peter, and joined Bingley Harriers aged just nine. His father came into fell running from the sport of mountaineering, first competing in the Fellsman Hike in 1974, an event which he eventually won seven years later. Jebb Senior consistently performed well in long, rough mountain races like the Karrimor, Capricorn, Mountain Trial and the Ennerdale Horseshoe. The amateur Buckden Pike race was inaugurated by him in 1982 and he remained as organiser for 20 years, until former Bingley Harriers clubmate Allan Greenwood took over in 2003.

The first race Rob Jebb himself entered was the Buckden Pike junior race, which his father had allowed him to enter even though he was technically under-age. Finishing one place from last he nevertheless enjoyed the experience. He recalled to me that:

> My father was my early inspiration as a junior and also my coach, but I also trained with the Harriers on Tuesdays for a long run and

on Thursdays for speedwork, having joined them in 1984 at the age of nine.

He didn't really show great promise as a junior, never winning a race, although he was second several times, at Blackstone Edge and Pen-y-Ghent in 1991 and at Burnsall in 1993. The latter two races had been won by clubmate Matt Whitfield, son of the 1987 English fell champion, Bob Whitfield. An indication of Jebb's potential can be seen in his tenth position in the 1993 under 18 boys' championship.

Rob Jebb swiftly moved into the seniors, as the next year he scored in Bingley's winning three-man team in the Sheepstones Relay. In 1995 he was first junior at Skiddaw, and an excellent nineteenth (Senior) at Ben Nevis, commenting: 'I had first run the Ben two years earlier as an under-age 18-year-old, having been inspired to enter by watching my father and Ian Holmes perform in it.' He started training harder and returned the following year to come fifth in this classic, with other highlights of that season including second at both Wansfell and the Glen Rosa Horseshoe on Arran, fifth in the Langdale Horseshoe, and sixth in both the Jura and Duddon races. He had achieved his first race win earlier that year in the Keighley Hill Runners' Winter League race from Goose Eye, a seven-mile route out to Keighley Moor Reservoir and back. During the summer he secured his second win in the short up-and-down event at Halton Gill, where he set a new record. That was after cycling 40 miles to reach the venue, plus 40 miles back.

He improved even further the following year with a win at Loughrigg, second at Boulsworth, third at both Ben Nevis and Burnsall, and fifth at Wasdale and Langdale. This indicates that Jebb had become a fine runner over all types of terrain and distance, though the longer races perhaps remained his forte. In 1998 his dedication was rewarded with sixth place in the British fell championship and third in the English. He also represented England in the Knockdhu International race that year, finishing seventh, and won the Tour of Pendle and Withins Skyline races.

The next season started well with a victory at Ovenden Moor. Seconds in the Ben, Callow, Donard-Commedagh and Welsh 1000m Peaks gave Jebb second place in the British Championships (and third in the English). Year 2000 finally produced a Buckden Pike win, and among other races a second at Dunnerdale, third in the Ben and fifth in the Three Peaks. Stretching his horizons, he competed in the tough Mount Kinabalu race in Borneo, where he came fifth on a course shortened due to torrential rain. In retrospect he felt that he was saying 'yes' to too many races, as international racing beckoned. He had finished twenty-eighth in the European mountain running champs in both 1999 and 2000.

Jebb's form returned in 2002, after the break for the foot and mouth epidemic the year before. He managed to win the Grasmere Guides Race the day after moving house to Cumbria from Yorkshire, with partner Sharon Taylor winning the ladies race. Jebb won five championship races that year to make him joint runner-up in the British Championships with Ian Holmes. His ambition was achieved in 2003 when he won the British Championships, just failing to get the English title too, as he was not able to get the required win in the last event at Langdale. To show his superb form that year, he won Slieve Bearnagh, came second at Stuc A Chroin in the British Championships, and at Holme Moss in the English. In non-championship races he won his first Ben Nevis race, Coledale Horseshoe, Wadsworth Trog (in a course record) and the local Kentmere Horseshoe, together with overall victory in the Lakeland Classics Championships (the long 'A' events). He repeated the British Championship success in 2006, having also won the World Skyrunning Series in 2005, and won the English Championship in 2008. He had a setback in 2011 when he had to have surgery on a persistent unstable shoulder injury.

Jebb names his favourite races as Ben Nevis, the Three Peaks, Jura and all the Lakeland Classics. These choices are perhaps not surprising given that Rob has won the Three Peaks race four times, and Ben Nevis four times. He also runs brilliantly in shorter races, being a proud eight times winner of the Grasmere Guides race. As well as selection for the two European Mountain Running Championships he has been selected for the World Mountain Running Championships for England in 2003 and 2007.

Rob Jebb has organised his own training, originally with advice from his father, then later occasionally from Dennis Quinlan. Jebb claims that his bike riding has allowed him to gain a largely stress-free endurance base, and that it aids his climbing strength and keeps him motivated outside the fell running season. Jebb acknowledges that climbing is his strength and that his preference is for runnable courses such as those at Fairfield and Kentmere.

His crossover to cycling started in his mid-teens and by 17 he had entered the Three Peaks cyclo-cross event. He has now won the event eight times, as well as finishing highly in the National cyclo-cross champs. Bikeradar. com reporting[83] on his seventh victory in the Three Peaks cyclo-cross when he also broke the course recorded:

> It's been two years since Jebb equalled Tim Gould's record of six victories in the difficult 61km-long event, which includes the climbs of Ingleborough, Whernside and Pen-y-Ghent. Last year's event was cancelled as a precaution because of a foot and mouth disease scare. But, 24 months since his last Three Peaks win, Jebb was more determined than ever to make the record his own – something he did comfortably. 'It was a great day, as ever,' he said. 'I couldn't have wished for better. I didn't have a puncture and I didn't have any problems. It couldn't have gone better. I went really hard over Ingleborough and got a gap on Nick Craig, who was on my wheel. I didn't kill myself on the descents, but I knew I had a chance at the record, so I kept the pressure on.' Jebb clocked in at 2 hrs 52 mins 22 secs, beating his own 2003 record by 42 seconds and finishing more than six minutes ahead of Nick Craig.

Due to the halt in fell racing in 2001 he took to road racing on the bike and achieved an international vest and a ride in the Tour of Ireland, but crashed on Stage 3 and retired with a dislocated shoulder. Both training and racing on the bike are kept basic with Jebb. In an interview in *Cycling News* (in 2008[84]) he said:

> I don't mind it [training in the dark of winter]. I start work pretty early and finish just as it starts to get dark. I get out on the road in the dark some nights, extend my rides to work some days, and do the dreaded turbo trainer sessions when it's too bad outside.

His cycle race tactics seem pretty simple too:

> I just tend to go out and race as hard as I can, I figure that most of the time in a cyclo-cross the strongest rider will win.

Every May the Fred Whitton Challenge takes place in the Lakes. It is a gruelling 112-mile sportive challenge bike ride around the Lake District. It starts and finishes at Coniston, and the route takes in all the major road passes in the Lakes, including the climbs of Kirkstone, Honister, Newlands, Whinlatter, Hardknott and Wrynose passes. Rob Jebb jointly holds the record for this event, sharing a time of 5 hrs 40 mins 40 secs with James Dobbin, from the 2008 event.

Finally then, back to Jebb's fell success, and to one possibly niggling annoyance. Despite winning Grasmere eight times, he has never quite challenged the record for the course. His fastest time is a full 15 seconds off it, which may not seem much but does show what a strong record it is. Has Jebb been obsessed with trying for the record? In an interview in *Cumbria* magazine he claims not to have been, saying:

> sometimes if you try too hard it all goes wrong. You're better off being relaxed. There have been times when I have tried too hard – not in Grasmere – but in others. Some races, yes, you could get obsessed. Pressure can get to you. You make mistakes. I prefer to be more relaxed and just turn up and run.

In the same interview he comments on the attitude of fellow fell runners:

> You know they won't give an inch. Yet they will never see you stuck. Once on the Duddon Horseshoe I ran with Gavin Bland from Thirlmere when I was a youngster. Then he said he was going to start accelerating. But first he told me the crucial short cut to take before he left me in his wake.

Conversely, brothers **Alistair and Jonathan Brownlee** are world class at their chosen sport of triathlon, but often claim to be happiest out running in the fells, and frequently do just that. Alistair is the elder of the two and was the first to make an impact on the world stage, but is now joined by his younger brother, and training partner. To many observers, they are the numbers one and two triathletes in the world right now.

Alistair Brownlee went to school in Bradford (the Grammar School), took up his place at Cambridge University, but eventually moved to the University of Leeds to gain a degree in Sports Science and Physiology. He is now a postgraduate at Leeds Metropolitan University.

Early in his career he was a successful fell and cross country runner, achieving silver at the National Cross Country Championships as a Junior.

He has also won the Yorkshire Cross Country title on several occasions. The move back to Leeds coincided with him concentrating on triathlon. He is coached at Leeds Metropolitan University's Carnegie High Performance Centre by Malcolm Brown, and by Jack Maitland, who was a top fell runner in his prime and who competed in the Commonwealth Games triathlon in 1990. Alistair Brownlee represented Britain at the Olympics in 2008 in the triathlon, finishing in twelfth place and first British competitor, having been in the lead until 3km to go, where his strength deserted him.

He was introduced to triathlon very early by a member of his family. On his own website[85] he states:

> Dad was a runner and Mum was a swimmer and then my uncle, Simon, introduced me to triathlon. I still continue to do cross country and fell run but triathlon is what I want to really achieve in.

Significantly, he also claims that if he wasn't a triathlete he would be a fell runner, and that his heroes are Haile Gebrselassie and Joss Naylor. Interviewed for *Mud, Sweat and Tears* in 2009[86] he explained how it all fitted together.

> I do as many cross country races as I can in the winter and a few fell races from time to time. I try to do the Yorkshire fell champs every year and a few when my triathlon season finishes, like the FRA relays and Dave Woodhead's races. I would like to do more but the summer months are quite busy for me! I really enjoy fell and cross country running. I think it's great fun, good for me and a way to break up the monotony of winter training. I like to try to run well in the major champs in the new year (Yorkshires, Northerns, Nationals, BUCS, Inter-counties) although my fitness seems to be a bit hit and miss.

When asked if fell running was something that he could see still being a big part of his schedule and whether the World Mountain Running Championships might figure at some point in the future, he replied:

> Yes I would definitely like to do some more mountain running in the future. I went to three world trophies as a junior and loved the experience. I think up hill only races in particular could fit in well.

I just need a bit of luck with scheduling of the trial races and triathlons. You never know, it would be great to have a different focus for a year somewhere along the line.

In the time since then his triathlon focus has obviously been even more specific. Despite that he did run some fell and cross country races as part of his 2011/12 winter regime, even though this was already build-up time to the Olympic triathlon in the summer of 2012. On the last day of December of 2011 Alistair won the relatively local Auld Lang Syne fell race – from his brother Jonathan. After the race he said:

on the rough descent back down to the Pennine Way I took my chance. Out of Sladen Beck I just kept pushing, knowing that Jonny never gives up. I crossed the line, tired, exhausted and knackered, but very happy to win the race for the third time.

Then on 7 January 2012 Alistair won the Yorkshire County Cross Country Championships at Wakefield. Once again Jonathan was second (by four seconds), with both just over a minute ahead of the bronze medalist, in what is always reckoned to be a tough county champs. A measure of Alistair Brownlee's fell running pedigree is the fact that he holds the course record for the Withins Skyline fell race, with a time of 41 mins 28 secs from 2006.

Jonathan Brownlee, who is two years younger than Alistair, has a very similar profile to his elder brother. Jonathan also attended Bradford Grammar School, and is studying history at the University of Leeds. He is a member of Bingley Harriers, and coached by Malcolm Brown and Jack Maitland, like Alistair. He is the two-times World Sprint Triathlon Champion and is the former Under 23 Triathlon World Champion (from 2010). In 2011 he finished second in the world following the conclusion of the ITU (International Triathlon Union) World Championship Series in Beijing, and in 2012 won the series.

In his *Guardian* 2012 Olympic Blog[87] in January 2012 Jonathan wrote:

The goal for the next few months is to keep plugging away, and not get injured. But it's hard this time of year. Because while Christmas is over, the season is still a long way away. That's why I have a few cross country races lined up in the next few weeks, which will be useful for two reasons: first it splits training up and ensures I don't get stale. I'll taper down for races, and then push on again after they are done. Second, it gives me a better indication of where I am. Training is one thing, racing is another. On New Year's Eve I finished second to my brother Alistair in the Auld Lang Syne fell race at Haworth. Fell running presents a different challenge, but it's one I enjoy. It's hard up those hills – especially when the ground is sticky and the mud seems to cling permanently to your ankles – and you use completely different muscles on the way down too. But I'm a big fan of the sport: it's real back-to-basics stuff. With triathlon you're dealing with high-end equipment, the media side of things, and everything else that comes with being a professional sportsman. Fell running has this purity to it: it's basically running in a field.

In the comments on the blog someone asked why he still went fell running when there was an added risk of injury. He replied in his next blog posting:

The poster had a point – but it's about risk management. Yes, my quad muscles get sore after fell running but it would be a shame to jack something I enjoy immensely. Similarly mountain biking is not that different from normal cycling – my arms have to work a little harder and they get a little sore – but it's vital for me to not only train different muscles but to keep it varied. There are just under six months to go before the big race at London 2012; that's an awful lot of swimming, biking and running to get through. Anything that mixes things up a little, providing it is safe, has to be a good thing.

As well as his second place at Auld Lang Syne Jonathan Brownlee won the Chevin Chase in December 2011, and came an excellent fifth in the Inter-Counties Cross Country Championships in Birmingham in March 2012, considering this a natural part of his own Olympic preparations. He came back to win the Auld Lang Syne race in December 2012.

Despite their current world status both Brownlees seem to keep their feet firmly on the ground, regularly returning to their roots. In 2011 they jointly nominated fell race organiser Dave Woodhead for the Yorkshire area 'Unsung

Heroes Award', which is part of the BBC Sports Personality of the Year Awards. Dave Woodhead (with wife Eileen) has organised many fell races over the last 30 years, including Auld Lang Syne. Commenting on nominating him, in the *Keighley News*, Jonathan said:

> Dave is a race organiser but he's way more than that, he's one of the most enthusiastic people I've met in my life. Fell running for some people is seen as an extreme sport, but he converts it into a sport for fun. I race all over the world but I still love turning up to Dave's races and getting muddy.

Alistair and Jonathan are now mega-stars, having won Gold and Bronze respectively in the triathlon at the London Olympic Games in August 2012. Over the years they have garnered a name for sporting behaviour and keeping an eye out for other competitors. A story by a friend of Alistair's[88] tells of how they met on one of the summits in the Dales where the triathlete was out running and his friend was out walking. Politely, Brownlee stopped to have a friendly word.

> They were chatting away when a pack of other runners appeared among the distant bilberries, each with a number card on his chest, like Alistair's. 'Ah,' said Yorkshire's latest gold medallist, 'I'll have to go. I'm in a race.'

Dave and Eileen Woodhead acknowleged the importance of the 2012 Olympic triathlon event by organising the Brownlee Gold Run, a short fell race on Penistone, which was followed by participants viewing the events of the Olympic triathlon on the big screen in the Old Sun Hotel. One hundred and seventy seniors (and 45 under 10s in a shorter race) competed in the event, and the whole event was highlighted on local television.

One direct result all this new fame is that they will no longer be sharing a house, as Jonathan noted in his blog[89]:

> As for long-term ambitions, I'm moving out of Alistair's house and into my own place soon. And, longer term, I'm definitely looking at Rio 2016 if I still love the sport and all the training. I'll only be 26 then so hopefully I'll be in my prime. Who knows, maybe I can give Alistair a run for his money.

Boff Whalley managed to mix the seemingly incompatible life of a musician on the road with his love of running on the fells. Ron Fawcett had one life as top climber before switching to fell running. I leave you with some thoughts on this move, which may have its own issues. Fawcett described some in *Rock Athlete*:

> Being tall with long thin legs I struggle uphill compared to shorter lads with a bit more muscle in their thighs. I'm quicker on the flat, however. I'm also known for being reckless in descent, which is tough on ankles that are rather battered after so many breaks and strains. I'm always going over on them and then have to rest up for a while. My Raynaud's disease is a bit of an issue as well, and in cold weather I have to wear gloves, and have even resorted to mountaineering mitts in harsh conditions. On longer races, where I'll need some sugar to keep me going, I like to carry some jelly babies in my bumbag.

So, pack some jelly babies and enjoy your fell running. We now move to find out how the enjoyment of sport has been reported over the years in the various media.

A conversation with: **Rob Jebb,** Bingley Harriers

I am sitting in the front room in my 'writer's retreat' transcribing one interview when the next interviewee taps on the window. It is Rob Jebb, who lives a few doors down from my friend Mike. Yesterday we had met him while we were watching the Coniston fell race, where his partner Sharon had come third, and he had agreed to come round for a chat the next day. His training on that day seemed to have consisted of pushing the kids in their double buggy up the rough start/finish track in the Coniston Coppermines valley. Now, this afternoon, he had taken a break from a heavy-duty weights session – he is deeply involved in some kind of rockery construction in his back garden – after also doing a longish bike ride in the morning. After he had gone, I realised that I hadn't even offered him a cup of tea or coffee.

'I train hard as I still enjoy it. The enjoyment motivates me.'

Rob Jebb came into the sport of fell running through his father. 'My dad, that is how I got into it. I always liked it, more for the social side. I'd been going to Bingley Harriers twice a week, and racing at weekends, since I was about nine years old. We used to go away on buses as juniors, about 20 of us. I just liked it, I wasn't any good really.'

They did cross country and road relays. Fell running was more something that he did for himself. 'Just going to do the juniors races where my dad went really. My dad won the Fellsman. My brother has only been running about two or three years from nothing and has reached a good standard in a short space of time, and is doing really well. I had no success as a youngster. I wasn't winning at county level, but I got into the odd team.'

At 17 he started improving, and started doing senior races at that age. He was doing Borrowdale at 18. 'I didn't win my first race until I was 21. I trained, but not properly. I was just enjoying it, doing the usual, going out, drinking, riding my bike.'

He started to improve, thought he could improve more, and that is when he started training harder. 'One of my best friends is Chris Caris, we went to school together. He doesn't do fell, but has been Northern Cross Country champion, and first Brit in the London Marathon. We trained together. Matthew Whitfield, Bob's son, is a year younger than me, and he was the best junior fell runner when I was younger. My father encouraged me, but never pushed me. I did it because I wanted to do it.'

Rob recalled that Bingley were such a successful club with the runners that they had, that success breeds success. 'You wanted to match them, you go training with them and were bound to improve. Road was never my cup of tea. I was in the winning Northern road relays champs team once. I did the 12-stage, and have only ever done one 10km. I just like fell running. If you are at a 10km you can't be at a fell race.' His 10k was in a respectable 31 mins 47 secs.

When he was really young it was Billy Bland and Kenny Stuart who were amongst those that inspired him. 'I remember them from when I was a kid. For me it was my dad, and Barry Peace that inspired me. Then a big influence was a guy called Ian Ferguson from Bingley. Andy Peace and Ian Holmes, who I looked up to. Ian is ten years older than me, and his consistency over time impresses me. Billy Bland's long records are something else, and Kenny Stuart's Ben Nevis record. Andy Peace's Three Peaks record. Some of them *change, the course and terrain changes. Courses get longer and changed, pitched paths can make descending slower.'*

Rob has personal race favourites but just likes racing, having won all the classics. *'Wasdale twice, Ennerdale twice, Borrowdale once, Langdale, Duddon. Of those I've won, Ben Nevis is one of my favourites, I've won it four times. Three Peaks I have won four times and I hate that race. It means a lot to me. It is an absolute classic, especially for a Yorkshireman, even though it is horrible. I just don't like all the fast running in between the peaks. I just love Lakeland races.'*

He thinks there are certain races like those mentioned, plus Grasmere, that are classics. *'I've won Grasmere eight times so I can run short too. Although I think I prefer rougher stuff. Although I have won Fairfield four times, and have got within four seconds of the record, so can run round it.'*

He says he is not the best downhiller, and is a better climber. *'I am not the best at one particular thing, but I am jack of all trades but master of none. Someone like Simon Booth who is a fantastic long distance runner would never win Grasmere. I am not as fast as some on short ones, but I am good overall. I think that's good.'*

Rob never raced against Billy Bland at his prime, nor John Wild or Kenny Stuart. *'Those guys were born with talent. They had an ability to run well over rough terrain. If you go training every day over rough ground you will probably be good at it. People talk about Keith Anderson as the best descender. In my time Gavin Bland, Simon Booth and Ian Holmes are the best at descending by a long way. For climbing Matthew Whitfield and Andy Peace, and maybe myself.'*

Rob Jebb has competed in International races, but is not especially enamoured with them, as he explained. *'I've done the World Trophy twice, and the Europeans twice. Done both uphill and downhill versions. Not so good at it. I think I was forty-ninth both times in Worlds, and in top 30 both times in Europeans. It never suited me. I never liked it. I remember going to the Europeans and they changed the course the day before because people complained. They made it zig-zag rather than straight down. That is why I have never pursued it. It has changed unrecognisably. I think maybe there should be like a home international for fell runners.'*

Nowadays Rob coaches himself. 'When I was younger we used to have coaches at the club. Dennis Quinlan was a big influence. He made me believe *in myself, and he did coach me for a couple of years. I just used to run with others as well and go training hard with them.'*

In his view it is not rocket science, although he did do track sessions when he was younger. *'Nowadays I may go to Kendal to do some flat work on grass now and again. I have had VO2 max test but I have forgotten the figures. It was before I was 20, someone just gave me chance to do it at the time. I don't use a heart rate monitor either.'*

Rob has always liked cycling, but did no competitive cycling when he was younger. *'It is expensive. I did a bit of Cyclo-cross on my dad's bike. I did the Three Peaks Cyclo-cross when I was 17. Enjoyed it, but didn't really start doing it till I came to Lakes. I just found that with no street lights I didn't like running on road. You can also train on a bike indoors. I have done some time trialling on the bike. Circuit of the Dales, the Shap race, for instance. Only done a few so that tells a tale. I did alright, on a standard road bike.'*

Having just supported some running friends on a Three Peaks attempt on which we did the Seathwaite-Scafell Pike leg predominantly in the night, I was interested in Rob's views on running with a headtorch. *'I have been doing that. It has revolutionised training really. I do it with Helm Hill Runners sometimes. Nice to go on the hills in the dark. Not done any night races though, they are becoming quite popular.'*

I wondered whether winning the Three Peaks on a bike or running gave Rob the most pleasure. *'Both really. Proud of fact that I have won both. Myself and Andy Peace are only ones to have won both. That is something really. I just love it, it is quite a unique event. When I first won it, it was the thing I most wanted to do in my life. Now after eight it is just something I am proud of. I do it now just because I like it. Also if you are well known for something it is good to keep that going.'*

Although not for him, he was aware of those that had tried to mix fell and marathon running. *'Dave Cannon may have done it because he wanted to run for England, so I was told. Kenny wanted to do it. Keith Anderson went to the roads. There is more for fell runners now though. Someone like Andi Jones for instance is a mountain runner not a fell runner. He has never won a Lakeland race as far as I remember.'*

Rob is trying to compete in the British Championships these days, but isn't particularly enamoured with the current setup. *'It is hard. For instance at Coledale Horseshoe, there was a fantastic field with everyone there, some had a bad run and they were out, and they won't do other races. I would like to see more races count so you have a second chance. It would improve fields, I am sure. It won't go back to 15 races though.'*

He has been very successful on the bike, setting best times for the Fred Whitton Challenge[90] and Three Peaks Cyclo-cross events. The weekend after our conversation he was doing the Slieve Bearnagh British Championships fell race on the Saturday and flying back to do the Fred Whitton on the Sunday (for his sponsor). *'I have the equal fastest time for Whitton. I was with a guy called James Dobbin, who had been national hill climb champion. We set off in a group of 20, whittled down to us two trying to batter each other all the way. In the last few miles we hadn't though. It is not strictly a race, and you couldn't really sprint in, so we finished together. We rode hard all the way, giving it some, trying to get rid of each other, but it never happened. So, we got joint title and equal fastest time.'*

The Three Peaks Cyclo-cross time came because he was battling Nick Craig and conditions were quite dry. *'Three Peaks is unique as it is over a set course, so there is a record. Normally in cyclo-cross you cycle for an hour and a lap of wherever it is held. I have represented Great Britain in two World Cyclo-cross champs. That was one of the best things I have done, riding with the pros. It was in Belgium and Italy. When it was foot and mouth year I cycled in Tour of Ireland as I was doing road racing then.'*

Rob has been reasonably injury-free, although he has dislocated his shoulder more than once, doing caving the original time. *'I have done it more times running than cycling. Eventually it got so loose it was coming out so easily I had to have an operation. It should be sorted now. I have had no injuries on the bike, in fact I have been lucky to have no other injuries.'*

Despite winning Grasmere multiple times Jebb hasn't managed to beat the record. *'I have been 15 seconds off it. I think I could have done better. Those boys, that is all they did, those short races. I have usually done Borrowdale shortly before Grasmere. I did Burnsall the day before my fastest time. I never thought the record was possible, so have never set out to beat it. They often didn't use to cut the grass. It could be waist high.'*

He prefers Lakeland races, although he has raced quite a bit elsewhere, especially in champs races. *'I have never done Rivington Pike. I won Pendle, and the half Tour for instance. I don't choose to go there, they are not my favourite races. I don't really like the moorland type of races. Sometimes they are in the Championships though. I don't get to Scotland enough. Although I've won at Carnethy five times, and the Isle of Jura.'*

He has to fit his training in with work, having a family, and partner Sharon, who also is a top fell runner and wants to train herself. *'Priorities change once you have a family. I ride the bike to and from work. At least once a week I go for a ride straight from work. Then come home and play with the kids. I'll go for an hour run and Sharon will go for an hour. Usually a long run at weekends. I train hard as I still enjoy it. Daft as it sounds I think I might still get better. The enjoyment motivates me.'*

Rob reckons that having six months out with the shoulder may have been good for him. It has made him keen again. *'I train a lot with Tom and Mark Addison, who are young and really keen, that rubs off on me. I am fit and pretty happy. I want to do well in the championships. I want to do well at Jura and the Three Peaks Cyclo-cross later in the season. I just did the Three Peaks race and came seventh, which was fine in a good field. I thought I had run alright, but not good enough.'*

The Bob Graham Round and other endurance events interest him, but he knows what it takes out of you. *'I would rather do some races than do that. I don't know if I will ever do the BGR. It doesn't float my boat, but I'd love to be able to say I'd done it, but that is about it. There are so many things to do, and I know that doing that you would miss out on so much more. I could probably go and potter round, but I wouldn't want to do that.'*

He acknowledges that his navigation is rubbish. He doesn't get a compass out, saying he'd rather run in the wrong direction. *'My dad was proud of his navigation though. I was once leading Borrowdale by a couple of minutes and ran to Kirk Fell instead of coming off Great Gable the right way. I like to reconnoitre and like to know where I am going. I have had loads of disasters. I have done Karrimor but didn't do the navigating. You'd think I'd learn.'*

So, what ambitions does someone have, who has achieved as much as Rob has? *'Remaining consistent. I like racing and doing well. I would like to win Three Peaks running race again, but that may not happen. I have won everything I've wanted to really. I'd go and have a go if there was something out there. I'd like to do a better time at Borrowdale.'*

CHAPTER 19

Reporting the Sport

The difference between literature and journalism is that
journalism is unreadable and literature is not read
Oscar Wilde

Throughout its existence organised fell running has struggled with its profile in the wider world. There have been those that have felt that it should be kept as a niche sport, with only a dedicated inner core of competitors and races. Extreme versions of this view extend as far as saying that publicity is not good for the sport. This view is taken by those who think that it might be swamped by large numbers of competitors, that race limits would be reached, inexperienced race entrants might cause safety issues to organisers, and that rights of access to courses might be jeopardised.

Even in researching this book there has been a marked resistance to disseminating information about the sport via a book from some within the FRA. Indeed the FRA website has this statement on the page explaining the benefits of joining:

> The Environment: Fell running is perhaps unique amongst sports
> in that it does not seek to attract ever greater numbers of participants.

The sport has not been reported very thoroughly over the years. Before the formation of the FRA in 1970 it was often only local papers that provided reports of events. In researching this book I have only been able to refer to a small number of books that were published before 1970. Of these, one of particular note was *Some Records of the Annual Grasmere Sports, 1852-1910* by Hugh Machell. This book was published in 1911, which gives a further indication of the significance of that particular sports institution. Secondly, there was *The Ben Nevis Race: A Short History of the Famous Marathon* by Charles Steel. This was published in 1956, by which time it had been run for over half a century.

One of the first writers to bring events described within this book into the mainstream of literature was Thomas Firbank. His book *I Bought a Mountain* was first published back in 1940, and is itself a classic evocation of the experience of an incomer buying and running a sheep farm in Snowdonia. In the book he devotes a chapter to their breaking the Welsh 3000s record. In 1961 Harry Griffin included a chapter on the Guides racers in his book *Inside the Real Lakeland*, and continued to include related topics in his later output.

As has been seen, the sport exploded in the 1960s and 1970s, with seven new races being added to the calendar in the first decade and 32 in the latter decade. Publishing on the sport to some extent matched this trend. The other books referred to in the research for this book are noted in the References section.

Obviously the establishment of the FRA and the issuing of an FRA newsletter meant that this would be the first place to look for information about the sport from then on. In that first FRA magazine/newsletter there is a note about reporting in *Athletics Weekly*:

> For several years, up to and including 1969, an excellent review of the preceding years activities in the Fell running world appeared in A.W. Enquiries of A.W. reveal that the author of this first-class resum was in fact anonymous, and despite speculation in several quarters, no one is able to provide the name of this obviously knowledgable writer.

Readers were then asked to help identify the writer and encourage them to write material for the new FRA magazine. It is not clear whether they were identified, and whether they carried on with their anonymous *AW* reports. What I do know is that as a subscriber to *Athletics Weekly* for over 20 years I can report that its aim of providing what its strapline calls 'the best coverage of the No. 1 Olympic Sport' very rarely encompasses more peripheral athletic activities. Randomly looking at a recent issue of *AW* I see that six fell races were in the results section, including the well-known Tour of Pendle, yet none have more than the first three places listed. I certainly can't remember the magazine profiling any of the significant fell runners at any time in my period of subscribing.

For a while there were significant sections in the orienteering magazine *Compass Sport* that reflected events in fell running. Starting up in 1980, it had at the time a strapline of 'the magazine for orienteering, fell running, wayfaring & associated sports'. There was a considerable overlap of people competing in orienteering and fell running at the time and several are listed in the magazine as contributors. The magazine listed results of, and reported on, many fell races in each issue. It also had a decent amount of good in-depth material. One such example is a three-part series entitled *A guide to the guides* by Roger Ingham over three issues in 1983-4. Then in 1990 a new magazine called *Up and Down* (strapline: fell racing – hill running – mountain marathons) appeared, but it only lasted a dozen bi-monthly issues before having financial issues and folding. While it lasted it had good results and reportage, race previews, training advice and profiles, while maintaining a slightly irreverent approach to the sport – particularly in its 'Fellternative' column.

Boff Whalley was the main progenitor of the Fellternative column, which as he explained to me actually started as a separate 'magazine'.

> In the late 1980s the football fanzines were just starting. Me and my friend Adie from Pudsey and Bramley decided to do a fell running fanzine. We really enjoyed doing it but found it hard to shift, despite the maverick nature of the sport. But fell runners are often really tight, and so we would be at races trying to sell it for 50p. People wouldn't even look at it, although it was the only alternative to the *Fellrunner*. Well then *Up and Down* magazine came along and asked if we wanted to incorporate it in that, which was great. They were very brave printing all the stuff that we wrote in the 'Fellternative' columns in the magazine.

Certainly for a while in the 1970s and 80s some of the major broadsheets employed sportswriters who had an affinity with the sport of fell running.

The British Library/Newspaper Library collection has been the source of some of the writing of such well-known journalists as Chris Brasher, John Rodda, and Norman Harris, writing respectively in the *Observer*, *Guardian*, and *Times/Sunday Times*. Sadly, nowadays even mainstream athletics loses out to sports like football in the broadsheets, and doesn't get decent coverage, except for the big events like the Olympics and World Championships.

Nowadays it is often websites that provide the coverage of sport, and these are also able to provide the instant gratification that seems to be required in today's society. The FRA website has an excellent online calendar of events, and also results links, plus information about their championships, and international events. It also has a useful library service, whereby members can loan some of the standard books on the sport. If you have not got a copy of the seminal Bill Smith book *Stud marks on the summits*, which is long out of print, you can view an electronic copy that is provided at the website[91]. Other websites that have proved to be fruitfull (*Mud, Sweat and Tears* being one) are listed in the References.

Finally, what prospects are there in the more visual media? There are countless amateur video clips on such websites as YouTube, which often concentrate on particular races or endurance challenges. However, they are almost always of poor quality and aren't narrated. In the same way as there aren't a significant number of books on the sport, there also aren't really many videos and DVDs. If you look hard enough there are DVDs of the British and English Championship races going back to 1997-8, but these necessarily tend to be from fixed camera positions showing a stream of runners coming by. Some of the later ones have higher production values, better photography and sometimes 3D map animations courtesy of Tracklogs, and interviews with leading contenders. PWT Productions in Kendal are behind many of these DVDs and are a good place to start looking.

As to any videos concentrating on individuals, particular races or historical aspects or compilations, it doesn't happen. Presumably this is because there 'just isn't the market'. Having said that, two that are out there are fairly recent ones concentrating on a couple of Joss Naylor's epics. Firstly *Naylor's Run* which was filmed when he celebrated his sixtieth birthday by attempting the 60 highest Lakeland peaks in 36 hrs. The run was almost 110 miles long and involved nearly 40,000 feet of ascent. It details his support network, and shows him at some of the checkpoints, as well as traversing some of the more tricky terrain. If memory serves, he starts to have trouble with his foot and at one point is seen to rip off a toenail that is troubling him with his bare hands.

Secondly, *Joss Naylor: Iron man* is a DVD celebrating his 50 years of fell running. On the longest day of 2009 he set off from Mungrisdale in the northern fells of the Lake District to run home to Greendale in the Wasdale valley. This was a distance of 35 miles, over 20 Lakeland Peaks, with 18,000 feet of ascent, and was completed in under 15 hours – at the age of 73. Naylor has never liked the tags thrust on him by others, such as Iron Joss and the Bionic Shepherd, so when asked to describe himself in it he says '….. a car with clapped out suspension'. Seeing him descending some of the fells in his unique crouched style in this DVD you can see what he means. Both DVDs were made by Eric Robson's company Striding Edge Productions, which is based in Wasdale. They give a reasonable insight into the extreme exploits of Joss Naylor, particularly when you consider how old he was when both were made.

A conversation with: **Boff Whalley,** Pudsey and Bramley AC

A quick holiday detour brought me to Leeds to interview Boff Whalley. His recommendation of the café in the West Yorkshire Playhouse was a good one. My pessimism over traffic and finding the place was unfounded and I got there far too early. A quick phone call got Boff to agree to meet me slightly earlier, which was fantastic as we talked on for ages. After turning off the dictaphone we shared publishing stories. His book Running Wild was at proof stage and he was looking forward to it coming out after a long gestation. I'll be interested to hear if his planned champagne launch atop a Yorkshire peak actually happened. When we finished I left him to go off to a read-through of his latest play.

'*There is a sort of playfulness of throwing yourself off down a scree slope.*'

Boff Whalley is someone whom I would struggle to categorise, and I suspect he would like that fact. He is a musician, playwright, author, and accomplished fell runner. His early sporting career was pretty unimpressive. He very briefly ran at school, but was not encouraged, so he gave up literally after a few weeks. *'Me and friend Dan decided to do the Bolton Marathon, at the age of 20. It was heralded as this great spectacle of mass participation, it looked really interesting.'*

It was the same year as the first London Marathon (1981), but Bolton was the biggest one in Europe at the time. *'We thought it would be a good laugh, so we bought some really rubbish training shoes and just did the distance. My first race was a marathon. It was good fun, but didn't give me any taste for running, and certainly didn't encourage what I like about running in any way.'* For Boff it was just a spectacle and he gave up straight afterwards, for about six years, and moved over from Lancashire to Leeds.

In about 1986 his dad, who had told him about this thing called fell running, showed him a load of slides, which he found not to be interesting at all. *'He would be saying "this is Kenny Stuart, who is the best runner", and I'd be thinking "yeh whatever".'* Despite this, his dad invited him to watch a race above Skipton. He came over from Burnley and they went to Simons Seat, above Bolton Abbey, on a drizzly evening. *'There was one lad there who I recognised as a punk, and he had a pink mohican. He was amongst these 200 runners and I never thought much of it. They set off up this thing, into the mist and got covered in mud. They came back down the hill and the mohican lad won – it was Gary Devine.'*

Boff had got to know him a bit as he was the bassist in a local punk rock band at the time. Boff was just starting a band and had made an album. *'I saw this spectacle of muddy enjoyment. It was in the countryside, and I just thought I want to have a go at it. The fact the he won it looking like a maverick made me think it was not an elite thing. I think in road running you tend to see people who are in incredible shape, checking their watches all the time, and they all have similar haircuts. It never attracted me. Fell running can be a rag-bag of different people.'*

He remembers seeing Andy Styan, who had a vest with a hand-stitched sign on his back saying 'speed kills'. *'Lovely, badly done but beautiful. It is not about equipment, it is about going up and enjoying yourself. That was it, I was hooked.*

Splashing around in mud, I think we lose that as adults, that sense of connection. People don't go out in the rain unless they are completely protected.'

His father took photos for ages, and always had been a walker. He had a go at fell running, and he was never a brilliant runner, but he loved it too eventually. When he first got into fell running Boff remembers that he went and borrowed people's magazines. *'All these beautiful old A5 typewritten magazines. Looking through all these results I suddenly realised who these guys like Kenny Stuart and Billy Bland were. I met up with Gary Devine at a gig. I said "I know you, you play in this punk band, but also do this fell running".* He said come and have a go, so Boff went for a run with him. He recalls it was one of those runs where you run with someone and they are chatting all the way and you are absolutely out of breath. *'At the end he said "come and do a race". I didn't have any shoes or anything so borrowed some.'*

His first fell race ever was Burnsall. He says it was great, eventually finishing well down but loving it. *'Coming down you suddenly reach this five foot dry-stone wall. People scrambling over it to get into the last fields. It is not as if anyone helps you or opens a gate, it is just a wall to get over. My version of sport growing up was all very clean and tidy, and homogenised. Suddenly to be involved in this thing when you are in the rough and tumble of it was great.'*

Gary Devine was a member of Pudsey and Bramley, so Boff went to meet some of the guys. *'I'd be asking what I needed. They'd say a pair of fell running shoes and a bum bag. I remember pictures of myself in early races with a cagoule and a balaclava. I remember being more impressed by people who were a bit strange and interesting. People like Rod Pilbeam, who did well in the World Mountain Cup, never caught my imagination as he was "just" a great athlete. Whereas people like Ian Holmes who always liked a laugh and a drink, and didn't mind not winning races and got involved in things, he was more interesting. Quite a few at that time at Bingley, and at Pudsey, were terrible party animals but incredible runners too. I liked the fact that fell running was pretty classless. There was a real spread in fell running. Football at the time was pretty working class. It was rare to get a footballer that was clever and articulate and interesting. That is a terrible broad sweep of the brush, but sometimes these footballers don't know the world. Fell runners were all sorts of backgrounds, and as soon as you are blathered in mud it doesn't matter what you do.'*

Before Boff got involved in music he had a few jobs. He was a postman for a while, worked for a local newspaper, in a local shop, all sorts of stuff. For about ten years the band made no money. He came across to Leeds to go to the University. Formal education and Boff just didn't get on. He was there for just for a year and dropped out. *'The concept of learning and education I absolutely love, but I never chanced to drop into something that suited me. The band coming together just took over anyway.'*

When he started running he had quite a lot of time and he used to train with Ian Holmes, Gary Devine and Scoffer Schofield, amongst others. Very quickly, as soon as the band started touring and became professional, he realised he really would struggle to train enough to be a really good runner. *'But, that was fine. I made that decision and I loved it. For instance the summer is really good for a band, with festivals and that. For about 12-15 years I missed almost every weekend for June, July, August, and September as far as running was concerned. When the clubs were going off to Sierre-Zinal and the classic English summer races, I just missed them all. That is fine, because along the way I have dipped in and out all the time.'* He would do anything, short or medium, and has also done some of the longer races.

He did the Bob Graham Round not because of the challenge, mainly because of the history and culture of it. *'I thought OK I don't do that long really, but it is a really important that I did it. I did a bit more long training and reconnoitred it all, and had people helping me. On the last leg Gary was going to do it but couldn't because he was ill. He said he would find someone, but I did worry. Anyway, for the last leg Billy and Gavin Bland turned up saying "Scoffer told us we had to come here". Networking, beautiful. I know Gavin a bit and towards the end he was saying "you could put a sprint on and get under 23 hours". I said "look, I'm not interested I am just enjoying it, inside 24 hours is fine".'*

Boff reasons that if you are really good it alters the way you look at running, but if you are a bit below that you don't have that problem. *'I don't have to ever think if I went out twice a day, and did track, I could be really good. I am never going to be as good as these people, so why not just enjoy it.'* The mass of fell runners aren't going to challenge for prizes or win races. They just love it, and then can still be competitive. *'The BGR was one of those things I always thought I had to do. I read 'Stud marks' when I first started and read the whole thing.'* He didn't know Bill Smith but went and spoke to him once just because of who he was. *'His book, although incredibly dry, was still an inspiration. The historical stuff in his book is great.'*

So, a plan was set. *'The whole Bob Graham story is so beautiful. I thought I will do it when I am forty. I turned forty and was really fit. I did Winter Hill and did really well, coming third or something. I thought "this is going to be a great year".'*

Two weeks later foot and mouth struck and that was it for the year. It didn't matter, as he just worked around it. *'The BGR was a great day out. I did Broad Stand, I was terrible, I am not a climber at all. I had been reading Wordsworth and Coleridge for my book. There is a great passage by Coleridge about his descent of Broad Stand[92] with very limited equipment, and I had this in my head as I am doing it. I am thinking there are all these ropes, and my helpers are saying "clip that to this, pull on that one, put your foot in that". I had no idea, I couldn't even look down. I was terrible, but I enjoyed it.'*

Boff comments that the Romantics, both the writers and artists, came along and said you can enjoy the countryside for no reason at all. *'Sometimes I'll be doing a run, say a two-hours hard mountain run, and I am thinking this is the most relaxed I am all week. On my own, it is the only time I am not bombarded with communications and everyday life. It is so beautiful, and yet others might think it is the hardest thing to do.'*

He explains why he thinks fell running is really different. *'One year I did Ben Nevis and a runner from Leeds University who didn't do fell running, but was a really class runner, turned round at the top in the top three places and got to the top of the zig-zags on the way down, and watched people go straight down and just stood there and said "I am not doing that". He tiptoed down and came about 150th.'*

Some people can encompass road and fell terrain. *'I also imagine, this may be rubbish, that once you start making money from running marathons that your training suddenly becomes very intense, and this can be a lot of pressure. Keith Anderson was running for Ambleside and was an incredible athlete as well as fell runner, he switched to road running and made some money for a while, but disappeared quite quickly, I don't know why. Billy*

Bland famously was first to the tarmac at Ben Nevis something like five times, yet only ever won once. He was purely a fell runner though.'

If he is racing he is really competitive, but can usually have a conversation with someone in a long race, or look at the view. *'I remember doing Ben Lomond and looking out at the top and saying "that is fantastic". Others just hit the top and headed off down. Could they not take two seconds to take it all in. In road running you have no reason to talk ... what would you talk about? The shops? A friend from Rochdale did the Mountain Trial and was so tired he stopped by a nice rock for 20 minutes and had a little sleep, and then carried on.'*

It used to bug him when his dad used to say to him when he was doing well in races that he was really lucky being athletic like that. *'I used to think that it wasn't luck, I trained really hard for it.'* On reflection though, his view is that he is much better at coming down. *'There is a sort of playfulness of throwing yourself off down a scree slope or something. You twig quite early that fell running is a craft you have to adapt to, running down rocky slopes. If it is really bad weather, snowing and sleeting, and there is a horrible descent coming up and I think I will do alright and proper athletes might struggle and I'll get past them.'*

He claims he thought about asking for advice on training at one time, but never got round to it. *'It depends whether the band is doing much. We have just moved to Otley which is great for running, basically out the back door and up the hills. Once I lived in London for a year and used to run a couple of miles to Hampstead Heath and run around there. I trained with Highgate Harriers doing track and interval sessions and didn't enjoy it. I came up to do a race up here and there were quite a few good runners and I came second. I thought "how did that happen", but it must have been those intervals. I still decided it wasn't worth it. I have been lucky with injuries mind, particularly since I stopped doing any road running. If I have to train in dark instead I might put a head torch on and train round the canals or the parks.'*

When asked what he would do if he could only do one more race EVER, he reckoned it would have to be a really long one, so he could enjoy it for a very long time. *'One of the Lakeland Classics, as I haven't done them enough. Something like Wasdale, which is a great day out.'*

As far as his achievements are concerned he struggled a little, not because they aren't any, more because he isn't really goal-oriented. *'A few races I have won have not been particularly great. I think the best thing is being part of the Pudsey and Bramley team winning a relay race or something. You watch other people and then you contribute. We have the record for a team relay on the Pennine Way, which we took off Bingley, which was great. The organisation and goodwill that went into it, and then the feeling at the end when we were all in the pub together. I did an Ilkley Moor race the other day which is in commemoration for Will Ramsbottom, who was a Pudsey member who died climbing. On the start line they got someone who knew Will to say a few words about him, which was poignant and sad, but might seem like the last thing you want to hear at the start of a race. It was Jack Maitland who talked, he only spoke for about 30 seconds and it was brilliant. It felt like it was what the sport is about. When I was thinking about writing a book I didn't want to write about me but more about how to connect what it is about fell running and about the world we are celebrating, and how it is life-affirming.'*

He described some of the background to his most recent book. *'I had all these weird things in my head for ages, about why we go out on the mountains. I recently attended the eightieth anniversary of the Kinder mass trespass. After the speeches everyone went for a big ramble. Me and my wife went for a run over Kinder plateau and I was thinking this is what it all about. Connecting the running with the politics that allows us to go out on the fells and not be shot at by gamekeepers.'*

A couple of years ago Pudsey asked him to design an image of famous club members for their website. *'I was really stuck because there have been so many of them, where do you stop. There is Jack Maitland who still holds some records, Gary Devine, and Pete Watson who won Burnsall six or seven times in a row. He was an early cross over from cross country to fell running, and he still trains kids at the club, and is an iconic club member. Then there is Sarah Rowell, who is an incredible athlete who prefers to run on the mountains. Then people start saying there is Rob Hope, and what about so and so. Then you think about what people did for the sport rather than being fell champions. The club was a cross country club originally. I wrote a history of the club on its centenary recently[93].'*

Looking more widely at the sport Boff considers the biggest change to the sport to have been putting the race calendar online and making the sport more accessible. *'There is much more to the sport than races. I must run alone around 20 times or more for each race I do, and I rarely see anyone else running when I'm out on the fells. Having 800 to 900 running the Three Peaks is absurd, much as I love the race and its tradition. Recently I did my first evening race of the year at Rossendale and you didn't pay to enter, no prizes, beautiful sunset, coming back muddy amongst about 120 other like-minded people.'*

Endnote

The Inca runner was fearful that the host of spirits around him
would desert him if he did not behave and think properly
Thor Gotaas

The sport currently faces several issues, including falling numbers in some lesser known races, yet paradoxically having some over-subscribed gems; possible problems over the environment and access; losing out to other sports such as trail running and adventure racing; and wanting to retain a low-key profile for the sport.

Taking the last of these issues first, the FRA website states:

Our sport has a relaxed low-key atmosphere where friendships are easy to make and the hills are there to be enjoyed.

The following also appears on the FRA home page:

The Environment: Fell running is perhaps unique amongst sports in that it does not seek to attract ever greater numbers of participants. The reason for this policy is that we have to balance our sporting interests with the impact on the environment. The sad fact is that the hills of Britain simply will not cope with ever increasing pounding of feet. Protecting the environment is one of our primary aims. We continually liaise with agencies and land owners over access and racing over environmentally sensitive areas. The Fell Runners Association will continue to protect your interests in these and many other matters.

While researching this book I asked for some information[94] from the FRA Committee, having explained the pitch of the book. The reply I received from the FRA Committee was:

> It may be helpful if I make it clear that the policy of the FRA is to avoid media exposure of and publicity for the sport. The prospect of yet another book about fell running is not welcomed and the FRA Committee will not wish to co-operate in providing assistance.

This is possibly a unique attitude from a sport's governing body – to actively avoid publicity and to discourage someone with a love of the sport (and a member of that body) from writing about that love.

There are other problems. A look at the News page on the FRA website on a random day in February 2012 showed the following:

- As a result of access problems, Todmorden Harriers had to cancel this race which should have taken place on Sat. Feb. 25th. There were no plans to reinstate the event in future.
- Edale Skyline race was full and entries on the day would not be possible that year.
- As a result of the anticipated increase in demand resulting from the cancellation of the Noon Stone race on the same day, the low-key Bleasdale Circle race was now pre-entry only with a limit of 120.

Those messages encapsulate some of the problems being faced by the sport. On the one hand issues of access are increasingly becoming problematic, despite the hard work that the FRA has been doing in this area. In some ways it mirrors problems seen in other sports. For instance in mountaineering, the governing body – the BMC (the British Mountaineering Council) – have long faced issues of negotiated access, particularly with crags and quarries that are in private ownership, yet are often the closest and easiest for physical access for keen rock climbers. There have of course been many examples of individuals and groups ignoring both the law regarding access, and the advice of the BMC.

Equally there are problems in athletics where road races are concerned. Race organisers are finding that increasing numbers are putting pressures on the communities they take place in. Specifically, there are some problems with road closures and police support. Only the biggest road races are able to get road closures to be granted. Several road races have decided that the less helpful attitude of the local police, or imposition of high charges for police presence, has necessitated their termination or move to off-road venues instead – fuelling the rise of trail running in the process, which is now seen as 'fell running lite' by some.

Finally, the tricky issue of numbers of participants. Figures for race entries can be traced over time but obviously give a patchy picture. For instance, in 2010, Steve Temple of the University of Manchester analysed[95] the numbers of entrants at races in the Hayfield area of the Peak District over the last decade or so:

Race	Period	First date	Last date	Difference
Kinder Downfall	1999-2009	232	279	+47
Lantern Pike	1996-2009	203	246	+41
Cracken Edge	1996-2009	57	229	+172
Kinder Trog	1999-2009	104	205	+101
Mount Famine	1999-2009	106	154	+48
Kinder Trial	2003-2010	90	130	+40
Famous Grouse	2004-2009	52	108	+56
Lamb's Leg	2000-2010	61	59	-2
May Queen	1998-2009	52	53	+1
Lantern Pike Dash	2005-2009	40	40	0

The trend appears to be a reasonable increase in numbers for the larger races, but with static entry numbers in the smaller ones.

Elsewhere, in October 2001 *Fellrunner* published an article entitled 'Will Long A Races Survive?' This prompted debate on whether the steadily falling entries for races such as Ennerdale and Wasdale might lead to their extinction, and on what could be done to help them survive. Brian Martin, the then FRA statistician, and Selwyn Wright, organiser of the Three Shires Race, developed the idea of a Grand Prix to raise the profile of, and encourage runners to return to, the long Lakeland classic races. Wright submitted an article for the same issue of the magazine suggesting that his race might be included along with others such as Duddon Valley, Langdale and Borrowdale in a new Lakeland Long 'A' Championship. While the primary focus of the Championship would be to keep the great Lakeland races alive, its second purpose would be to recognise the performance of runners who excelled in such events.

In 2002 the idea came to fruition as the Lakeland Classics Trophy, based on the six races noted above and also including the 21-mile and 5,500 feet Dockray Helvellyn race. The concerns expressed in the original article seemed to be coming true because 2002 actually saw the last running of the Dockray Helvellyn race and in 2003 the Ennerdale race was cancelled because of very low entries. Fortunately, since 2002 the number of runners who have wished to compete in the great Lakeland classic races has grown and those completing the series had increased from 38 (four female) and 12 teams in 2002 to 104 (13 women) and 14 teams in 2008. The Challenge Trophy has always been about supporting the individual races rather than being an end in itself, but it has rekindled interest in races such as the Wasdale and Ennerdale, as the following figures show:

Year	Wasdale	Ennerdale
2002	54	30
2003	53	cancelled (low entry)
2004	49	85
2005	*141*	95
2006	128	*224*
2007	105	105
2008	125	129
2009	*194*	95
2010	121	*278*
2011	140	90

[Note: the italic entries are years that the race was included in either the British or the English Championships]

I am sure though that the good races will survive and that a responsible attitude to the environment can indeed see the sport prosper. I do think that attitudes have to change and that the sport should welcome all those who want to take up the challenge to compete that it provides. We should be celebrating the variety of events and competitors that there are, be proud of the fact that great Olympic Triathlon athletes like the Brownlees like participating when they can, and that fell champions like Rob Jebb can excel also at top cycle events.

To plagiarise the title chosen for this book: it's a hill, let's get over it.

Postscript

The road to injury is paved
Adam Chase

As I was completing the manuscript for this book I got to thinking about whether I had answered some of my own questions.

It seems to me now that fell running and marathon running are **very** different activities, and that it is not the case that someone who is very good at the one should necessarily be able to perform well at the other. The training and performance demands are more diverse than at first might seem. Kenny Stuart and Dave Cannon were unusual in their ability (and desire) to translate their fell endurance background to deliver quality marathon performances. Having said that, others like Ron Hill and Jeff Norman managed to combine the events from both strands throughout their careers, whilst others have had limited success in trying to cross the boundaries between fell and road running.

While I was writing this manuscript, Boff Whalley's book *Run Wild* was published. Having read it over one weekend I realise that I have written predominantly about **fell racing** and not really explained why I love **fell running**. I will leave him to put the case for what he calls wild running (which he does very well in the book) and will just close with this quote from him:

> Off-road running is a metaphor for life – on the assumption that we don't know exactly where we're going, we may get lost, we'll probably have to stop somewhere to take stock of the magnificent surroundings, we may spend huge amounts of time clambering over,

under or through things, and by the time we're almost finished we'll be too busy marvelling at what we've just experienced to notice we got to the end.

I have tried to take stock of my experiences and feelings about fell running, inter-woven with an account of the sport from its beginnings to the present day. I could apologise for the mass of dates and times, but I do feel they are important to tell that story. However, I do hope that the conversations with, and comments from, some of the main players in the sport included herein are able to give some insight into the ways that runners train (both on and off the fells). It should also be possible to see how this may have changed over time, and may vary significantly between different individuals. I now feel there is a case for fuller biographies of some of the athletes mentioned. That is for another project, or perhaps for another author.

Although I no longer race on the fells I still have an immense love of being out amongst them. Just recently I was supporting some friends on an International Three Peaks Challenge. On the Lakes leg we set off from Seathwaite in the dark and I walked up most of the Scafell route to help with the navigation. Leaving them to do the last bit of ascent I set off back down as the sky lightened. I had the marvellous sight of a wan sunrise appearing over Borrowdale underneath the glowering cloud cover, as I came back alone off the end of the Corridor Route. As I descended further Airy's Bridge, which we missed crossing upper Styhead Gill on the way up, became suddenly visible. At the other end of a day, and a very long time ago, I have very distinct memories of a very easy training run from Kendal Youth Hostel out to Scout Scar. As my training partner and I ran up to the viewing platform there we saw the whole vista of a glorious sunset over the Western Lakes spread out before us.

So, an end to racing, but not to being out enjoying the fells. Maybe I'll meet you out there one day.

References

Listed here are the main sources accessed in researching this book. It can also be seen as a useful reading list for those wishing to delve deeper into the sport of fell running.

A seminal work on the early days of fell running is *Stud marks on the summits* by Bill Smith, with its sub-title of *A History of Amateur Fell Racing 1861–1983*. Latterly Richard Askwith's *Feet in the Clouds* has expanded on the subject by trying to answer the question posed on its dust jacket: 'What makes a good fell-runner?' The best biography of a runner is probably *Joss: The life and times of the legendary Lake District fell runner and shepherd* by Keith Richardson. In fact, if Richardson hadn't got there first this book might not actually have been written, as I was originally planning to write a biography of Naylor myself. Much of the factual matter included here has been checked against these volumes, although these and other sources don't always agree on specific details, particularly early dates and times.

The following also proved useful during the research:

BOOKS:

Bellamy, Rex. *The Four Peaks*, Warner, 1993

Brander, Michael. *The Essential Guide to the Highland Games*, Canongate, 1992

Brown, Pete. *Man Walks into a Pub*, Pan, 2010

Clayton, Roy and Turnbull, Ronald. *The Welsh Three Thousand Foot Challenges*, Grey Stone, 2010

Davies, Hunter. *A Walk Around the Lakes*, Orion, 2000

Fawcett, Ron. *Rock Athlete*, Vertegrate Graphics, 2010

Firbank, Thomas. *I Bought A Mountain*, New English Library, 1972

Fixx, James F. *The Complete Book of Running*, Penguin, 1981

Gotaas, Thor. *Running: A Global History*, Reaktion Books, 2012

Gray, Dennis. *Rope Boy*, Littlehampton, 1970

Griffin, Harry. *Inside the Real Lakeland*, Guardian Press, 1961

Griffin, Harry. *Long Days in the Fells*, Robert Hale, 1975

Harvie, Robin. *Why we run: a story of obsession*, John Murray, 2011

Henderson, Jon. *Best of British: Hendo's Sporting Heroes*, Yellow Jersey Press, 2007

Hill, Ron. *Long Hard Road: Nearly to the Top*, Ron Hill Sports, 1981

Hill, Ron. *Long Hard Road: To the Peak and Beyond*, Ron Hill Sports, 1982

Hooper, Peter. *Best of the Fells*, self-published, 2010

Jones, Bill. *The Ghost Runner*, Mainstream, 2011

Lomas, Roy. *Grasmere Sports. The First 150 Years*, Roy Lomas, 2002

Machell, Hugh. *Some Records of the Annual Grasmere Sports*, 1852–1910, Charles Thurnam, 1911

MacLennan, Hugh. *The Ben Race. The Supreme Test of Athletic Fitness*, Ben Nevis Race Association, 1994

Miller, Michael and Bland, Dennis. *See the Conquering Hero Comes. An Illustrated History of the Grasmere Sports Senior Guides' Race*, Bland, 1973

O'Sullivan, Moire. *Mud Sweat and Tears*, self-published, 2011

Pearson, Harry. *Racing Pigs and Giant Marrows. Travels Around the North Country Fairs*, Abacus, 1997

Shepherd, Nan. *The Living Mountain: A Celebration of the Cairngorm Mountains of Scotland*, Canongate Canons, 2011

Steel, Charles. *The Ben Nevis Race. A Short History of the Famous Marathon*, Charles Steel, 1956

Symonds, Hugh. *Running High*, Hayloft, 2004

Turnbull, Ronald. *Long Days in Lakeland*, Grey Stone, 1998

Wainwright, Alfred. *Pictorial Guide to the Lakeland Fells – book 4: Southern Fells*, Westmorland Gazette, 195996

Wallechinsky, David. *Complete Book of the Summer Olympics*, Aurum, 2008

Watson, Peter. *Rivington Pike. History and Fell Race*, Sunnydale, 2001

Weeton, Ellen and Hall, Edward. *Miss Weeton: Journal of a Governess, 1807–1811*, OUP, 1936

Whalley, Boff. *Run Wild*, Simon and Schuster, 2012

Wilson, J. *Reminiscences in the Life of Thomas Longmire*, Skelton, 1885

Woods, Rex. *Grasmere Giants of Today. A Pictorial Record*, Spur, 1975

Woods, Rex. *Lakeland Profiles*, Sidmouth, 1977

BOOKLETS:

Blackburn, Marjorie. *Our Traditional Lakeland Sports*, Ambleside Sports Association, 2000

LDMTA. *Fifty Years Running: A History of the Mountain Trial*, Lake District Mountain Trial Association, 2002

Smith, Roger. *42 Peaks. The Story Of The Bob Graham Round*, self-published, 1982

Naylor, Joss. *Joss Naylor MBE Was Here. A Personal Account of the Complete Traverse of the 'Wainwright' Lakeland Peaks*, KLETS

As well as the books noted, there are magazines that have provided articles, results and opinions that have helped shape the resulting work. In particular the Fell Runners Association magazine *Fellrunner* has been invaluable in providing background information, as have the FRA committee minutes around the negotiations with AAAs and other organisations. Similarly, orienteering's *Compass Sport* magazine, and the short-lived magazine *Up and Down*, have given different perspectives, slightly removed from the 'official' line of the FRA. Further library research has turned up material in journals and regional publications such as *Cumbria* magazine, the *Westmorland Gazette*, the *Craven Herald*, the *Lancashire Evening Post*, as well as the national broadsheets like the *Guardian*, *Observer* and *Sunday Times*.

Finally, it has to be acknowledged that in this day and age much material is to be found on the internet, with the usual caveat about accuracy and impartiality. Particularly fruitful were those websites listed below:

Fell Runners Association (FRA): http://www.fellrunner.org.uk/

British Open Fell Runners Association (BOFRA): http://www.bofra. co.uk/index.php

World Mountain Running Association: http://www.wmra.ch/

Bob Graham Round: http://bobwightman.co.uk/run/bob_graham. php

Mud, Sweat and Tears: http://www.mudsweatandtears.co.uk/

Grasmere Sports: http://www.grasmeresports.com/

Burnsall Classic: http://www.burnsallsports.co.uk/

Like the classic races at Grasmere and Burnsall, many other fell races have their own websites now, as do some individual runners.

Appendix 1 –
Fell running and music

You wouldn't think that there would be much connection between fell running and music, but the following are three notable, but slightly quirky, links.

Italian composer Maurizio Malagnini recently wrote a new piece of music celebrating fell running in the Lake District. *Running in the Clouds* is a musical diary including memories of Joss Naylor. Announcing it on the BBC website[97], Malagnini said:

> The music takes us through the most energetic and heroic moments of the ascent. It culminates in the final movement, A View from Yewbarrow. Here, Joss is lost in the mist until the wind blows away a cloud and uncovers an incredible view from the summit.

The music was commissioned by BBC Radio 3. Richard Wigley, general manager of the BBC Philharmonic and a keen fell runner, said:

> The inspirational challenge created by Bob Graham is matched by the inspiration of an orchestra in full flight; the full flight we experience when our minds are allowed to float free from daily life.

Extracts of the work were featured in a BBC Radio 4 documentary, broadcast in December 2011. The programme followed two stories: the development of Malagnini's music and the attempt of two runners seeking to complete the Bob Graham Round. The full work received its world premiere with the BBC Philharmonic at Westmorland Hall, Kendal, on 14 January 2012, and was recorded for future broadcast by BBC Radio 3.

At the other end of the musical spectrum are Boff Whalley's band Chumbawamba, described rather grandiosely by Last.fm as:

> an English musical group formed in 1982 in the Leeds squatting community. They have, over a career spanning nearly three decades, played punk rock, pop-influenced music, world music, and folk music. Their vocal anarchist politics exhibit an irreverent attitude toward authority; the band have been forthright in their syndicalist, pacifist, communist, multicultural, and feminist social stances.

Despite all that, they have written two songs that put both Joss Naylor and Bill Smith into popular culture. The lyrics are reproduced here thanks to permission from the band (who have taken a certain amount of artistic licence with their subjects):

Joss[98]

Joss Naylor of Wasdale
Greatest fell runner of our time
Running the mountains
And working the farm
Cutting the bracken
Constructing walls
Studded farm boots
Attacking the fells

Then one day in '78
The final twist in the tale of Joss the Great
Four slipped discs, a career's culmination
Joss took a job at Windscale power station
Well, they say you can tell now
When Joss is out running
'Cause he glows
'Cause he glows in the dark

Stud marks on the summits[99]

Business bought the athletes out
With gold medals and role models
Drugs and media and national pride
Why join in when you can watch it on TV?
So out of the stadiums!
Into the hills!
Out of the armchairs!
Onto the fells!
Staggering through mud and peat
Gasping breaths and sucked-in cheeks
Bogs like lead to clutch your feet
Through the rivers, over peaks
So out of the stadiums!
Into the hills!

Out of the armchairs!
Onto the fells!
Studmarks next to summit heather
Everything suddenly comes together
No audience viewing-figures
Just you against yourself
So out of the stadiums!
Into the hills!
Out of the armchairs!
Onto the fells!

When I talked to Boff Whalley, he reflected on how the album containing these songs came about.

> Sometimes you are sitting in the pub and have crazy ideas but never pursue it because they sound stupid in the morning. I believe you should sometimes make those ideas happen. Chumbawamba did that sometimes, and once we were in the pub talking about this thrash/metal/hardcore band that brought out an album with 100

songs on. So we were saying let's do an album with 101 songs on it, just to say we have done it. Then let's do it all on one topic. Sport, no one ever writes songs about that in rock and roll. So '101 songs about sport' was born. The following morning we decided to do it. We spent several months writing the songs, a few of which are about fell running. Fell running was much more obscure in about 1987 than it is now, and people must have wondered what we were about. The record label had a charcoal drawing of Joss Naylor. I imagined all these kids jumping up and down at our gigs having bought the album and wondering 'who is that guy on the label'.

Possibly even further out on the musical spectrum are the pupils of Ambleside Primary School. In 2000 the Year 6 pupils composed and performed a song during a folk music workshop in school. It said on their website at the time:

It is a special reminder of our wonderful location at the heart of the beautiful English Lake District and tells the story of the traditional Guides Race that takes place during the Grasmere Sports each year.

Appendix 2 – Course Records

The following is an incomplete list of course records, as at May 2014. The information is compiled from various sources, including *Stud marks on the summits*, the FRA website, and recent race results. It covers the main races that were established early in the history of the sport. The last column shows a calculation of the number of feet of ascent per mile, a very rough indicator of severity of courses (obviously biaised towards shorter courses). This shows Grasmere, Burnsall and Wansfell as potentially the toughest with their 600 feet per mile of ascent. The two lowest scorers are the two Skylines, at Withins and Chew Valley, with 143 and 154 feet/mile respectively

Name	Category	Length (miles)	Assent (feet)	Men's record	Women's record	First held	Feet/mile
Grasmere Guides	AS	1.5	900	F. Reeves – 00:12:21 – 1978	P. Maddams – 00:15:33 – 2010	1852	600
Hallam Chase		3.5	1,000	T. Wright – 00:19:42 – 1968	J. Turnbull – 00.24.22 1988	1863	333
Rivington Pike	BS	3.25	700	J. Wild – 00:15:53 – 1981	C. Greenwood – 00:19:38 – 1987	1893	215
Ben Nevis	AM	10	4,406	K. Stuart – 01:25:34 – 1984	P. Haworth – 01:43:25 – 1984	1899	441
Eccles Pike	AS	3	817	A. Wilton – 00:19:26 – 1996	O. Bush – 00:24:53 – 2011	1928	272
Burnsall Classic	AS	1.5	900	J. Wild – 00:12:48 – 1983	C. Greenwood – 00:16:34 – 1983	1932	600
(Slieve) Donard	AM	6.5	3,300	R. Hope – 01:02:01 – 2007	A. Mudge – 01:11:28 – 2007	1945	508
Bradwell	BS	3.7	750	A. Thake – 00:24:00 – 2011	P. Vazey-French – 00:27:12 – 2009	1946	203
Hope Wakes	AS	5.9	1,480	S. Bond – 00:40:58 – 2011	L. Gibson – 00:50:34 – 2011	1946	251

Name	Category	Length (miles)	Assent (feet)	Men's record	Women's record	First held	Feet/mile
Eldwick	BS	3	550	D. Slater – 00:16:01 – 1981	C. Haigh – 00:17:45 – 1985	1947	183
Bamford Carnival	BS	4.5	1,000	S.Bond–00:28:07 – 2010	F. Smith – 00:31:30 – 1999	1949	222
Three Peaks	AL	23.3	5,280	A. Peace – 02:46:03 – 1996	A. Pichtrova – 03:14:43 – 2008	1954	227
Pendle	AS	4.5	1,500	J. Maitland – 00:29:44 – 1984	C. Greenwood – 00:34:25 – 1993	1956	333
Pendleton	AS	5	1,500	K. Capper – 00:30:38 – 1983	C. Greenwood – 00:36:36 – 1984	1956	300
Eildon 2 Hills	AS	3.5	1,500	K. Stuart – 00:25:48 – 1984	T. Calder – 00:30:28 – 1990	1962	429
Creag Dubh	AS	4.5	1,225	J. Brooks – 00:27:07 – 1997	A. Mudge – 00:32:21 – 2006	1964	272
Skiddaw	AM	9	2,700	K. Stuart – 01:02:18 – 1984	S. Rowell – 01:13:29 – 1989	1966	300
Fairfield	AM	9	3,000	M. Roberts – 01:15:11 – 2000	J. McIver – 01:28:21 – 2008	1966	333

Name	Category	Length (miles)	Assent (feet)	Men's record	Women's record	First held	Feet/mile
Chevy Chase	BL	20	4,000	R. Hackett – 02:40:00 – 1992	T. Calder – 03:04:20 – 1991	1967	200
Ennerdale	AL	23	7,500	K. Stuart – 03:20:57 – 1985	J. McIver – 04:01:33 – 2008	1968	326
Roseberry Topping	AS	1.5	715	R. Bergstrand – 00:10:20 – 1992	G.Hale–00:13:36 –1990	1968	477
Manx Mountain Marathon	AL	31.5	8,000	L. Taggart – 04:22:45 – 2007	J. Lee – 05:13:03 –2007	1970	254
Carnethy	AM	6.2	2,500	G. Bland – 00:46:56 – 1999	A. Mudge – 00:54:20 – 2002	1971	403
Wasdale	AL	21	9,000	W. Bland – 03:25:21 – 1982	J. McIver/J. Lee – 04:12:17 – 2008	1972	429
Langdale	AL	14	4,000	A. Styan – 01:55:03 – 1977	H. Diamantides –02:23:25 –1992	1973	286
Latrigg	AS	3	950	K. Stuart – 00:16:37 – 1984	V. Wilkinson – 00:20:00 – 2005	1973	317
Wansfell	AS	2.5	1,500	K. Stuart – 00:18:56 – 1984	S. McCormack – 00:23:00 – 2013	1973	600

Name	Category	Length (miles)	Assent (feet)	Men's record	Women's record	First held	Feet/mile
Ingleborough	AM	7	2,000	M. Croasdale – 00:44:15 – 1991	C. Greenwood – 00:53:01 – 1998	1973	286
Bens of Jura	AL	17	7,700	M. Rigby – 03:06:59 – 1994	A. Mudge – 03:40:33 – 2008	1973	453
Saddleworth	AS	3	950	R. Wilde – 00:18:50 – 1978	C. Greenwood – 00:22:49 – 1984	1973	317
Edale Skyline	AL	21	4,500	G. Bland – 02:34:39 – 1999	S. Newman – 03:09:44 – 2000	1974	214
Borrowdale	AL	17	6,500	W. Bland – 02:34:38 – 1982	M. Angharad – 03:14:37 – 1997	1974	382
Blisco Dash	AS	5	2,000	J. Maitland – 00:36:01 – 1987	H. Fines – 00:45:26 – 2013	1975	400
Kentmere Horseshoe	AM	11.9	3,300	S. Bailey – 01:22:36 – 2004	T. Brindley – 01:42:40 – 2004	1975	277
Holcombe 2 Towers	AS	4	1,300	D. Kay – 00:30:53 – 2010	D. Campbell – 00:40:31 – 2011	1976	325
Stoodley Pike	BS	3.25	700	I. Holmes – 00:18:10 – 2007	L. Jenska – 00:21:24 – 2010	1976	215

Name	Category	Length (miles)	Assent (feet)	Men's record	Women's record	First held	Feet/mile
Snowdon	AM	10	3,065	K. Stuart – 01:02:29 – 1985	C. Greenwood – 01:12:48 – 1995	1976	307
Withins Skyline	BM	7	1,000	T. Adams – 00:39:26 – 2013	J. Waites – 00:48:39 – 2006	1977	143
Wrekin	AS	5.5	1,700	J. Wild – 00:34:27 – 1980	C. Greenwood – 00:40:47 – 1986	1977	309
Dale Head	AS	4.5	2,210	M. Kinch – 00:41:32 – 1995	S. Rowell – 00:51:16 – 1995	1977	491
Belmont Gala	BS	4.5	1,000	N. Wilkinson – 00:30:15 – 1993	V. Wilkinson – 00:33:48 – 2008	1977	222
Hades Hill	BS	5	1,200	R. Graham – 00:31:14 – 2007	E. Flannagan – 00:38:38 – 2007	1977	240
Lantern Pike	BS	5	1,050	R. Wilde – 00:29:12 – 1977	C. Greenwood – 00:34:50 – 1984	1977	210
Coniston Fair	AM	6	2,400	A. Dunn – 00:52:36 – 2006	J. Lee – 01:02:16 – 2007	1978	400
Edenfield	BM	7.5	1,600	B. Taylor – 00:44:34 – 2010	C. Abraham – 00:53:08 – 2010	1978	213

Name	Category	Length (miles)	Assent (feet)	Men's record	Women's record	First held	Feet/mile
Duddon	AL	18	6,000	I. Holmes – 02:42:35 – 2007	J. McIver – 03:11:26 – 2008	1978	333
Turnslack	AM	8	2,000	J. Brown – 01:03:24 – 2008	M. Laney – 01:17:25 – 2004	1978	250
Gisborough Moors	BL	12.5	2,600	M. Speake – 01:19:09 – 2010	C. Greenwood – 01:35:26 – 1987	1978	208
Hodder Valley Show	AS	4.4	1,650	T. Addison – 00:48:36 – 2009	D. Atkins – 01:05:11 – 2011	1978	375
Whinberry Naze	BS	4	750	A. Norman – 00:22:13 – 2005	L. Whittaker – 00:27:46 – 2002	1979	188
Sedbergh	AL	14	6,000	K. Anderson – 01:57:11 – 1991	N. White – 02:25:21 – 2006	1979	429
Mytholmroyd	BM	7	1,350	K. Gray – 00:44:03 – 2006	K. Pickles – 00:54:29 – 2010	1979	193
Great Hameldon	BM	5	1,000	R. Hope – 00:36:12 – 2004	A. Green – 00:43:41 – 2007	1979	200
Chew Valley Skyline	BL	13	2,000	G. Devine – 01:47:31 – 1989	C. Haigh – 02:02:31 – 1989	1980	154
Otley Chevin	AS	3.5	900	I. Holmes – 00:17:04 – 2001	R. Bamford – 00:20:08 – 2011	1980	257

Name	Category	Length (miles)	Assent (feet)	Men's record	Women's record	First held	Feet/mile
Llanbedr-Blaenavon	AL	15	4,500	J. McQueen – 01:59:01 – 1999	M. Angharad – 02:19:03 – 1996	1980	300
Thieveley Pike	AS	4.3	1,300	R. Hope – 00:30:44 – 2006	N. White – 00:35:41 – 2006	1980	302
Tockholes	BS	5.8	1,100	R. Thomas – 00:37:37 – 2003	V. Peacock – 00:44:24 – 2003	1980	190
Buckden Pike	AS	4	1,500	C. Donnelly – 00:30:51 – 1988	C. Greenwood – 00:36:32 – 1993	1982	375
Coniston	AM	9	3,500	I. Holmes – 01:03:29 – 1996	M. Angharad – 01:20:51 – 1996	1982	389

Appendix 3 –
Fell Running Champions

BRITISH CHAMPIONS – MEN

1972	Dave Cannon	Kendal
1973	Harry Walker	Blackburn
1974	Jeff Norman	Altrincham
1975	Mike Short	Horwich
1976	Martin Weeks	Bingley
1977	Alan McGee	Keswick
1978	Mike Short	Horwich
1979	Andy Styan	Holmfirth
1980	Billy Bland	Keswick
1981	John Wild	RAF – CFR
1982	John Wild	RAF – CFR
1983	Kenny Stuart	Keswick
1984	Kenny Stuart	Keswick
1985	Kenny Stuart	Keswick
1986	Jack Maitland	Pudsey & Bramley
1987	Colin Donnelly	Eryri
1988	Colin Donnelly	Eryri
1989	Colin Donnelly	Eryri
1990	Gary Devine	Pudsey & Bramley

1991	Keith Anderson	Ambleside
1992	Steve Hawkins	Bingley
1993	Mark Croasdale	Lancs & Morecambe
1994	Mark Kinch	Warrington
1995	Mark Kinch	Warrington
1996	Ian Holmes	Bingley
1997	Ian Holmes	Bingley
	Mark Roberts	Borrowdale
1998	Ian Holmes	Bingley
1999	Gavin Bland	Borrowdale
2000	Ian Holmes	Bingley
2002	Simon Booth	Borrowdale
2003	Rob Jebb	Bingley
2004	Simon Bailey	Mercia
2005	Simon Booth	Borrowdale
2006	Rob Jebb	Bingley
2007	Rob Hope	Pudsey & Bramley
2008	Rob Hope	Pudsey & Bramley
2009	Rob Hope	Pudsey & Bramley
2010	Tim Davies	Mercia
2011	Morgan Donnelly	Borrowdale
2012	Joe Symonds	Kendal
2013	Rob Jebb	Bingley

BRITISH CHAMPIONS – LADIES

1979	Ros Coates	Lochaber
1980	Pauline Haworth	Keswick
1981	Ros Coates	Lochaber
1982	Sue Parkin	Holmfirth
1983	Angela Carson	Eryri
1984	Pauline Haworth	Keswick
1985	Pauline Haworth	Keswick
1986	Angela Carson	Eryri
1987	Jacky Smith	Dark Peak
1988	Clare Crofts	Dark Peak
1989	Ruth Pickvance	Clayton le Moors

1990	Trish Calder	Edinburgh
1991	Trish Calder	Edinburgh
1992	Clare Crofts	Dark Peak
1993	Angela Brand-Barker	Eryri (née Angela Carson)
1994	Angela Brand-Barker	Eryri (née Angela Carson)
1995	Sarah Rowell	Pudsey & Bramley
1996	Sarah Rowell	Pudsey & Bramley
1997	Angela Mudge	Carnethy
1998	Angela Mudge	Carnethy
1999	Angela Mudge	Carnethy
2000	Angela Mudge	Carnethy
2002	Andrea Priestley	Ilkley
	Louise Sharp	Keswick
2003	Louise Sharp	Keswick
2004	Tracey Brindley	Carnethy
2005	Jill Mykura	Carnethy
2006	Natalie White	Bingley
2007	Janet McIver	Dark Peak
2008	Angela Mudge	Carnethy
2009	Phillipa Jackson	Keswick
2010	Phillipa Maddams	Keswick
2011	Philippa Madams	Keswick
2012	Lauren Jeska	Todmorden
2013	Victoria Wilkinson	Bingley

ENGLISH CHAMPIONS – MEN

1986	Dave Cartridge	Bolton
1987	Bob Whitfield	Kendal
1988	Shaun Livesey	Rossendale
1989	Gary Devine	Pudsey & Bramley
1990	Shaun Livesey	Rossendale
1991	Gavin Bland	Borrowdale
1992	Brian Thompson	Cumberland FR
1993	Mark Croasdale	Lancs & Mor.
1994	Mark Kinch	Warrington
1995	Mark Kinch	Warrington

1996	Ian Holmes	Bingley
1997	Mark Roberts	Borrowdale
1998	Ian Holmes	Bingley
1999	Gavin Bland	Borrowdale
2000	Ian Holmes	Bingley
2002	Ian Holmes	Bingley
2003	Ian Holmes	Bingley
2004	Simon Bailey	Mercia
2005	Simon Bailey	Mercia
	Rob Hope	Pudsey & Bramley
2006	Rob Jebb	Bingley
2007	Simon Bailey	Mercia
2008	Rob Jebb	Bingley
2009	Simon Bailey	Mercia
2010	Rob Hope	Pudsey & Bramley
2011	Lloyd Taggert	Dark Peak
2012	Simon Bailey	Mercia
2013	Simon Bailey	Mercia

ENGLISH CHAMPIONS – LADIES

1986	Carol Haigh	Holmfirth
1987	Vanessa Brindle	Clayton le Moors
1988	Clare Crofts	Dark Peak
1989	Clare Crofts	Dark Peak
1990	Cheryl Cook	Clayton le Moors
1991	Cheryl Cook	Clayton le Moors
1992	Jacky Smith	Dark Peak
1993	Carol Greenwood	Calder Valley
1994	Andrea Priestley	Fellandale
1995	Sarah Rowell	Pudsey & Bramley
1996	Sarah Rowell	Pudsey & Bramley
1997	Mari Todd	Ambleside
1998	Angela Brand-Barker	Keswick (née Angela Carson)
1999	Janet King	Cumberland FR
2000	Sally Newman	Glossopdale
2002	Andrea Priestley	Ilkley

2003	Louise Sharp	Keswick
2004	Louise Sharp	Keswick
2005	Sally Newman	Calder Valley
2006	Natalie White	Bingley
2007	Janet McIver	Dark Peak
2008	Natalie White	Bingley
2009	Phillipa Jackson	Keswick
2010	Lauren Jeska	Todmorden
2011	Lauren Jeska	Todmorden
2012	Lauren Jeska	Todmorden
2013	Helen Fines	Calder Valley

Reference notes

[1] In *Running: a global history*

[2] The spelling varies in different accounts

[3] http://gillonj.tripod.com/thecelebratedpedestrian/

[4] Calculations throughout the book are based on the National Archive currency converter website: http://www.nationalarchives.gov.uk/currency/results.asp#mid

[5] See Chapter 11 for more on the World's Greatest Liar contest

[6] http://www.amblesidesports.co.uk/frame1.html

[7] Usually considered to have actually been in 1868 by most sources

[8] Ron Fawcett is a British rock-climbing legend. He was one of a number of leading climbers who in the 1970s were responsible for climbing's evolution from amateur pursuit to professional endeavour.

[9] The original definition of an amateur athlete was 'a person who has never competed in open competition, or for public money, or is a mechanic, artisan or labourer' – as noted by Robin Harvie in *Why we run. A story of obsession.*

[10] There are various spellings in different historical sources. It is from Sölva How – after the Norwegian King. Even now the Ordnance Survey label it as Silver How and Silver Howe in different map products.

[11] The fifth Earl of Lonsdale, Hugh Cecil Lowther, known as the Sporting Earl, as well as being a patron of the sports meets, was also famous for cleaning up boxing and instituting the Lonsdale belts.

[12] Stories of sportsmen being fortified with brandy abound, from Captain Webb on the first swim crossing of the English Channel in 1875, to marathon runners at the 1896 Olympics. More recently, on the day he died in the 1967 Tour de France, British cyclist Tom Simpson was seen to drink brandy in the early parts of that stage. The post mortem found that he had taken amphetamines, and a diuretic combined with the alcohol proved fatal when taken on such a hot day.

[13] He dropped the first part of his given name, which was McConchie.

[14] On Ordnance Survey maps it is sometimes Butter Crag, and sometimes Butter Crags.

[15] This was a different athletic club to Horwich RMI Harriers and AC, which was formed in 1924.

[16] The best sweep style timing devices could record to the nearest 1/16th of a second at the time.

[17] It should be noted that Pauline Haworth became Pauline Stuart when she married Kenny Stuart in 1985. Her maiden name is used throughout the book in describing her early records and performances.

[18] http://www.bingleyharriers.org.uk/html/eldwick/eldwick.htm

[19] Book Four: The Southern Fells

[20] A great thing about the Ordnance Survey sponsorship was one of their prizes. Presented to the first six men and the first three women were framed copies of various OS map covers, painted by Ellis Martin. These are classics and are much sought after nowadays. The maps with his cover art can be found in secondhand bookshops, but if you find an Ellis Martin original then you are made. Even more unlikely is a find of an original Frank Patterson line drawing. These superb works of art adorned articles in *Cycling* magazine for 60 years from 1893, but most of the originals were destroyed in a fire in the Second World War.

[21] Later to become more famous as Pauline Haworth, and then Pauline Stuart

[22] Rosemary Cox/Harrold ran for Enfield Harriers, and held the British Record of 2-50-54 (set in 1978) for the marathon prior to Joyce Smith. She was also my marathon-training partner for a couple of years in the early 1980s.

[23] Bill Teasdale held the record for the professional race at 46 mins 35 secs from 1952.

[24] http://www.snowdonrace.co.uk/services/servicesView.aspx?serviceid=2&folder=1

[25] http://www.pikeracers.com/page14.htm

[26] The full story of this epic run over 303 mountains is told in Hugh Symond's fascinating book *Running High*.

[27] http://www.theomm.com/

[28] http://www.slmm.org.uk/

[29] http://www.lamm.co.uk/

[30] www.durhamfellrunners.org.uk/resources/lamm2011a.pdf

[31] Björkliden Arctic Mountain Marathon

[32] http://www.dragonsbackrace.com/

[33] http://www.durhamfellrunners.org.uk/marathon.htm

[34] In *Reminiscences of Joe Bowman and the Ullswater Foxhounds*

[35] Ted Dance and Dennis Weir had completed it in 4 days 23 hrs 20 mins, north to south, in 1970.

[36] http://users.ox.ac.uk/~ouac/info/history.pdf

[37] *One more kilometre and we're in the showers*, Tim Hilton, Harper Perennial, 2004

[38] Much information in this chapter is from the published minutes from the FRA AGMs and committee meetings.

[39] An anonymous *Athletics Weekly* contributor used the Road Runners Club scoring system of 10 for a win down to 1 for tenth place to unofficially score the 1968 fell racing season, with Mike Davies coming out on top. The same system was used for 1969 with the 'winner' being Pete Watson. If used for 1970 and 1971 it would have resulted in wins for Jeff Norman and Dave Cannon.

[40] www.marathonguide.com

[41] http://www.carnethy.com/ci_newsletter/int_angelam.htm

[42] The current tallies for all these six can be seen in Appendix 3. The data was in an article in the June 1989 *Fellrunner*.

[43] In 1983 Mike Cudahy final broke the three days barrier, with his 2 days 21 hrs 54 mins 30 secs, going south to north.

[44] *A Coast to Coast Walk*, A. Wainwright, *Westmorland Gazette*. Wainwright's guides have been republished recently by Frances Lincoln.

[45] http://www.lakestay.co.uk/wasliar.html

[46] http://www.independent.co.uk/arts-entertainment/the-legend-of-iron-joss-1336177.html

[47] No one actually beat Billy Bland's time for Duddon, and the course was shortened a couple of years ago

[48] It is a two-part interview which is available at: *www.youtube.com/ watch?v=TR3qGaAvAxE and at* www.youtube.com/watch?v=0ucfAjKL_7c

[49] http://www.weshamroadrunners.com/Memories/MemoirsofaFellRunner_DoughBrown_March07.htm

[50] http://www.ldsamra.org.uk/accidents.aspx

[51] FRA *'Safety Requirements for Fell Races' are available in full at*: http://www.fellrunner. org.uk/pdf/committee/fra_safety_requirements.pdf

[52] *Long Hard Road: Nearly to the Top* and *Long Hard Road: To the Peak and Beyond*

[53] http://highgateharriers.org.uk/hh_aa_interviews.php?i=89#89

[54] Gerard Nijboer won in 2-15-16

[55] http://www.runnerslife.co.uk/guest-runners/the-norman-family

[56] http://www.runnerslife.co.uk/andi%20jones/blog/fell-and-mountain-running/829

[57] Subsequent drug revelations cast doubt on the validity of this mark for Armstrong

[58] http://www.topendsports.com/testing/records/vo2max.htm

[59] Clayton had a marathon personal best time of 2 hrs 8 mins 33.6 secs

[60] http://bobwightman.co.uk/run/bgr_history.php

[61] In 1980 Roger Baumeister topped this with a double BGR in 46 hrs 34 mins 30 secs, although he did it Keswick to Yewbarrow clockwise, then reversed the route to Keswick and on to Yewbarrow again, before turning round again and finishing clockwise back to Keswick. Joss Naylor, Selwyn Wright and Martin Stone were among his pacers.

[62] http://www.runbg.co.uk/Bob%20Graham%20record.htm

[63] This was written in 1998 which of course was before hand-held GPS devices were readily available; they now give a reasonably accurate figure of how far completers actually travelled.

[64] http://www.bobgrahamclub.org.uk/

[65] *Bob Grahams – The Bland Way* by Tony Cresswell appeared in the July 1983 *Fellrunner* magazine.

[66] http://www.mh.k313.com/mh/fell/bg/fastestBG.html

[67] *Lancashire Evening Post*, 4 June 1976

[68] It is worth noting that the original concept was to use the shortest day of the year.

[69] http://www.durhamfellrunners.org.uk/resources/Winter_BG_28th_Feb_2011.pdf

[70] http://www.theepicentre.co.uk/blog/summer-comes-to-a-winter-round

[71] http://www.theepicentre.co.uk/blog/bob-graham-round-1-2-2-12

[72] http://bobwightman.co.uk/run/bgr_winter_rounds.php – presumably Mann is going for Ashworth's 18 hrs 45 mins time.

[73] http://www.ramsaysround.com/finishers/

[74] Mike Hartley completed all three rounds consecutively in 3 days 14 hrs and 20 mins from 13-16 July 1990. His times were: Charlie Ramsay Round 21 hrs 14 mins; Bob Graham Round 23 hrs 48 mins; Paddy Buckley Round 33 hrs 30 mins, dozing fitfully in the car journeys in between.

[75] Charlie Ramsay established the Ramsay Round in 1978, and Paddy Buckley devised his eponymous round in 1982.

[76] http://www.heraldscotland.com/running-in-heaven-1.832035

[77] http://www.ukclimbing.com/news/item.php?id=68133

[78] http://www.williamhillmedia.com/manvhorse.asp

[79] Mick Woods is now a top athletics coach, leading his athletes from Aldershot Farnham & District AC to many international athletic honours. He holds the record (jointly with Taff Davies) for the 24-mile Snowdon leg of the Three Peaks Yacht race, set in 1983.

[80] http://www.wmra.info/

[81] http://www.youtube.com/watch?v=YXs1dOLJa6Q&feature=player_embedded

[82] http://www.bbc.co.uk/news/magazine-16548236

[83] http://www.bikeradar.com/news/article/uk-cyclo-cross-rob-jebb-breaks-three-peaks-record-18770/

[84] http://autobus.cyclingnews.com/cross.php?id=riders/2008/interviews/rob_jebb_jan08

[85] http://www.alistairbrownlee.com/profile.htm

[86] http://www.mudsweatandtears.co.uk/2009/03/08/5-mins-with-alistair-brownlee

[87] http://www.guardian.co.uk/sport/london-2012-olympics-blog/2012/jan/19/jonny-brownlee-cold-weather-training

[88] http://www.guardian.co.uk/uk/the-northerner/2012/aug/07/leeds-brownlee-brothers-gold-olympics-yorkshire

[89] http://www.guardian.co.uk/sport/2012/aug/07/olympic-triathlon-bronze-jonathan-brownlee

[90] http://www.fredwhittonchallenge.org.uk/

[91] http://fellrunner.org.uk/studmarks/

[92] Samuel Coleridge reputedly recorded the first recreational rock climb in the Lakes in 1802 by descending Broad Stand by hanging from its rock and dropping on to the narrow ledge below.

[93] http://www.pudseybramley.com/page2.htm

[94] It was a request for access to the archive of *Fellrunner* magazine

[95] http://www.cs.man.ac.uk/~temples/hc/race-stat.html

[96] Wainwright's guides have recently been republished by Frances Lincoln.

[97] http://www.bbc.co.uk/news/uk-england-cumbria-16143800

[98] http://lyrics.wikia.com/Chumbawamba:69._Jos (lyrics reproduced with permission of the band)

[99] http://lyrics.wikia.com/Chumbawamba:14._Studmarks_On_The_Summits

Index

Places and Races

People and Organisations